René Girard. Photo by Herlinde Koelbl.

CONVERSATIONS WITH RENÉ GIRARD: PROPHET OF ENVY

Edited by Cynthia L. Haven

BLOOMSBURY ACADEMIC
LONDON • NEW YORK • OXFORD • NEW DELHI • SYDNEY

BLOOMSBURY ACADEMIC
Bloomsbury Publishing Plc
50 Bedford Square, London, WC1B 3DP, UK
1385 Broadway, New York, NY 10018, USA

BLOOMSBURY, BLOOMSBURY ACADEMIC and the Diana logo are
trademarks of Bloomsbury Publishing Plc

First published in Great Britain 2020

Cover design: Louise Dugdale
Cover image © Michael Sugrue

A catalogue record for this book is available from the British Library.

A catalog record for this book is available from the Library of Congress.

ISBN: HB: 978-1-3500-7517-7
PB: 978-1-3500-7516-0
ePDF: 978-1-3500-7515-3
eBook: 978-1-3500-7514-6

Typeset by Deanta Global Publishing Services, Chennai, India
Printed and bound in Great Britain

To find out more about our authors and books visit www.bloomsbury.com
and sign up for our newsletters.

CONTENTS

Contents

René Girard grew up in Avignon. In this photograph, taken circa 1930, he sits beside his sister Marie, brother Henri, and his mother, Thérèse Girard. Photograph is used courtesy of the Girard family.

Novelist Raymond Federman, René Girard, and Professor Albert Cook at a gathering at the home of Provost John Sullivan at the State University of New York at Buffalo, New York, 1974. Photograph by Bruce Jackson is used with permission.

Professor Albert Cook and René Girard enjoy a party at Arts and Sciences provost John Sullivan's home in Buffalo, New York, 1974. Photograph by Bruce Jackson is used with permission.

René Girard holds a seminar on the ideas that would eventually become *Violence and the Sacred* at Buffalo in spring 1971. Photograph by Bruce Jackson is used with permission.

INTRODUCTION
SOCRATES IN THE DIGITAL AGE

It's been said that there is no such thing as talking and listening, only talking and waiting. It was not so for René Girard.

The great French thinker, who died in 2015 after an illustrious career spanning continents and disciplines, enjoyed conversations more than most. No wonder, then, that so many of his most prominent works are in the form of an interview.

Girard's capstone, *Things Hidden since the Foundation of the World*, is in Q&A form. So is *Evolution and Conversion: Dialogues on the Origins of Culture* and also his last major work, *Battling to the End*. Some of his minor works are dialogic as well—Maria Stella Barberi's long interview in *The One by Whom Scandal Comes*, for example, and his excellent conversation with Michel Treguer, *When These Things Begin* (short excerpts from both, showing the playfulness as well as the intensity of his thought, are included in this volume). One might even consider that his published letters with the Innsbruck theologian Raymund Schwager[1] were conversational—across thousands of miles.

Girard's colleague Sandor Goodhart told me Girard the professor was "doggedly dialogic." He added, "He likes working *with* people on things. He always spoke in terms of 'us,' 'our' project. What 'we're' doing. He had a sense of discovery."

Literary theorist Mikhail Bakhtin described why that might be so: "Truth is not born nor is it to be found inside the head of an individual person, it is born *between people* collectively searching for truth, in the process of their dialogic interaction."[2] And while that interaction can take place between the living and the dead, or in poems exchanged between long-distance lovers, or in cybersphere, it is uniquely effective between people conversing face to face. Socrates knew this: he brought people into conflict, and considered himself the "midwife" of the truth that was born that way. To answer any of the big questions in life, and many of the smaller ones, we need to collaborate and work together.

Dialogical format liberates thinking and takes it out of the straitjacket, according to Stanford Professor Robert Pogue Harrison, whose interviews are also included in this volume. We continually complain about the boringness of the lecture format, but for the most part we still deal in mind-numbing monologues—whether in lecture halls, dissertations, on YouTube, or on the nonfiction best-seller lists.[3]

I can attest to the power of Girard's interviews: my own introduction to his corpus was not through his books, but through his interviews. I've included in this volume some of the interviews that spurred my early questions—for example, Lévy's "War Is Everywhere," and Meotti's "The *J'Accuse* of René Girard: The Audacious Ideas of a Great Thinker." Others, such as Philippe Godefroid's "Opera and Myth," drawing Girard out on Wagner and Mozart, were a delightful discovery.

Contemporary French thought (Derrida, Foucault, Lacan), Heidegger, and Nietzsche figure more prominently in some of the earlier Q&As than in the later ones—particularly the *Paroles Gelées* and *Birth of Tragedy* interviews. Mark Anspach and Laurence Tacou explore anorexia in their conversation, but the discussion quickly opens out into a more general critique of society and modern culture. Michel Treguer's interview is provocative, diverse, and very accessible for a general reader—as is the transcription of Robert Harrison's two-part radio interview with Girard. Five chapters are translated from French originals, and one from Italian and another from Portuguese. The first chapter in this volume is the discussion following the talk at the landmark 1981 "Disorder and Order" conference, and shows Girard engaging with a range of colloquists, rather than a single interlocutor or pair of interviewers.

Some readers may find a few of the exchanges too academic; others will find a discussion of Derrida's "Plato's Pharmacy" beyond their ken; and those who dismiss the Hebrew Bible as a fanciful text written by an ancient people with too much time on their hands will find some of the biblical exchanges pointless. But all should find something of interest, enough to familiarize themselves with one of the major thinkers of our era.

Girard clarifies, contradicts, or amplifies earlier comments as he encounters a different question, or addresses a different audience, for a different interviewer—for example, a question in Rebecca Adams's interview draws him into a beautiful elucidation of "positive mimesis." The reader is warned not take anything he says as *ex cathedra*—but rather as a snapshot of a moment, what he thought at a particular time in a particular context, even as he contradicts himself within the volume.

In these interviews, over years and decades, Girard gradually becomes Girard, like an image slowly appearing in the developer of an old darkroom. (Yet, paradoxically, in the earliest of these interviews, he was already in his late fifties—already fully himself.) The back-and-forth allows the reader to eavesdrop on published conversations—to listen to him, as I did, in the early days when our friendship introduced me to his thought.

The time to do this book is now: many of these articles, once available online, have disappeared behind paywalls or dead links. The *Birth of Tragedy* interview, encompassing some of his early philosophical preoccupations, had to be exhumed from off-campus storage; others required an interlibrary loan. Still others, such as the excellent *Anorexia* interview, are available only through the books that published them years ago. And all require you know of their existence in the first place.

There will be inevitable repetition within these interviews, as the same or similar questions are asked. I have adjusted for typographical and spelling errors, and to conform to *The Chicago Manual of Style*, but for the most part these interviews are "as is." But how much revision occurred before they were published is another question.

* * *

None of the interviews in this book are directly from Girard himself: they've been prepared for the printed page which takes them already one step away from the spoken word. Yet some began as live audio interviews, which is a different world altogether, and one with its own protocols, possibilities, and limitations.

Robert Harrison's 2005 interviews for his *Entitled Opinions* radio show and podcasts were untranscribed until we prepared them for publication in England's *Standpoint* magazine and Germany's *Neue Zürcher Zeitung*, with an eye to later publish them in this book. Harrison and I worked over the manuscripts carefully, but minimally and delicately—Girard was no longer alive to correct any missteps in nuance or concepts. Harrison and Girard had been close friends, lunching at the Stanford Faculty Club twice a month. "I knew him so well that our conversations were something that carried into the studio," Harrison said.

While we knew he would have wished his words smoothed out for readability and clarity, we couldn't second-guess his editorial pencil. Harrison was concerned: the over-the-top assertions, the trial balloons, the banter, the wit and the laughter, the intimacy, the layers of irony are lost on the flat page, and words said in one context could be misread in another. "He was having a grand old time shooting the breeze. It's great on radio," he said. "People love to hear declarative sentences without qualification—but

I worry. It can backfire." (Surely one could argue that Socrates ran the same risks, even before the era of podcasts and the printing press.)

Neuropsychiatrist Jean-Michel Oughourlian recalled a very different process when he, along with psychiatrist Guy Lefort, was interviewing Girard for *Things Hidden since the Foundation of the World*. The conversations at the State University of New York at Buffalo took place during 1975 and 1976, and continued in Baltimore when Girard moved to Johns Hopkins University, but that was only the beginning. They were reworked and augmented with a range of earlier writings and interviews, including material Girard had intended to include in *Violence and the Sacred* and had decided to hold for later publication.

The hours and hours of tape recordings needed to be processed in a pre-digital way: "I would listen to the tape recording, writing it down by hand, then handing it to a secretary to type," Oughourlian recalled. His secretary typed a manuscript of about 580 pages, probably on an old-style manual typewriter. Girard rewrote it, and added a text he had prepared that became Book 2. Then, the back-and-forth continued—by snail mail, by subsequent conversation, by phone calls, by meetings—to winnow what they had gathered into a workable manuscript. It was a five-year process. "Gradually, gradually, gradually" the manuscript came together. Together they reviewed the whole manuscript during the summer of 1977, and *Des choses cachées depuis la fondation du monde* was published the following year.

Goodhart, who had worked with him since 1969, was on hand for the interviews in the Cheektowaga Sheraton Hotel, in an old steel mill area. "There was something slightly absurd about sitting in this abandoned place in Buffalo talking about ideas that could change the way we think about the world." Yet he recalls having "a sense of him as a star," and the conversations were punctuated with "a momentary insight you spend the rest of your life trying to figure out," he said. "We often called it the 'Midas touch.'"

While the interviewers were full participants in the discussion, they were not the author of the concepts: "The work was dialogic in its presentation, but not in the ideas. Was he doing warmed-over Hegel or warmed-over this or that? He wasn't. He was like the director of a play: 'You'll talk about this and then, you'll ask me this and you'll ask that—and let's have Sandy here and he'll talk about Freud and Shakespeare,'" Goodhart recalled, remembering how he was occasionally asked to join the conversations. "Most of the ideas were his. Obviously, he had so much more knowledge, especially in anthropology and the Bible and Gospel texts, myths all over the planet, Levi-Strauss. I was of course more a pupil—learning, more than anything else," Goodhart said.

Oughourlian recalled the circumstances somewhat differently: While it wasn't like the combative interviews of *L'Esprit*, neither was it a prepared feast, where the interlocutors were diners but not cooks. "It wasn't simply Socratic, either. Something in-between. The comparison with Socrates seems to be very valid—except that Socrates asked more questions than he answered, whereas René had more answers," he said.

The words from the foreword to *Things Hidden* are stern: "We quite deliberately left out all concessions to the reader which it is customary, and wise, to make in the presentation of so ambitious a thesis." The authors wished instead to preserve the "character of the discussion."[4] It's a solemn warning to pay attention to the nature of the colloquy, and also beware the power of ideas.

Some have later turned against the ideas they once embraced. Lefort, who had been one of the interlocutors for *Things Hidden*, was among them, but he was hardly alone. As Girard's audiences grew, the harvest could be uneven. Professor Bruce Jackson, a colleague from Girard's days at State University of New York, Buffalo, told me the story of one disciple:

> I had a PhD student who was intensely consumed by René's ideas about sacrifice. I remember several arguments in which I reminded him: "It's fine to use the ideas, but you're being inhabited by them." . . . He saw René in everything, like someone who has just discovered God or fallen in love. He was working on bullfighting, an apt topic for *Girardisme*. Then, he suddenly turned against René—not personally, but the ideas. He wrote a raging, awful paper on what was wrong with everything René had said.

"I was in the curious position of arguing for René," he told me. "I work very hard not to suggest to graduate students what they *ought* to think. My practice is pretty much helping them trust themselves and pointing them to stuff that might complicate their thinking. That time, I got argumentative at a basic conceptual level."

"I told this guy he's just flipped the signs: he was gone too far the other side. As I recall, he relaxed a bit before we fell out of touch. The whole thing had that kind of religious arc to it: the true disciple who is then the one ready to light the kindling under the bound feet."

But having had the good fortune to have enjoyed the friendship of the "prophet of envy," such stories make me smile. René Girard was a gentle and kindly companion and, as Michel Treguer noted, a remarkable man:

> I got into some lively arguments with him over the airwaves of France Culture. But there was something very strange about even these debates—the tit-for-tat and the aggressive verbal sparring that would have led any other thinker to sever ties with me once and for all left René Girard as serenely benevolent, interested, curious, amicable, and affectionate as ever. Not at all like the others, that one.[5]

Notes

1. *René Girard and Raymund Schwager: Correspondence 1974-1991*, eds. Scott Cowdell, Joel Hodge, Chris Fleming, Mathias Moosbrugger and trans. Sheelah Treflé Hidden and Chris Fleming (New York: Bloomsbury Academic, 2016).

2. Mikhail Bakhtin, *Problems of Dostoevsky's Poetics*, ed. Caryl Emerson (Minneapolis: University of Minnesota Press, 1984), 110.

3. "How Literature Thinks Me," Robert Harrison, Rosina Pierotti Professor of Italian, in conversation with Dylan Montanari, February 10, 2014, Piggott Hall, Stanford University.

4. René Girard, *Things Hidden since the Foundation of the World*, trans. S. Bann and M. Metteer (Stanford, CA: Stanford University Press, 1987).

5. René Girard, *When These Things Begin: Conversations with Michel Treguer* (East Lansing, MI: Michigan State University Press, 2014), x.

CHAPTER 1
"THERE ARE REAL VICTIMS
BEHIND THE TEXT."
Disorder and Order/1984*

In 1981, René Girard organized the "Disorder and Order" symposium at Stanford with his colleague Jean-Pierre Dupuy. He wrote that it was "a daring encounter between humanists of many countries and scientists with unconventional views not only on the diverse conceptions of disorder and order in their various disciplines, but also on the often illusory nature of the cultural fragmentation that affects us and from which we all suffer."[1] Girard's own presentation on mythology discussed how myths move from social disorder to order, from mob violence and murder to social unity after the scapegoating of a sacrificial victim, who is blamed for the chaos. This is the discussion that followed.

—ED

Ronald Hilton [Humanities Special Programs, Stanford]. Professor Girard has suggested a kind of dichotomy between the revenge of the organized tribe against the creator of disorder, and the mass, the *turba*, as though it were as simple as that. I think it is more complicated, because you should bring in the term *agent provocateur*. Those of us who have seen *agents provocateurs* realize how it works: I remember during the student disturbances here, on White Plaza, there was a mob of students, the Plaza was full, and standing next to me was a bearded character, obviously not a student, and he began shouting, "Shut it down! Shut it down!" Two girls nearby began shouting, "Shut it down, shut it down!" and within two minutes the whole of White Plaza was shouting, "Shut it down, shut it down, shut it down!" It was a perfect example of an *agent provocateur*. Now, Mr. Girard spoke about the Indians of the Northwest, quoting Lévi-Strauss. Mr. Girard is very well-

*From *Disorder and Order* (Stanford, CA: Stanford Literature Studies, 1984), 89–97. Reprinted with permission.

known as a specialist on the Christian religion. He mentioned the Gospels, but I would like to ask him to apply what I have just said to certain episodes in the Gospels. Firstly, the stoning of the woman caught in adultery; secondly, the condemnation of Jesus Christ; and, thirdly, the condemnation or the killing of Saint Stephen. Were those the work of organized society, or were they the work of the mob, or were they the work of *agents provocateurs*? In the first case the *agents provocateurs* were the Pharisees and the Sadducees, in the second case, likewise, and probably in the third case as well, although the *agents provocateurs* can come from outside the society as in Iran and other places, and so it is much more complicated than just the dichotomy you suggest.

René Girard. I think we already have an example of the "passions" that I said would be aroused. I am not sure I understood the first question, but I would be very glad to comment about Stephen's stoning, especially because in my last book I have devoted about a dozen pages to this episode. I think that stoning is very important as a form of ritual execution which occurs in many primitive societies. If you look at forms of primitive execution in primitive societies you will see that they are always of a type that manages to involve the entire community without involving anyone too directly. No one in particular is responsible and revenge is discouraged. In the case of Jewish law, of course, the first two witnesses are supposed to cast the first stone, which will bring us back to another text of the Gospel, but I feel that the essential point of stoning is that it is a collective form of murder. I think, by the way, that the "primitive legislator," who is supposed to elaborate primitive legislation, including forms of collective execution, must be a collective scapegoat. Another well-known form of execution by the whole tribe is the action that consists not in throwing the suspect from a cliff, but in moving very slowly towards him at the edge of that cliff until he finally throws himself off "voluntarily." The purpose is to have the equivalent of the social transcendence that a judiciary system provides. You have a survival of this, I think, even in firing squad executions when one or two of the guns of the riflemen are not loaded.

Now, in the case of the Gospels, the examples chosen are extremely good because mythology is not present. The adulterous woman who is condemned by her society and is about to be executed would normally be stoned, and she would be stoned by that whole crowd which becomes mimetically incited to do so. The fact that Jesus interrupts the process literally sets up the opposite mimetic contamination, since they leave not *en masse* but one by one, beginning with the older members. So I think that this is one of those texts in which the so-called "rumor" is publicized, namely the fact that the victim of such an act, even though he or she is a legal victim, is in reality the victim of a kind of mob action. In the case of the Passion, of course, the same would be true. The text of the Gospel constantly emphasizes the fact that no one is really guilty, and *agents provocateurs* are not really very important, contrary to what Mr. Hilton believes. Judas is very unimportant, the denial of Peter is not very important, the politics of Pilate are not very important – what is important is that whatever the particular motivation of every individual participant, all these motivations ultimately resemble so many rivulets running together to form a big river, all flowing in the same direction. I recently gave a reading of the death of John the Baptist in which I show that this death also illustrates that same mechanism. If we look at the Old Testament, we find very much the same thing. Consider the story of Joseph, which I always take as an example. In the story of Joseph we have eleven brothers, one of whom is expelled and cast out. But instead of adopting the point of view of the eleven brothers, the text adopts Joseph's viewpoint. In the second episode, Joseph is accused of having committed adultery with the wife of his protector, which is the equivalent of the incest of Oedipus, and the whole crowd of Egyptians accepts that accusation and they punish it, and they put Joseph in jail. But the text of the Bible tells you that this *official message*, which is the myth is not to be believed. It is some kind of mythology the Egyptians believed in but not the Jews, not those who wrote the story of Joseph. All these texts are perfect examples of what I am talking about in the sense that the illusion of the mob is denounced as illusion instead of being accepted as true, as in the case of our Dogrib myth, which, I believe, uncritically reflects the perspective generated by a mob phenomenon.

Hilton. Mr. Girard, you didn't discuss the case of Christ, where the crowd was divided. You didn't bring up the question of the role of Christ and the Sadducees urging the crowd on.

Girard. Well, the crowd is divided at the beginning, but finally it becomes mimetically united. Finally, the entire crowd unanimously says the same thing, and it is important that the supreme power, Pilate, the man with the power to kill, is led by the crowd and does not lead it, so it is obviously a situation where it is not the political power that decides, but the crowd that supersedes this political power. It is the same in the case of John the Baptist; Herod is forced against his will to follow the guests at his banquet who side with Salome and demand the head of John the Baptist.

Jane Arnold [News & Publications, Stanford]. I hope I have so far understood you as not to make my question a repetition of anything, but it often seems to me that of these legends, the most important are those that had the most important consequences for culture and for order. The victim of the mob is already a sort of leader figure, as in the case of Jesus, as in the case of Oedipus, or becomes a leader and an establisher of a new order, as in the case of the Dogrib woman. Could you comment on this dual role of being both the leader and the victim?

Girard. Yes, I think there are reasons for choosing victims. In normal circumstances the victims can be leaders. The tendency for crowds to turn against their own leaders is something we observe every day. There are also other reasons for which victims are picked. They are picked because they do not belong to the majority religion or because they look different. The interesting thing for me is that, if we start examining mythology carefully, we find that the reasons why certain people are picked as victims have not changed. Some of these attributes are difficult to see, because they are not transcultural. For instance, the problem of Judaism in a Christian society is not transcultural; no equivalent phenomenon can be observed in mythology, but the man who limps tends to be regarded askance in a very backward crowd; there is a tendency to move against the man who limps that is already visible in animals. If you look at mythology, you will see that all the infirmities that can still attract persecutors are attributes of great mythological heroes. You will see that in late mythical elaboration there is a tendency to minimize or eliminate entirely these features of "supernatural" beings. They are also great leaders, but the question of whether they become great leaders before or after their death is, I think, in a sense a moot point. It is a question that in most instances cannot be answered and that in a way is fairly irrelevant. I would say that poor people are oppressed; the indigent are persecuted; also the sick, the crippled, and the plague-ridden, and so forth, but great leaders are too: all extremes in a society, everything outside the system is a target for persecution. In a way the great leader is at the center, but the center is somewhat like the eye of a cyclone. It is a quiet center, and when trouble enters, the system tends to collapse and reform around a victim. This is my view. Therefore the tendency to victimize leaders is quite real but it is only a small part of the story. In the last analysis, the victims are random, I think, because even if there is no one in a crowd with a distinguishing feature of the types that polarize crowds, there will still be a victim beyond a certain point of tension, the selection of whom will depend on such insignificant factors that they must be called random.

[**Question**]. I have the impression that the myths and rituals that appear in hunting societies are different in a qualitative way from those that appear in farming societies, and perhaps the former are not quite so malignant as the latter. I feel this ties in with the sacrifices of Cain and Abel, but I wonder if you have any comments to make on this?

Girard. I do not think that it is right to pose first the question of "malignancy" – I feel we should try to talk in a dispassionate way. I think it is quite true that hunters usually have no human sacrifice of the type found in agricultural societies. Certain anthropologists in a certain period in the past made a great deal of that. I really think that hunting techniques, like every other technique, originate in sacrifice. Primitive hunting is always a sacrifice. If you think of hunting big animals and so forth, you will see that the organization demanded by hunting, which is extremely complex, is taught to human beings by sacrifice. I am trying to say that sacrifice is the birth of the order of culture, and I mean this seriously. This would be an example of it. We usually see rituals behind social customs when these customs are rigid and inconsequential. When we see a society go into a great ritual disorder because there is less and less sunshine at the beginning of the winter, we are tempted to say, "Ho ho, these fools, they believe that the sun is a god, and that by going into a great agitation, they are going to force the sun to behave in a friendlier way." But if you look at techniques of winemaking, cheesemaking, metallurgy, all of the great Neolithic techniques, you will see they are all associated with the ritual, and the type of prohibition that would prevent all action is really the opposite of ritual, which demands that things be mixed and that something be done with them. When something occurs such as the fermentation of a product that generates an alcoholic beverage or creates a new food, we claim the purpose is "economic," but if we examine the ritual process associated with winemaking we must discover that this is the same ritual process as in seasonal ritual or, by the way, funeral ritual, because dead bodies are submitted to exactly the same type of techniques that in other instances result in food processing. Therefore there are good reasons to believe that ritual has a tremendous plasticity that may result in institutions very different from each other, some of which can be truly productive.

Carl Rubino [Department of Classics, University of Texas at Austin]. I would like you to comment on something that was suggested to me by your talk. What do you see now as the difference between myth and history? The reason I ask is this: Voltaire said, "history is written by the victors!" and you seem to suggest, in both your last book and today, that myth is a kind of fake history written by the victors, and real history, as in the Bible, is written by the losers.

Girard. That is a very good question, which was already asked and answered by Nietzsche. However, there is no chance that I will repeat the response of Nietzsche, who sided with the victors, that is, against the truth of persecution. Ultimately, Nietzsche felt that history should be remade by the victors, and that the problem with our world is that the victims talk too loudly. I think it is the greatest depth of Nietzsche to have recognized that. It is also the ugliness of Nietzsche, his explicitly anti-Jewish, anti-Christian stance, that he sides openly with the victors, rather than with the victims.

It is wrong, however, to believe that the victims, spontaneously, have a perspective that is fundamentally different from the perspective of their persecutors. In Greek tragedy, the victims speak but they speak in a vengeful fashion whereas in the gospel they do not; nor do they agree with their persecutors. There is something amazing about our reading of the witch hunts in the sixteenth century. You know, interpreters often do not believe any longer in what they are doing, because they hold that there are as many messages as there are interpreters, and that every interpreter has a new message. This is perfect for professors of literature who want to keep writing forever about the same texts with no practical consequences whatever. In the seventeenth and eighteenth centuries, when intellectuals started to reject the witch hunts they did something that professors of literature would not dare to do; they read records of witch hunt trials and interpreted them in a dogmatic fashion, against the authors, against all witnesses. Everybody directly involved in these trials maintained that the witches were guilty, and usually the accused herself said she was really a witch. Perhaps she had been tortured, perhaps she had not, perhaps it was a way for her to be part of the system and to assert her individual existence. And then historians, two centuries later, came and dared say, "This is nonsense. We have the only correct interpretation which makes nonsense out of all this." The historian is right, of course, and the nihilism of modern interpretation regarding the problem of representation has to face the truth of that interpretation.

Are we going to give up the difference between magical thought and its demystification in the name of a greater skepticism which really destroys all the basis of interpretation today? I don't think we can. That is why I think we have to go back to this amazing feat of modern interpretation, which I consider the greatest of all and which, in spite of that, is never defined – its specificity, which I am trying to define now, is not something that has interested the specialists of interpretation. I think history is the possessor of that interpretation, and the structuralists do not see this. The most advanced reading, the most advanced interpretation, is in the hands of the historians, but they do not perceive their own superiority; and they do not know how relevant they are to the understanding of mythology, because they have been intimidated out of their wits by nihilistic "theory," especially in France.

Gerald Weisbuch [University of Aix-Marseille II]. Listening to your talk, I asked myself whether the ideologies of revolution have something to do with myth as you analyze them.

Girard. I am not sure I understand your question.

Weisbuch. There is a general mythology held by the political left that real change can be achieved only through violence, and so there is some sort of myth of foundation of a new order.

Girard. Well, I agree to a certain extent. The articles of such people as Vincent Descombes on the French Revolution aptly describe the French Revolution as a founding myth. At the same time one has to be very careful, we live in a world where biblical aspects are necessarily present and interfere with the operation of violence and the sacred.

Rubino. I want to say two things. When you say that history is the interaction between the discourse of the losers and the discourse of the winners, you leave yourself open to the kind of free play which the textualists will drag in on you.

Girard. You use the word "discourses" – I would not use this word in the current sense. I would emphasize the *reality* of victims behind the interaction behind the discourses. Language is important, but it is also an event in the world. What is amazing about these records of persecution in the Middle Ages is that they are distorted and include fantastic elements. Yet, in spite of the fantastic elements, we say there are real victims behind the text; there is a real historical event. In other words, there is a type of text for which it is possible to say, "because certain things are obviously false, the likelihood of other aspects to refer to real victims is increased," which is really amazing from the standpoint of interpretation, but unquestionable. If you find in a text the common, vulgar prejudice of the persecutors, and then these naïve persecutors say, "We have killed these people," you have a good reason to believe they speak the truth. In order to make sense out of the text you must trust them in respect to some things and not in respect to others and then everything fits, and you have a perfect reading. It is not merely for moral reasons that we have stopped burning witches; it is also for intellectual reasons. We looked at this text, and we realized that the part of the text that is necessarily false makes it highly probable that the rest is true. Any one text could be a forgery but the total number of texts is such that we can be absolutely sure that most victims were real. I am not going back to some kind of historical reading – it is still a structural reading, but in order to have the right structural reading, you must postulate the reality of the victim. Only real persecutors say certain things and tend to distort their victims in a certain fashion.

Rubino. May I say one more thing? When reading your last book about the Bible, and listening to you again today, it strikes me that the Bible is too simplified a concept, even within your own discourse, because the Bible is also the product of an appropriation and it is also in a sense the discourse of the victor, because what you refer to as the Old Testament was not the Old Testament until it was appropriated by the Christians.

Eric Gans [Department of French, University of California at Los Angeles]. I've known René for a very long time. I was one of his first Ph.D. students, I imagine, and I have been led by Professor Girard's work to take an interest in some of the questions he has raised. It seems to me that the question previously asked about the differences between the mythologies of hunting societies and agricultural societies is extremely relevant, and I am not quite sure that René's answer to it was altogether adequate. It would seem to me that one could postulate that in hunting societies, which were essentially egalitarian, there is a different use for mythology and a different use for ritual than in agricultural societies, which rather quickly become hierarchical, and that the difference in the mythology would seem to reflect a different ideology of the whole complex of myth and ritual, which is to say that, instead of saying that hunting comes from sacrifice, because one can always show ritual aspects in the hunt, it would be much simpler to say that sacrifice in a sense comes from hunting, with the understanding that in the early hunt there is no distinction to be made between hunting and sacrifice. This is not simply a trivial question because it poses the whole question of the relation between the competitive and what you might call the "aggressive" or the purely metaphysical which is, I think, at the heart of Professor Girard's theory of desire and also of his theory of cultural structure. In other words, if you start with the hunt you start with something that is good to eat or, at the very least dangerous and has to be eliminated. It is easy to see how the animal that is hunted could then evolve into a human victim in terms of ritual – in other words, after the hunt, you tend to imitate the hunt, you tend to have someone play the role of the animal, and as society becomes more complex, and in particular, as it becomes more hierarchical, the usefulness of having a human victim becomes greater, and eventually usurps the purely competitive role of the animal. I don't intend to give a speech, and I intend in any case to put this all in a book, but I would at least like René to respond to this on a preliminary level.

Girard. One thing I will say about your first point is that differentiation or asymmetry as a definition of society does not imply hierarchy; all societies are segmented, therefore differentiated, but in a society which has two *moîtiés* there is not necessarily a hierarchy between the two. I do not really think there is too much difference between a hierarchical society and a segmented society. What you say about hunting coming first is very nice, I think, and very good, but, if you look at the evidence – well, if I accepted your theory, I could no longer connect my theory of desire with my theory of victimage. [*Laughter.*] Half of it would be destroyed. Speaking more seriously, there is no real evidence for your view.

Note

1. Foreword to *Disorder and Order: Proceedings of the Stanford International Symposium (Sept. 14–16, 1981)*, ed. Paisley Livingston (Stanford, CA: Stanford Literature Studies, 1984), v.

CHAPTER 2
OPERA AND MYTH
Philippe Godefroid/1985

While most of the interviews in this volume follow a question-and-answer format, interviewer Philippe Godefroid chose to reproduce only René Girard's replies, which he organized into a monologue. The result drew René Girard out on an unusual topic – opera, and its relationship to myth.

—ED

I'm always drawn to the same problems: anything having to do with mimetic desire, with the role of violence and the sacred, with sacrifice, anything having to do with scapegoating. This means I'm mostly interested in the structure of works, in everything that's communicated not through words, but through the way dialogue or events are organized. I could give you two examples: one from an opera that has become a myth, although nobody can say exactly how or why (*Don Giovanni*); the other a more obvious choice because of its reworking of mythical material (Wagner's oeuvre).

It's the structure of *Don Juan* that I find particularly noteworthy. My generation came of age after the war, and we read, for example, Roger Vailland's *Don Juan*. I'm always surprised by how much all of these historically recent Don Juans are focused on death, on hell. That has always seemed totally uninteresting to me. It's also uninteresting when these seducers become womanizing machines—especially in a world where balconies and chaperones no longer have any meaning, and hell has even less meaning.

So in Mozart's oeuvre, I tend to look for the collective aspects, which are tied to the characters around the main hero, and to see how everything takes on meaning at the moment of Don Juan's death. According to my traditional criteria of interpretation, we're justified in wondering whether Don Juan isn't really and truly mythical, in the sense that his death effects

*From *L'Avant-Scène Opéra* 76 (1985): 115–16. Reprinted with permission of Philippe Godefroid. Translated by Trevor Cribben-Merrill.

a restoration of order, which is underlined by the final quintet (this quintet should never be omitted from stagings of this opera). An order that has been disrupted, a balance that has been disrupted, is reestablished. But disrupted by what? The immediate response would be: by Don Juan himself, since he's the one who pays the price for the disruption. But maybe that's too hasty. Instead we should see that the disorder concerns the way the couples are organized. What's striking is the complicity of the three women: it's obvious in what Donna Anna recounts to Don Ottavio, with the famous "*Respiro!*" Obvious, too, in Zerlina's attitude. And it's undeniable when you see how Donna Elvira keeps returning, motivated solely by her desire to intervene in Don Juan's life. I'd be tempted to see in the Don Juan–Elvira couple a mirror image of the Célimène–Alceste couple in Molière's *Misanthrope*...

We could argue, then, that Don Juan's death is mostly about establishing the myth of the innocence of women – all the more so since the relations between the sexes appear to me to be very equal here, or at least more equal than Leporello's facile myth of Don Juan would have us believe. Moreover, what we know about the idea of the couple in Mozart and Da Ponte (from *Cosí Fan Tutte* and *Les Noces de Figaro*) suggests that for them there's no order in the couple – no immutable order that is, outside of a social order. All you have to do is put on a disguise, or a mask, or deal out the cards differently, and the course of love changes direction. So we're in a game of doubles, where individual identity is less important than rivalry and where strength matters less than the fear of weakness which it gives rise to—a fear that Anna artfully plays on with Ottavio. This idea is even more strongly confirmed when Leporello takes Don Juan's place (masks yet again) and becomes a seducer, which leads to his caning by the group.

All of these collective aspects are typical of the 18th century. They were masked by the nineteenth century, which pinned everything on Don Juan, without looking for another guilty party. In the process, it boils everything down to one individual versus the world, versus God, versus Hell. This erasure of the mimetic aspect and of collective violence glosses over and completely transforms what's really at issue. The 19th century took at face value the figure of the Commendatore, who even in the 18th century might just be a logical attempt, through the intervention of a divinity (in the broad sense of an sublime guarantor of a more material order), to cover up the true circumstances of Don Juan's demise. This sort of intervention is everywhere in mythic narratives like these. To finish the opera with it is to get a cheap thrill from yawning abysses, to scare people so that they're unable to see clearly.

As for Wagner's *Ring*, obviously you'd have to analyze it in greater depth than is possible here. Let's be content with questions pertaining to the structure of this huge work. I'm tempted to say that there are two *Ring* cycles: the group formed by *Das Rheingold* and *The Walküre* on the one hand, and by *Siegfried* and *Götterdämerung* on the other. In *Das Rheingold* the mimetic reading is just too obvious. It's right there, naked, explicit, since the work is based entirely on the mechanisms of desire and doubles. Starting with the first scene, the gold is transformed into the ultimate prize, the absolute source of conflict. Back in the "open air" it will give way to Freia and her golden apples, but it's quite obviously the same mechanism. Loge's speech says as much, and Alberich, referring to the power of his ring, explains it solely by its ability to arouse the desire for gold (gold accumulated, multiplied)—and the curse of the ring sends the same message, because it is exchanging and circulating the gold that breeds conflicts, not its mere existence. Reciprocity must therefore be abolished. Logically enough, that's what *The Walküre* tries and—at least in a certain sense—fails to do, even as the series of violent episodes continues. This series, however, is all the more interesting because the ring is no longer circulating (meaning that desire is already strong enough to do without an object): the momentum of events takes over, and this tends to bring us closer to the world of human beings. In theory, with Siegfried we should find the "new man" capable of breaking the cycle of reciprocities. But no: all the mythological "stuff" from the Prologue reappears—and several characters, too—and is activated.

In particular, the Tarnhelm: the helmet of metamorphoses, which abolishes identities (*niemand gleich*) but also, by erasing differences, makes everyone look alike. As for the hero himself, he conquers authenticity only through murder, just like Sartre's Orestes. In fact, the return of all the symbols condemns the whole enterprise, such that Siegfried manages only to make doubles multiply around him. The two final installments of the *Ring* are a modern remythologization, where true responsibilities are glossed over until the final deconstruction (Brünnhilde's speech, set up by the Norns' scene). It's interesting to note how, in the 19th century, as awareness of mythic violence grows, the temptation to remythologize the individual as such is so strong. In the end, it's the same mechanism as in Don Juan. What's most incredible is that Wagner wrote his libretti in the opposite order to the one in which they were performed—and that the mechanisms of concealment and revelation differ depending on whether you read the work from A to Z or from Z to A.

More generally, all of this is typical of Wagner's constant hesitation between implementing a sacrificial scheme and an anti-sacrificial one. He hesitates between primitivism and Christianity. If the *Ring* were everything it should be, the mythology/Christianity duality would be stated more fully, as it is in all the other works. This duality could be summed up as follows: "The knight crosses himself, and mythology disappears." But the trick lies in deciphering all these "signs," which are sometimes deeply hidden, and sometimes very obvious.

CHAPTER 3
TECHNOLOGICAL POWER IN THE POST-SACRIFICIAL WORLD
Scott A. Walter/1985*

The Stanford-based magazine Birth of Tragedy, *published between 1980 and 1988, was inspired aesthetically by fanzines of the New York hardcore punk variety, as well as the Beat poets. Its publisher, Eugene S. Robinson, recalled that the magazine was designed to be ethically, intellectually, and emotionally difficult to digest, adding "but Girard, a heavyweight in his own distinctly quiet way, did not only meet our expectations editorially, he aggressively exceeded them in an interview that crossed all kinds of hard philosophical lines. And he did so with a grace and élan that impressed even the hardcore crazies on our staff."*

— ED

Birth of Tragedy: In *Violence and the Sacred* you wrote that modern society is an anti-culture, would you say that we are in a sacrificial crisis?

René Girard: That's right, yes. You know people make fun of those people who say well, the modern world is in shambles or chaos, and so on. People have been saying that since the sixteenth century. But in a way it is always true, I would say, instead of being always false. It's always true, in the sense that every new form of art breaks down distinctions that, before, were the rule.

And our world, I think, can take it better than any other world could, so, in a way, it's power. It's power of innovation. You see what I mean, that it is no longer, it [modern society] no longer encounters the barriers to thinking that the primitive society would. The interaction of the old primitive world is collapsing more and more, and the Judaic and the Christian – which are

*From *Birth of Tragedy* 3 (May–July 1985). Published as "Interview with René Girard." Reprinted with permission of Eugene Robinson and Scott A. Walter.

fundamentally anti-sacrificial, you see – the Judaic and the Christian never really triumph in our world. They are always shunted back, even by the people who claim they represent it. Do you see what I mean? But at the same time they have a deep influence on the world.

To talk about that, I always talk about what happened at the beginning of the modern world, when the witch hunt trials stopped. A society which doesn't burn witches is the exception. In order to invent science, in my view, you have to stop burning witches first. You don't stop burning witches because you have invented science. No. It's for religious reasons you stop burning witches.

These religious reasons may look like anti-religious reasons. Some people rebel against sacrificial interpretations of Christianity. But theirs is still a Christian inspiration. Our world, I think, is essentially a conflict between this Judeo-Christian inspiration and more primitive forces which are closer to something we might call "human nature." To such a world you cannot simply apply the principles of analysis outlined in *Violence and the Sacred*. In my opinion, this book has no relevance to our modern society.

BOT: And yet you mention modern society many times …

RG: Yes, symbolically … if you want. Why is Greek literature still significant in our world? I think it's because the "sacrificial" remnants in our society, the leftover sacrificial rules, are always breaking down and symbolically, our relations often resemble those of Greek tragedy. But we rarely kill one another.

BOT: These remnants are like Nietzsche's "shadows of god"?

RG: The shadows, yes, if you want. Complex forces shape our world, and we cannot talk about it as neatly as we can talk about *primitive* institutions. I wish we could – I'm a highly systematic individual, you see, and I'm quite different from many of my colleagues. We live in a world today, especially in the humanities, where the very notion of truth has become the enemy. The idea is you must have plurality. So, today, the interest of plurality takes precedence over the search for truth. You have to say ahead of time that you don't believe in truth. In most of the circles in which I move, decency is equated with a skepticism verging on nihilism. Engineers know there are solutions that work and solutions that don't work. Well, in the humanities, we are also looking feverishly for solutions but we are not supposed to find any. In intellectual life today, there is a sort of paralysis, because people are so afraid of not being nice enough to each other – you know, offending the opinion of the next fellow, that they've given up the search for truth very often. Or they regard it as evil in itself, which I think is wrong. Do you see what I mean? It's going too far the other way. They are so afraid of dogmatism that they prefer to reject all possible beliefs. The number one imperative is the avoidance of conflict. We can only succeed through sterility.

BOT: You mentioned that today we have a power that ancient societies did not have. Were you referring to technological power?

RG: Yes, I mean undoubtedly the power of technology, because I think that a sacrificial society has built-in safeguards against excessive innovation. It is not true, of course, that all primitive people "respected" nature. Some of them burned an entire forest to grow one bushel of corn or something. But, nevertheless, in most primitive societies people were afraid of tampering with nature – even cutting off trees to open a plot of cultivable ground, because they feared there were geniuses and gods there. So they were terribly scared because the world itself was sacred – the water, the trees, the mountains, and so forth. This is no longer true in our world. The pagan gods were destroyed by monotheism and collective victimage has lost its magical power of deterrence. The result is a world in which natural forces are manipulated without religious inhibitions and technological progress becomes possible with all its beneficial consequences, and also its dangers, of course, if the beneficiaries do not abide by the golden rule. People will acquire power, more and more power.

BOT: The power that used to be in the sacred rituals?

RG: That's right. It will become the property of man, you know, usable energy. The question is what are the people going to do with this power? If they keep using it against each other, someday they are going to reach a point of no return, where it becomes non-usable, because the power is so great that you cannot hurt your neighbor without hurting yourself. Which is the case today with the nuclear winter, etc.

BOT: Reciprocity at the international level has always been a fact, even if unperceived, now and in the distant past.

RG: The thing which is interesting I think in our world is that an awareness of human vengeance as the supreme danger is back with us. Because if you go back to the great literature of the past, the Bible, Greek Tragedy, you see it's all dominated by the problem of revenge. In a world without judicial institutions, very small peasant communities, revenge, unleashed revenge, can destroy an entire community. Now, critics in the nineteenth and twentieth centuries didn't recognize that at all. They themselves, I think, were living in a world which was too protected. They had judicial systems. Revenge was under control, inside the community, and war was still remote. Curiously, our situation, which is very different from that of small primitive societies in other respects, is very similar in respect to vengeance. We are a world community, which is like a primitive village because the means of destruction today, in proportion to the world as a whole, are similar to what they were in the tragic world described by Aeschylus. Certain realities about human reciprocity are coming back to the fore.

BOT: Such as the reality that the whole community is in danger?

RG: The whole community is in danger, yes. And that there are no possibilities of sacrifice to ward off the threat.

BOT: You have written that there is a lack of law in Western society. Would you care to explain that?

RG: First, there is a lack of international law. But today mutual deterrence is a *de facto* international law that can be transgressed only at the cost of terrifying destruction, complete annihilation perhaps. This law has forced itself upon us as a result of our inability to entirely give up vengeance and violence in a world deprived of sacrificial protection. We love the increased power provided by the Judeo-Christian demystification of primitive religion but we failed in regard to the increased ethical responsibility that goes with it. We owe our increased power to an abandonment of magical thought that is rooted in our religion, ultimately. If we assume this power in a spirit of arrogant superiority, as the West has done, if we believe rationality alone can solve all problems, it doesn't seem to work, and suddenly people find themselves back into vengeance. So, there is a great danger of regression. Nevertheless, I think that our evolution is always in the direction of less vengeance, because we understand more and more the horror of it. At the same time, the danger I repeat is greater than ever, because of the enormous means we have. We live in a world where a great deal more is demanded of the communities and of each individual in terms of self-mastery. But at the same time, very often our world is one which abandons ethics, which abandons any ideal of self-mastery. We surrender to a philosophy of self-gratification that ends up in pure consumerism. It is a disturbing sign.

BOT: What similarities and differences exist between your thought and Nietzsche's concept of the master-slave relationship, outlined in *On the Genealogy of Morals* and his later writings?

RG: Well, I have been thinking about this recently, and I think that Nietzsche shared a great insight with his entire period, the great insight of modern anthropology which remains valid today in my opinion. He realized that all religions, including Christianity, are centered upon the same type of collective victimage.

He wrote several times that the "martyrdom" of Dionysus (collectively killed and devoured by the Titans) and the martyrdom of Jesus, the Christian Passion, are similar. The anthropologists also perceived that similarity and they concluded that all religions are more or less similar, including the biblical and Christian religions.

These anthropologists were positivists. They believed that the meaning must be the same if the facts are the same. They believed that a fact is inseparable from its meaning. They could see more or less the same fact everywhere and they believed that the meaning had to be more or less the same everywhere.

Not so with Nietzsche, who was no positivist. He could see that the same collective murder can mean two entirely different things if it is interpreted from the standpoint of the victimizers – the so-called masters – and from the victims – the so-called slaves. Nietzsche realized that victimage is everywhere interpreted from the standpoint of the victimizers except in Judeo-Christianity which views it, as a rule, from the standpoint of an *innocent* victim, especially in the Passion. This standpoint casts doubt, inevitably, on the justice of pagan "sacrifices." That is the reason Nietzsche accuses Christianity of slandering and of discrediting paganism. He reproaches Christianity for making human sacrifice "impossible."

This is the same Judeo-Christian difference I mentioned earlier. I think this difference is truly essential and my views could be defined as some kind of Nietzscheism in reverse. Nietzsche was terribly wrong to choose the deceptive violence of mythology over the biblical revelation of this same violence as deceptive victimage.

As a result of this dreadful choice which he pursued with an intellectual consistency worthy of a better cause, Nietzsche, in his last years, forced himself to become an apologist for the worst forms of cultural violence. In *Twilight of the Idols*, for instance, he glorified the cruel treatment of the Untouchables in the Indian caste system as something absolutely necessary to the production of a true elite, a genuine aristocracy. It is correct to assert that such positions anticipate Nazism and this kind of text was frequently quoted by the theoreticians of National-Socialism.

Personally, Nietzsche was a kind and humane individual. The reason he made such a terrible choice, which finally drove him to madness, or was already a symptom of his madness, lies with some of the secondary consequences of Christianity, such as he observed them in his own world.

A religion of the *innocent* victim, a religion that goes against the immemorial tradition of sacrifice in human culture, will produce a lot of hypocrisy, a lot of false compassion, a lot of *ressentiment,* as Nietzsche says, as soon as it is imperfectly embraced. Given the imperfection of real human beings, it is more or less certain that Christianity will be imperfectly embraced.

The terrible error of Nietzsche was to see these faults in our world not merely as the illegitimate child but as the father and creator of the biblical religions. You cannot have a parody of the victim's truth before the genuine article has first appeared into the world. This truth appears nowhere in mythology, it appears only in the gospels and "prophetic" text of the Bible.

Nietzsche correctly saw that the Christian world had weakened and interiorized revenge rather than given it up entirely, as recommended by the gospels. The medicine he proposed was worse than the disease. It was to go back to real revenge, which is a little bit like blowing yourself up because you have a mosquito biting you, or something like that. I think that resentment, hypocrisy, negative feelings in our society can be very dangerous, but they are nothing compared with the potential of destruction with real revenge. And now we can see it. In other words, what Nietzsche said about the superman is completely outmoded today, outmoded by the nuclear weapons. I think that even though it's fair for Nietzsche to say that the Nazis misinterpreted him, in a way there are many things in the later Nietzsche that can be misinterpreted.

BOT: Nietzsche's taking the side of the "masters" was not an aspect of Perspectivism?

RG: Perspectivism was all over the place in the days of Nietzsche. He didn't invent that. But, on Christianity and the Judaic, I repeat, he was extremely original. He saw the truth. But he was hostile to it, which had something to do perhaps with his being the son of a Protestant minister, reacting against his family. I think that there was something childish about his reaction. I don't say he was a Nazi, but you understand. I say he wrote in a manner that could provide an alibi for the worst excesses of the Nazis. It is the same thing with Sartre. Sartre was misinterpreted of course, but he spoke such a violent language that he influenced the people in Cambodia who perpetrated the genocide of their own people. I would not say you shouldn't read Sartre, and if you read him literally, you will see that he preaches violence. If you read Nietzsche literally, you cannot deny that he preached violence. There will always be people to interpret modern thinkers literally. I really think the ideologists in our world, the Marx, the Engels, the Lenin, the Nietzsche, or the Sartre, if you deny their responsibility, you deny the seriousness of their ideas. Nietzsche is both very great and very dreadful.

BOT: Moving even farther back in Nietzschean thought now, to the *Birth of Tragedy*, how do you view his separation of Apollo and Dionysus as conflicting elements in the Greek psyche?

RG: I think Nietzsche used the names of two different gods in order to describe two phases inside the same violent process that is the process of all mythology and ritual. If you observe the Apollo in the first two plays in the *Oresteia* of Aeschylus, you will see that he is not "Apollonian" in the Nietzschean sense at all. He is a dreadful god of revenge. But in the third play, *The Eumenides*, he looks much more peaceful and serene, he becomes Apollonian in the Nietzschean sense, because the time has come for the cultural re-ordering that is really a product of victimage. In the Aeschylean tragedy, the successful victimage is the murder of Clytemnestra and Aegisthus by Orestes.

Dionysus, in the scheme of Nietzsche, embodies the most violent aspects of pagan and primitive divinity. The embrace of these violent aspects, divorced from the reconciliation that follows, I must see as another sign of Nietzsche's irresponsibility or incipient madness. I believe it would have been interpreted that way by the ancient Greeks. The idea of embracing Dionysus "in the raw" would never have occurred to anyone in his right mind. It could only occur to a very blasé nineteenth-century esthete who was tired of the secure world in which he lived and wanted to conjure up the "dionysiac" forces that had been imprisoned by Western civilization.

If Nietzsche were back among us, he might be able to come back to his senses and rectify his thinking in accordance with later historical developments. But the ideas of some of his disciples are not too encouraging.

BOT: I think later on he recognized that Dionysus was life as well as death.

RG: That's right. It's very interesting to relate it to the Wagner of the "Ring" more than people have done. People read Nietzsche, and if they read Nietzsche they are philosophers and so forth, and Wagner is the villain. If they read Wagner they are musicians and Nietzsche is the villain, who did not understand Bayreuth. It's a very important moment in European culture, when that breakdown of Western ideals – of classical order [took place]. Before, they had Romanticism. Romanticism was still tame compared to Wagner and Nietzsche. Nietzsche and Wagner, I think, are the immediate forerunners of the collapse of Europe. From a cultural point of view it's great because it happens there and it takes form there. It takes the form of works of art. At the same time, it's a very negative moment. I don't think you can take it as an ideal, or as a guide. You can take it as a symptom, or as an example, or as a lesson for other things. But I think it is dangerous to see it as an ideal for youth, for instance, or as the title of your magazine, it's kind of scary. [*Laughter.*] Except, the history of American intellectual life, if you want, is different from Europe because America has suffered from passivity and intellectual – I wouldn't say stagnation – but in philosophy and these things ... I don't think it has the same meaning here. I think here it can have a good meaning.

BOT: What is your opinion on the influence of French thought in the U.S.?

RG: Last year they had the articles about French novels in the *Wall Street Journal* that infuriated the French. They say there hasn't been a French novel and so forth. In a way, in the humanities and the social sciences, French influence has never been as great as it is today, with French critics like Foucault and Derrida and that sort of thing. But they are all post-Nietzschean nihilists. In a way, they transmit Nietzschean nihilism to the American body politic. [*Laughs.*] I'm not sure it's very good. I'm sure it's undergoing a process of transfiguration when it reaches this country. I don't want to say they are sole Nietzschean. They represent something on their own which is weird, but ... The active groups in the humanities and the social sciences are influenced by these French views, which I do not share, even though some people feel I am very much part of it. [*Laughs.*]

BOT: What do you view as the sacred? What is the sacred?

RG: When I use the word sacred, myself, I use it as a translation of the Latin. It's a Latin word, *sacer*, which means cursed and blessed simultaneously. It means extreme violence and peace. It's really this ambivalence, and I really think it's a process through which human violence is transfigured.

Primitive societies and their religions exist, in my view, as a result of this transfiguration, and human violence finally absorbs itself through these victimage mechanisms that I'm talking about. The sacred is that process. I see it basically as a human process, which today we can understand. The paradox is that this demystification comes from the Bible. The holy in the Bible, especially as you get to the greater books of the Bible – it means something which has nothing to do with violence and which reveals the other sacred as what it is, as bad. For me there would be two forms of religion, and modern rationalism and atheism are sandwiched in between. That would be the paradoxical aspect of my view. So, personally, I am Christian, I am a believer, but I think there are aspects of rationality in the Judaic-Christian scriptures that inform us about certain aspects of our world, and that do so independently of religious belief. This reversal of the viewpoint of the persecutors who believe in their victim, to the viewpoint of the victim, can be expressed in purely rational terms. So, I don't think you have to be a believer to understand and accept certain of the things I say. But it makes it impossible to have a very naïve view of the Bible as superstition, like the eighteenth century had. Does that make sense?

BOT: The Bible is ignored, and as you said before, it has become another form of sacrifice.

RG: Yes, that's right, the expulsion of the text. It's especially true in universities. Or, the text is sometimes regarded in a very fetishistic way. Some of the old-style believers don't dare touch it and say every letter is true, period. Regard it as some kind of absolute... Intellectuals don't want to touch it, either.

BOT: So things aren't really sacred today?

RG: No, I think that the sacred in the sense of primitive religion is still present in our lives. For instance, when people are overly impressed by something, by power, there are aspects of the sacred. It's a mixture of fear and veneration that influences their behavior. You see that very much in totalitarian societies. Totalitarian societies are regressive in their very effort to get rid of the sacred through violent means. They tend to damage seriously the independent judicial institutions. They need scapegoats much more than we do. The trials in which the victim is forced to confess publicly are extremely significant. Their purpose is to restore the unity of the community through a *unanimous* condemnation of the victim, which is the very essence of "scapegoating."

BOT: That's an incredible phenomenon.

RG: It's a Job phenomenon. I think it's a sign of regression to primitive phenomena. It's very scary.

BOT: How does mimetic desire affect modern society?

RG: It affects society both in a negative and positive way, through fads and fashions, through sterile rivalries, and also through productive rivalries. When people talk about an economy of incentives, they rely on the channeling of mimetic desire into economic life. It's interesting in relationship with the socialistic world, which wants to do away with mimetic desire for ethical reasons, and ends up depriving economic life of all incentive. In their optimism, the socialists believed that, in a world where there would be no conflicts, no social conflicts, people would work with pleasure, in order to create for the good of the community. Unfortunately, it doesn't seem to be happening. They have deprived economic life of its most powerful engine and it's becoming so obvious today, that Russian style socialism is losing its attractiveness even to many third world countries such as China. In order to become economically productive (as it is in the Western world) mimetic desire must be both very intense and severely constrained by strict rules, which I would define as elaborate post-sacrificial devices. If you transgress the rules of this mimetic competition, for instance, if you shoot your competitor when he beats you at your own game, you will be arrested. It's a very complex world, where there are still prohibitions, but ones much less constraining than those ancient societies.

BOT: *Violence and the Sacred* is concerned mainly with Western and primitive concepts of religion. What is your view of Buddhism?

RG: I think it's all methods, recipes, working on oneself, in order to get rid of mimetic desire. Or the idea of the wheel of existence and so forth is very tied up with that. The purpose is to obtain complete peace of mind. This non-involvement is a very general trend in the great mystical religions of the East. There is some of this in the mysticism of medieval and early modern monasticism but, as a whole, it is not characteristic of the West because it is not characteristic of Judeo-Christianity. Buddhism sees that desire immediately involves you with other people. The endless process of rivalries and frustration they see very well. The difference with the biblical world is that they leave the world to itself. They know that not everybody will be a Buddhist monk. They know that there will be victimage. The Bible wants to go to the bottom of the social process, and uncover past victims.

The Bible has an ideal of non-desire inside society, rather than by leaving society.

BOT: Well, supposedly the end point of meditation, Zen meditation, is merging with the Buddha.

RG: That's right. Not with the Buddha personally because in Buddhism, Nirvana is an impersonal state and most people would say that pure Buddhism should not be defined as a religion. There is no concept of a divinity or it is unessential.

BOT: It's all around us.

RG: It's all around us, yes, that's it. But it's certainly cutting off whatever ties you down to the present situation.

BOT: In conquering mimetic desire, it seems you need to add the fourth element, which is time. Instead of everything occurring at once, our desires converging on the object while time disappears – if you sit back and let time pass, as Hamlet tried to do, you may break the circle of desire.

RG: You mean the conquest, the recovery of the time dimension, being contemplation, yes, that's true. I think there are aspects of contemplation in the East and West that are very similar to each other. But Western religions tend to want to act upon the world rather than withdraw from it.

BOT: And we have.

RG: And we have, yes, for better and for worse.

CHAPTER 4
THE LOGIC OF THE UNDECIDABLE
Thomas F. Bertonneau/1987*

Thomas Bertonneau's interview with René Girard took place on March 7, 1987, following Girard's lecture on "Sacrifice and Deconstruction," given under the sponsorship of the graduate students of the UCLA French Department and its journal Paroles Gelées. *Bertonneau, at that time a doctoral student in the UCLA Program in Comparative Literature, began the interview by invoking what Paul de Man refers to as "the Resistance to Theory," in an essay of that name.[1] "Just such a resistance had haunted my reading of Prof. Girard's work; and it had been evident in a number of questions put to him by his audience," he recalled. In an email, he wrote, "If I experienced any nervousness on the occasion of the interview, Girard immediately put me at ease. I conducted two other interviews for* Paroles Gelées. *Without mentioning any names, the contrast with Girard could not have been greater. That makes Girard stand out all the more in my memory."*

—ED

Thomas Bertonneau: Your lecture today had the same effect on me as your books, which I confess is ambiguous. On the one hand, your arguments persuade me; on the other hand, I'm so persuaded as to feel somewhat suspicious. A certain innate skepticism asserts itself which leaves me feeling uncomfortable. I might add that a poll of local readers reveals a similar response. Are you aware of the "resistance to Girard's theory," and if so, to what do you attribute it?

René Girard: Resistance to theory is really quite an interesting idea. But do you mean a resistance to theory among the theoreticians? [The interviewer assents.] One could, in fact, view contemporary theory itself as a resistance

*From the journal *Paroles Gelées* 5, vol. 1 (1987): 1–24. First published as "The Logic of the Undecidable: An Interview with René Girard" in *Paroles Gelées*. Reprinted with permission of Regents of the University of California, *Paroles Gelées*.

to theory ... But if your ambiguous reaction to my books is a fear of what you might perceive as a totalizing principle, then I would assure you that there is no such project in me – no impulse whatever to systematize. While I have undoubtedly developed a *kind* of system, and while there is no *refusal of theory* in me, the result was not intentional. To put it bluntly, my theory took me by surprise.

Bertonneau: Your remark takes *me* a bit by surprise. What exactly do you mean?

Girard: Mind you, I will need to be subjective in order to explain myself; so, of course, what I report may be a purely subjective illusion – I don't know . . . But when I first started working with mimetic theory [in the early 1960s] I noticed some pretty amazing effects. Quite suddenly, all these novels by Dostoyevsky, Zola, and Flaubert made sense. And yet it was still, somehow, diffuse. At that point the victimage theory presented itself to me. On the one hand I was flabbergasted, but on the other hand I was not surprised at all. Do you know why?

Bertonneau: It sounds as if something like Jung's Collective Unconscious was hard at work.

Girard: You are being ironic, of course. But whatever explanation you prefer to invoke, I felt that it was none of my doing. Eugenio Donato, who later became a deconstructionist, advised me to look into anthropology; he thought that I'd find a lot of material on mimeticism and victimage in anthropological texts. And, up until then, I had, in effect, rejected anthropology. Donato said to me, "Read it, you really ought to read it." So I read it, under his influence, I guess you'd say. That's when things started to fall into place. One, two, three! just like that. It came together so naturally that I simply couldn't be surprised. But, since Donato didn't understand victimage in the way in which I was beginning to understand it, the process wasn't exactly causal. I had no formal intention of providing a universal explanation of cultural development, and, if that's what it proved to be, then I only recognized it after the fact. I'm really just as startled by it as anyone else. But the fact that [the victimage theory] provides a useful explanation for so many things should not prejudice us against it. What if it is the product of my systematizing mind? Should we make that an *a priori* objection to my theory? If we make it an *a priori* that, should a theory move toward systematization, we won't accept it, then I suppose that we will have just that resistance to theory that de Man talks about. In fact, I myself felt that resistance for a while. That's the reason it took me eleven years to write *Violence and the Sacred*: I felt certain that there were errors in my theory, and I was always reading more in order to see whether I would have to make any adjustments. But research just kept confirming the original insight. After a while, I just had to say to myself: "Well, that's the way it is." Maybe there is a tendency toward system in me. I can't say, because, of course. I can't get outside of myself. It's as I said in my lecture: nobody is ever aware of himself as scapegoating another. It's always someone else who is guilty of scapegoating.

Bertonneau: How far is your interest in religion, or indeed the religious element, responsible for the defensive attitude many people seem to take toward your theory?

Girard: I would say ninety-eight-and-a-half per cent; maybe ninety-nine-and-a-half. The religious aspect wasn't there at the beginning, and maybe that's why some scholars can accept *Deceit, Desire and the Novel* but not *Violence and the Sacred*, let alone *The Scapegoat*. Eric Gans said something about me in his introduction to my lecture today that I would like to amend or correct. He suggested that there was a strategic aspect in the order of my work, that religion and, in particular, Christianity, was deliberately omitted from *Violence and the Sacred*. The truth is that when I wrote *Violence and the Sacred* I indeed wanted to include the religious element, to write a "two-sided" book. As I wasn't able to do that, I cut it out entirely. Time was passing and I wanted to publish the book.

Bertonneau: I had wondered about what I had perceived as the conspicuous absence of Christianity from *Violence and the Sacred*.

Girard: Yes … Much of what later became *Des choses cachées* goes back to '67 or '68, or around that time … *Des choses cachées* is really *Violence and the Sacred* plus the Christian element. In some ways I like *Des choses cachées* better than the earlier book. It's more logical, a bit more sound.

Bertonneau: Is it, in your opinion, a serious cultural problem that scholarship in general should reject a comprehensive interpretation of human institutions, such as yours, more or less because it contains a religious element?

Girard: Yes, I think it's a very serious problem. On the other hand, it may well be an inevitable problem. We should perhaps ask ourselves if, after all, the modern university, going back, I mean, to the French and British universities of the late Middle Ages, was founded on a religious principle. The easy answer would be yes. But sometimes I think not. It appears to me that the modern university expels the religious element more or less from the beginning – and perhaps for good reason. Religion is going to be divisive. There's no getting around that. We might well ask whether modern democracy is founded on a religious principle. Again the answer is no: modern democracy also expels the religious – not, perhaps, very graciously, and certainly not to the satisfaction of some parties, but certainly for good reason. And because of this I hesitate to criticize the universitarians for their suspicion of the religious, or even for their non- or anti-religiosity. The expulsion of religion may paradoxically be the unitive element of our world – yet one more embodiment of the victimage principle.

Bertonneau: To Americans at any rate, that expulsion and its positive results seem more or less invisible. There's this clamor on the political right to put religion back into public life, whatever that might entail, and so on.

Girard: We need more time. Do you see what I mean? We need the passage of more history before the necessity of this expulsion will be fully revealed. But it's becoming more visible all the time. And, to come back to what I said a moment ago about the problematics of non-religiosity: I think it's going to make things more difficult, rather than easier, at least in the short term. I think, really, that just this is what deconstruction is all about, and why it's not terroristic, as some of its opponents claim it to be. Deconstruction teaches us, far better than Heidegger, how to live in a "groundless" world, how to avoid the violence inherent in any kind of a foundationalist doctrine.

Bertonneau: I've been curious about your reading of Heidegger [in *Des choses cachées*], and this may be a good point to ask you about it. You react to him as I reported myself to have reacted to you, namely with both admiration and suspicion.

Girard: Yes, yes. And this is because there are so many repressive elements in Heidegger: what I would almost call a worship of the old sacred. That strikes me as pretty scary. I mean, look at his "Speech to the Rectorate" (1934),[2] and some of his other writings from the early or mid-thirties. I really think that they represent a kind of dark worship of this force that Heidegger calls Being— which really isn't a being. It's sinister. And yet there can be no doubt that Heidegger is a genius. Deconstruction owes a great deal to Heidegger. But when you turn to deconstruction, none of those dark elements that haunt Heidegger are present. Deconstruction is – certainly –

nihilistic in its post-modern and post-humanist way; but, as such, it belongs to the modern democratic world. There are no Nazi or fascist temptations, and probably no communistic ones either, in deconstruction. There's no center, so there's no temptation to centralize. It's the death of humanism. Heidegger, the French critics – Derrida, Foucault, Lacan – these all contribute to it.

Bertonneau: Your attitude toward the deconstructionists, like your attitude toward Heidegger, is ambiguous. In *Des chose cachées*, for example, you refer to post-structuralism as a *"vaste syndicalisme de l'échec."* That's a strong phrase. But, I take it, your position is not now so polemical.

Girard: The characterization was strong, yes, and my position has changed. I have become less polemical vis-à-vis my fellow French critics. This is to some extent because I've been so disappointed by the social sciences. I've come to feel that my natural audience is philosophers. Then again it may be that because of age I've become less polemical. It was a combination of these things, I suppose, that sent me back to Derrida to begin to read him again in earnest. I now feel that he must be credited with very powerful readings, and that this is a great thing. There aren't many readings carried out at [Derrida's] level. What he says should and needs to be said. Recently, you know, some books have been published which suggest that Derrida is nothing but Heidegger *rebouilli*, "warmed over," as you might say in English. Likewise with Foucault. It's just not true to say that Derrida brings nothing new or original to the space opened up by Heidegger. He does. And what he brings is creatively and powerfully original.

Bertonneau: People note that Heidegger, at least the early Heidegger, is not as much a textual exegete as is Derrida, and that, because Derrida is, apparently, purely exegetical, it follows that he can't be as original as Heidegger.

Girard: Or, in the same vein, they argue that Derrida doesn't limit himself to philosophical texts, and that he is, therefore, a literary exegete. In the case of "Plato's Pharmacy," for example, Derrida leans toward mythology. But in my opinion this is a great thing.

Bertonneau: The mention of "Plato's Pharmacy" suggests some questions about your theory. The accessory relation of criticism and philosophy to the concealment of the origins of culture in a scene of victimage, one of the strong features of your scheme, intrigues me. I can see how Nietzsche, for example, fits the pattern: where Christianity expels the old sacred, Nietzsche expels Christianity. But it's less easy to see where the post-Nietzscheans find their place. Where, for example, do we locate the concealment of origin in Heidegger?

Girard: I imagine that we would go to what Heidegger, in his text, calls the withdrawal of Being, his history of metaphysics. As I read that history, it moves in parallel with, or is even an allegory of, the movement away from the old sacred and its sacrificial gods. That movement is quite slow, of course, since the influence of the Bible on late antiquity is gradual; and it cannot be considered as a mere duplication of what people call religious faith. When Heidegger claims, then, that there is, for example, no such thing as a Christian philosophy; that, when the Christians start thinking, they simply appropriate Aristotle; and that, therefore, they can't be taken seriously as philosophers—he has duplicated the original expulsion. I sense in Heidegger's total expulsion of Christian thinking something both positive and negative. It reflects the exclusion of Christianity from philosophy, but that's exactly why Christian thinking could come into its own. That's why the Christian Logos was able to come into its own. By the way, I need to correct you on one point. Christianity doesn't duplicate the pre-Christian, the sacred, act of expulsion: it reveals expulsion and clears the ground for something new.

Bertonneau: In *Des choses cachées*, in the chapter on "The *Logos* of John," you discuss the distinction between the Greek or Heraclitean *Logos* and the Christian *Logos*, in the context, in fact, of Heidegger's derogation of the latter. Given that, for you, the history of the West since the time of Christ is articulated on just that distinction, I wonder if you wouldn't explain for me exactly how you measure it.

Girard: The text of Heidegger that I have in mind in that chapter is his *Introduction to Metaphysics* (1935).[3] Heidegger remarks that the word *Logos* appears prominently in the Gospel of John. That's why the Gospel of John has always been considered the most "Greek" of the Gospels. Now the Christians, Heidegger says, always claimed that the Greek Logos was the "little brother" of the Christian Logos. Then the philosophers made the counterclaim that the Christian *Logos* was the "little brother" of the Greek *Logos*. But nobody ever said that they were completely different. Heidegger was the first ever to say so. Heidegger claims that the Christian *Logos* doesn't mean "order" so much as it means "obedience." He also notes that the Christian *Logos* sometimes bears the name of *Kyrix*, which means "herald." In Heidegger's reading, the Son of Man came to earth to call people to obey the Father, casting the Father in the role of a kind of "chief of police." I can't agree with that. But Heidegger's separation of the two *Logoi* is nevertheless significant. As to how we are to understand the Christian *Logos* as different from the Greek: the Christians said of Christ that "he came into his own and no one recognized him," and, of course, no one would dream of a Greek Logos which wasn't visibly present or recognizable. Note that the metaphysics of presence is right there, in the Greek Logos. The Christian Logos, on the other hand, is *not there*. It isn't part of this world, or of the City of Man. That's what the text says. So Heidegger is righter than he knows; he just didn't carry his reading far enough. The *Logos* of John is the excluded *Logos*, or it's the *Logos* of exclusion which speaks about exclusion. Heidegger's definition of the *Logos* is that it keeps opposites together with violence. That's pretty interesting. It's the *Logos* of dialectics, of philosophy.

Bertonneau: It strikes me that there may indeed be some common ground between Heidegger's thinking and your own. This would be in what he calls *Unverborgetiheit*, "unconcealment," modeled on the Greek *Aletheia*. In *Des choses cachées*, you invoke a related concept, that of Apocalypse, which is almost a synonym of *Aletheia*. You describe modernity as apocalyptic. I suppose that just such texts as Heidegger's, or Derrida's, which seem to presage some great transformation in human thought, prompt your characterization.

Girard: Yes, but let me make it clear that by Apocalypse I don't mean the end of the world, which is the vulgar interpretation of the term. When I say that modernity is apocalyptic, I mean that it is revelatory. Certain of the *choses cachées* are being revealed. And I would say that I belong to the same epoch as these thinkers. The difference between their Apocalypse and mine is that mine finds its roots and, naturally, its nourishment, in the Bible and in Christianity. It goes back to the disavowal of the sacred at the beginning of our culture, Judeo-Christian culture. The argument *against* the sacred cannot, if it is to differentiate itself *from* the sacred, use the methods *of* the sacred. Our epoch is characterized by the ongoing revelation of the *human* origin of violence. I think there's a kind of systematic logic to it. A world without sacrificial protection will create all sorts of tools, more and more dangerous, which will threaten those who build them. Technology when applied to destruction functions this way: it reveals or disconceals the human origin of violence. Insofar as the Christian text anticipates this revelation, it is, precisely, apocalyptic. It declares that no violence comes from God, but that violence comes entirely from the human agency. It's one nation against the other; brother against brother. It's force; it's excess. For just these reasons, not only is ours an apocalyptic age; it's an age for which the apocalyptic text of John, and of the New Testament in general, is the most appropriate text. How can we deny John today? And yet there is the mystery that our culture does not speak much of it. All those cartoons which one used to see in *The New Yorker*, with a sort of beatnik character walking along with a sign that reads "Doomsday" —you don't see that much anymore.

Bertonneau: It was Stine, I think, who was famous for those cartoons in the early and mid-fifties. You'd have to dig into the archives to find them.

Girard: Yes, and it's actually rather interesting that they existed then, so close to the beginning of the atomic age. That shows that the situation was already what it is today. Some details may have changed. I'm never sure of the exact distinction between the atomic and the hydrogen bomb. But the *Angst* was already there. Indeed, I would say that people like Heidegger are forerunners of the modern temperament, discerners of a situation that has become more pronounced and more widespread. But my sense of it is, frankly, more optimistic than theirs. Sure, the year 2000 is close at hand, but that doesn't mean that the end of the world is imminent. It means that any radical religious experience in this world must be apocalyptic, must be conditioned by the possibility of total destruction. The ethical imperative today is dominated by that. Any thinking that fails to take into account the fact of the H-bomb will be partial thinking. Now, if it's only a reaction to the possibility of total destruction, it may well run to the superficial. But that too is part of our experience today, which is fundamentally historical. Whatever leaves out contemporary historical conditions must necessarily be banal or superficial. That's why I think a book like *Being and Time* is, to use the language of technology, obsolete. Today our existential experience includes the potential for complete annihilation. Everybody knows that that wasn't there in the 1920s or 30s. In 1986, one cannot read a newspaper without being made aware of man's self-destructive capacity.

Bertonneau: The notion of an ethical imperative is a Kantian notion. In your talk today you used another Kantian term, "the Transcendental." In *Des choses cachées*, you call your anthropology a "Fundamental Anthropology." Today, however, you called it a "Transcendental Anthropology." What, exactly, did you mean?

Girard: I meant "transcendental" in the Husserlian sense, because I said at the same time there was an empirical referent. I meant "transcendental" in the sense that there is a relation [between any particular aspect of culture and some original] ritual however distant. But, since the origin of the ritual has not been witnessed by the people who repeat it, or who manifest its meaning, what I'm talking about is on another level, a reconstructed level. "Transcendental" refers to that level. I mean "transcendental" in the philosophical and not in the religious sense.

Bertonneau: If I follow you, you're saying that your reconstruction of the originary sense is an eidetic reconstruction.

Girard: That's right – eidetic. I wish I had said eidetic instead of transcendental. Transcendental is subject to misreading, whereas eidetic is not.

Bertonneau: Since we're on the subject of terminology, let me ask about the distinction between two terms employed fairly consistently in *Violence and the Sacred* and in *The Scapegoat*, but particularly in the latter. I mean the terms "sacred" and "supernatural." These seem strongly distinguished from each other. In *The Scapegoat* you write that there is a pervasive and undeniable "supernatural" element in the Gospels which you would not wish to denigrate. How far is your reading of the Gospels articulated on these two terms?

Girard: It's not that I tried to use them systematically; but I wanted to show that there cannot be a humanistic reading of the Gospels. In other words, the Father cannot be reduced to some kind of psychological device. You can do this to some extent with Satan. You can call him a figure of mimetic desire, and there might not be much left. Not so with the Father.

Bertonneau: I'm not sure that I follow you.

Girard: One has to assume that everything Jesus says touches on a reality outside of this universe, something out of human reach, which nevertheless acts upon this world. Christ refers to "the One who sent Me." That's not the same as the sacred at all. That's the main thing.

Bertonneau: The supernatural can't be bracketed.

Girard: Not at all. It's part of the very substance of the Gospels.

Bertonneau: It may be that the question of the Gospels is once again the question of the resistance to your theory.

Girard: Yes, of course.

Bertonneau: It may be unfair of me to ask, but does one need faith, ultimately, to accept your theory?

Girard: As I see it, my argument is quite logical. If you understand the old sacred as a closed system, and if you understand the Gospels as a revelation of how that system works, then the Gospel cannot come from within the closure of violence. It can't come from humanity, and therefore it must come from without. If you think that God is violence, then, in effect, you have no god; you've only got your own mediated desires. Now, because violence reigns within its own closure, if God comes into the world of violence, he cannot remain there. The proof that he's God is that he's killed. But having behaved like the anti-sacred God, by submitting himself to death rather than imitating the pattern of violence, he has triumphed over violence. The whole scheme of redemption enters with the temporary presence of God. It's part of the logical sequence of what I would call the anthropology of the Gospels. You cannot contradict it at all. One doesn't need sacrifice, one needn't go back to the old sacred, in order to find transcendence, using that term now in the religious sense. The Gospels constantly recognize this by talking about the intermediate powers, what Paul calls the celestial powers. There are, maybe, these petty gods, but they are not at all identical with the true God.

Bertonneau: The Mosaic injunction against the worship of false gods makes sense in this context.

Girard: And the great continuative between the Old Testament and the New is the refusal of idolatry.

Bertonneau: In this negative proof of the transcendence of God, or of the supernatural, there is something that resembles Derrida's notion of metaphysical closure: we can posit the "other" of a system only as the notion of something outside that system.

Girard: I can agree to some extent. Mind you, Derrida says nothing about the Torah. But there is, in his assertion of multiple centers, none hierarchically valorized over any other, a certain non-violent skepticism. Yes, it's anti-idolatrous, like the work of all great negative thinkers — Nietzsche, for example.

Bertonneau: I suppose that to some extent we must read people like Nietzsche and even Heidegger as religious thinkers, while admitting that such a characterization is almost bound to be misunderstood.

Girard: I would exempt Heidegger on the grounds of what strikes me as his idolatry of Being, or perhaps on account of his cult of the ancient Greeks. Things like that worry me. Not to mention the cult which has formed around Heidegger himself. And maybe certain aspects of his readings of poetry could be considered cultic. I don't really know, however, what Heidegger's religious stance was. Nietzsche is a different case. His anti-Biblical stance is explicit throughout his writings, but it doesn't irritate me, even in spite of my own Biblical orientation. Heidegger, on the other hand, irritates me. This is purely personal. I mean, there are attacks against Heidegger which say, don't read him because he associated with the Nazis, he's tainted, and so on; but I can't buy that kind of simple-minded prohibition. Nevertheless, there is something in Heidegger profoundly sympathetic to some of the worst things to have shown themselves in our century. But he's like Wagner, uncanny because he's so frightening.

Bertonneau: I'd like to direct a question to what you call mimetic appropriation, which one member of the audience today tried to map onto a Marxian model of economic scarcity. The assumption was, apparently, that desire is always provoked by material conditions. As I read you, however, mimesis does not have to be articulated on anything material. Is that correct?

Girard: Yes. Let me explain. First of all, my mimetic theory is not by any stretch of the imagination a scarcity theory, and the Marxian commentators are fully aware of that. The *economic* commentators, on the other hand, are also aware of it, and a number of them are interested in its implications for their field of study. There's a book called *La violence de la monnaie*,[4] due, I think, to be translated into English. It's a theory of inflation, and in my opinion, it's quite good. The authors' thesis has to do with dominance patterns. You understand that in animals, when mimetic desire is played out, you have, as the result of the playing-out, a dominance pattern. The dominated animals will prefer to retreat rather than challenge the dominator. While dominance patterns aren't exactly the same thing as mimetic desire, they prefigure it. We ought not, therefore, confuse mimetic desire, or mimetic appropriation, with the struggle for goods which takes place in the situation of scarcity, as Marxist economics describes it. There's an interesting example that I like to use to illustrate this. It has to do with an experiment in which five children of about four years of age were placed in a room with five identical toys. The toys were of the mass-produced type and were indistinguishable from one another. Now, the first child chooses a toy. The other children, in fact, see no difference between the toys, and, as their behavior shows, the only criterion they have for preferring one toy over another is that someone else has chosen it first. It's rational. I mean, the first child may have seen something special about the toy he chose which is not yet apparent to me. It becomes the superior object and I have reason for desiring it.

Bertonneau: When you call such behavior "rational," I take it that you don't mean that it's particularly reflective, but that it has a certain unconscious but predictable grammar.

Girard: No, no, of course. I contend that most, if not all of the time, mimetic behavior is not aware of itself. But I don't know that much about mimetic desire. What interests me is the conflictual mechanism; and also reversals of mimetic desire: the fact that an obstacle becomes immediately desirable in some situations. All such phenomena, so-called, fall neatly into the mimetic pattern. That must be my systematic penchant at work again. Right now, as a matter of fact, I'm reading Shakespeare's comedies. I feel certain that Shakespeare wrote his comedies in the order of the conflictual configurations, as they ascend in complexity. You can base a logical theory of mimetic desire on a chronology of Shakespeare's comedies. The *Two Gentlemen of Verona* is the earliest and simplest version of mimetic desire. As you progress through the comedies, you have increasingly complex, and perhaps pathological, situations. I'd say that the comedies reflect Shakespeare's increasing understanding of the mimetic principle and are his discovery of mimeticism. The heroes of *Twelfth Night*, you know, are so defensive with one another; and they are quite unlike the heroes of *A Midsummer Night's Dream*. What I would call their pseudo-narcissism is much elaborated over the characters of the previous plays. Once Shakespeare elaborates all the stages of mimetic desire, he stops writing comedies.

Bertonneau: You say that mimeticism is almost always unaware of itself. This remark points up the fact that some kind of unconscious figures prominently, if not always explicitly, in your theory. How does your notion of the unconscious differ from the classic notions of the unconscious, say Freud's?

Girard: It differs from the Freudian unconscious in that there's no great treasure or mystery to be found in my unconscious. It is, you might say, a purely negative unconscious. Enmeshed in ritual, we see nothing. Insight comes only when we are jolted out of ritual practices, or out of our habits. I don't, in fact, like to use the term "unconscious," because it makes everyone think of Freud. And, then, of course, in some of these matters, I remain uncertain. The most that I can say is that up to a certain point in the historical development of the human condition, aspects of that condition remained concealed. Later, they "came to consciousness." The configurations of desire are, after all, supra-individual. The individual isn't much in mimeticism. It's always a pattern, a triune pattern, or something of that sort.

Bertonneau: For Freud, then, the unconscious is the repository of various drives and contents; for you, on the other hand, the unconscious is simply the lack of content —behavior without reflection.

Girard: I'm not certain that I could accept that entirely, but as an approximate formulation it's satisfactory. Somehow, you see, I think we need to get away from the Freudian idea of the unconscious. I mean, Lacan says that the unconscious is language, and that's a good way out if you want to get out of Freud. I can say no such thing, however. But you're right. Freud wanted the unconscious to be a kind of storehouse or determinant. And, if the unconscious is a store, well, somebody has got to mind the store – do you see what I mean? And then, Freud wanted to create a psychoanalytical school, and so forth. He lived in a more substantial – the deconstructionists would say a more metaphysical – world than our own. In those days, one believed in substance. I believe in substance. I mean, I don't deny reality. But what I'm talking about are patterns of human relationships that affect the view one has of reality. Just keep in mind, please, that there is a reality that remains unaffected. When the deconstructionists tell us, therefore, that the structure of something – it might be human culture – is decentered, then I think that they're wrong. I'd say that there are historical periods when structures are decentered. But if something is decentered now, then it was centered at some point.

Bertonneau: This is perhaps the crucial difference between your view of the Western tradition and Derrida's.

Girard: That's right. I would say that the elements of decentering were always there. Derrida would be correct [in pressing for what usually goes by the name of undecidability] insofar as a center always implies a desirable locus, a locus of power, and implies as well its counter-locus. Between the two points a tension will develop. Therefore one welcomes an approach that obviates the necessity of choosing. The verb "to decide" comes – I take it you know this – from the Latinism *decidere*, "to cut the throat." Decisions, then, always echo, however faintly, and reproduce, a certain originary violence. The logocentric demand that we decide partakes, to some extent, of the old sacred, or could at least be traced back to it. The sacred is always violent. But let me say this, that religion is always for peace.

Bertonneau: We're back in the topos of the sacred and the supernatural.

Girard: Yes, and the supernatural, in the Christian sense, respects freedom. Quite literally, it cannot make itself felt as a commanding force. To a certain world, therefore, it remains absolutely out of reach. [The supernatural] is incredibly dangerous to human, especially to bureaucratic, organization.

Bertonneau: You appear to share some common ground with some of the Christian existentialists – I'm thinking especially of Søren Kierkegaard, but also of Gabriel Marcel – in that you distinguish strongly between the Gospel message and its all-too-human appropriation by various and sundry institutions.

Girard: That's true. At the same time, I caution myself that it is deceptively easy to posture as a totally pure individual who can curse institutions because he belongs to none. That's the intellectual's position, isn't it? And I think that the intellectual is right to do that. At the same time, it can be rather facile.

Bertonneau: Especially in the usual case, where the intellectual is employed by some university.

Girard: Yet very often they do curse it and try to undermine it. I've heard some French scholars make speeches in which the first half is "How we can destroy the French University," and the second half is "How the Minister of Education asked me to found a New Department." [*Laughter*] It can get pretty ridiculous. We should avoid that. There's a tendency today to turn institutions into scapegoats.

Bertonneau: Is there anything else that *can* be turned into a scapegoat nowadays?

Girard: None that comes immediately to mind. [*Laughter*] Institutions are the only possible scapegoat today for people who, so to speak, know too much. You can always make the institution appear responsible, or reprehensible. If you make such an accusation, you will always sound pure. Do you see what I mean?

Bertonneau: I think so. An example might be the love-hate relationship between the American electorate and the institution of the presidency.

Someone suggested today that we don't elect presidents so much as scapegoats. It was meant as a joke, but there's some truth to it.

Girard: I'd say that this turning against institutions is almost a worldwide phenomenon. Look at the French and De Gaulle. Or look at Gorbachev blaming the Soviet bureaucracy for the woes of the Soviet economy. What does it mean to solve one's political problems? It probably means to have some sort of ... democratic regicide! [*Laughter.*] You will pardon me; I don't mean to be cynical.

Bertonneau: I'd like to ask a question about the development of your thinking. In *Violence and the Sacred* you appear to be much more interested in reconstructing the originary scene than in subsequent books. Is this a correct perception?

Girard: I think I've said something that bears on this. When I wrote *Violence and the Sacred*, I thought that my natural interlocutors would be the anthropologists. I reached some of them but not many; usually they've rejected dialogue. People have said that this is because I was too polemical with Levi-Strauss. Maybe. But it also has to do with my own training, which was first in history, and only later in literature. I'm not a philosopher, and it might be because I'm not a philosopher that I started to read anthropology from the viewpoint of its drama. I read it as I would Greek tragedy. Euripides, Socrates, and later Shakespeare and Racine—these were great mediators for me. At the same time, I was probably philosophically rather naive.

Bertonneau: As someone whose scholarly activity crosses so many boundaries, would you be willing to endorse the observation that modern academics is too confined inside special disciplines?

Girard: Yes, and, in fact, that's what I was thinking of when I warned against the dominance of what I called, borrowing Husserl's term, the regional ontologies. As a matter of fact, the greatest scholarship in recent times seems to have been generated by people who crossed disciplines: Levi-Strauss, Foucault and others. I would ask of myself today, what exactly is the status of my hypothesis? Is it anthropology or something else? Maybe I should try new titles. There has been a lot of misunderstanding as to what, exactly, I'm about. Your notion of eidetic anthropology is fairly interesting. At the same time, there's something static, or motionless, about phenomenology. But one should try new words.

Bertonneau: What you've said anticipates my next question and answers it, in part. Doesn't your theory lack a fully worked out epistemology? How, precisely, does desire affect the individual? How does it shape perception?

Girard: Since the individual figures in my scheme only as far as he is involved with other individuals, the epistemology of the isolated consciousness wouldn't make a great deal of sense for me. I feel that one of the advantages of my theory is its pragmatic effectiveness. You can generate explanations with it. You could say, coming back to our initial exchange, that it produces *too much*; but what is our business as intellectuals if not to explain things? Today great theories are unfashionable. In the last century they were rife. People felt that everything was amenable to explanation, so you had these comprehensive schemes in Frazer and so forth.

Bertonneau: And yet comprehensive explanations for human behavior, and for culture, have been put forth in recent times. Take E. O. Wilson, and his student Blaffer-Hrdy, for example.[5] They propose Sociobiology as a reductive explanation for all human actions, institutions, and so forth. In what relation do you stand to Sociobiology?

Girard: I object to the Wilsonian type of explanation, and my objections to it would not differ much from my objections to Levi-Strauss. Sociobiology disregards the specificity of human culture; it collapses man and animal. I am in fundamental disagreement with that. On the other hand, I think that Levi-Strauss and his followers are wrong when they say that ethology teaches us nothing relevant to humanity. That's why mimetic theory interests me so much: you can start with it at the animal level and trace it across the threshold of hominization right into human culture. That threshold is when the victim becomes the conscious object of attention by members of the community. The behavior is then no longer purely instinctual. You can take as many eons as you want to get to that point, but at least you've got something that takes into account the animality of man without making it triumph. You have cultural specificity, a break between animal and man.

Bertonneau: It strikes me that your theory insists on the fairly contradictory requirement that there be both a continuity and a dis-continuity between brute and true hominid. How do you reconcile the contradiction, or do you need to?

Girard: Any sound theory, you see, must have both continuity and discontinuity. It's not an either-or, it's precisely not a decision. The problem with the ethologists is that they don't have a break. The problem with the structural anthropologists is that they don't have any continuity. Both are obviously wrong. Ultimately, it seems to me, we must reveal these partialities because they prevent us from understanding our origins, and, therefore, prevent us from understanding our fate. If I am optimistic about that fate, it's because I am optimistic about the possibilities of recuperating our origins. Once we have done that, we have gained a position from which we can examine, rationally, the subject of ourselves, of our humanity.

Notes

1. Paul de Man, *The Resistance to Theory* (Minneapolis: University of Minnesota Press, 1986), 3–20. "If is a recurrent strategy of any anxiety to defuse what if considers threatening by magnification or minimization, by attributing to it claims to power of which it is bound to fall short." (p. 5)

2. Martin Heidegger, *Die Selbstbehauptung der Deutschen Universität* (Rectoratsrede [May 27, 1933]) (Reissue: Frankfurt am Main: Vittorio Klostermann, 1983).

3. See Martin Heidegger, *Introduction to Metaphysics*, trans. Ralph Manheim (New Haven: Yale University Press, 1957), 126 ff.

4. Michel Aglietta and André Orlean, *La Violence de la monnaie* (Paris: Presses universitaires de France, 1982).

5. E. O. Wilson, *Sociobiology: The New Synthesis* (Cambridge: Harvard University Press, 1975); Sarah Blaffer-Hrdy, *The Langurs of Abu: Female and Male Strategies of Reproduction* (Cambridge: Harvard University Press, 1977).

CHAPTER 5
VIOLENCE, DIFFERENCE, SACRIFICE
*Rebecca Adams/1993**

Rebecca Adams: Your work is highly interdisciplinary and sweeping in its themes and conclusions. At Stanford, you hold a Chair in the Department of French and Italian, but you also have an appointment in the Comparative Literature and Religious Studies. What is your intellectual training?

René Girard: I attended the *lycée* (public school) in my hometown Avignon; my higher education was in history. I am an *archiviste-paléographe*, in other words, a graduate from the École des Chartes in Paris, a school entirely dedicated to the most technical aspects of French medieval studies. (My father was the curator of a library and a museum.) When I was a student there, I was dissatisfied with the dry positivism of the school, but I was too young and ignorant to understand why I was such a mediocre student, and I wasted a lot of time. A few years after World War II I came to this country, and then I took a Ph.D. in contemporary history from Indiana University.

Many people see literary criticism as my original field but, in an academic sense, literary criticism is no more "my" field than anthropology, or psychology, or religious studies. If our "real" field is the one in which we are not self-taught, my "real" field is history. In everything that truly matters to me, however, I am self-taught.

RA: You chose to come to the United States after World War II and have lived here most of your adult life. What effect did the war have on you? And can you tell us about your intellectual background and development?

RG: During the war, in 1943, I was nineteen. My story is not a Paul de Man story – I was lucky enough to have parents who were very anti-German and

*From *Religion & Literature* 25 (Summer 1993): 9–33. Published as "Violence, Difference, Sacrifice: A Conversation with René Girard." Reprinted with permission of the University of Notre Dame. This interview was conducted in November of 1992 at the Academy of Religion Convention in San Francisco, where Rene Girard gave a plenary address on "The Satan of the Gospels."

pro-British. The idea of resistance therefore fascinated me, though I'm not going to say that I was any great activist. But the war affected me deeply, probably negatively in my feelings about Europe too, and that must be one of the reasons why I stayed in the U.S. when I later had the possibility of coming one year. My father was a very lucid, clear-minded man about political and historical affairs. I had intellectual friends, too, connected to the Surrealist school. But I felt at that time that the intellectual and artistic life was not for me, it was alien.

The first great literary influence on my thinking was Marcel Proust. What I saw in him was a certain approach to the study of human relations, which seemed more powerful to me, and, yes, more truthful, than the various philosophical, psychological, or psychoanalytical approaches with which I was getting acquainted at the same time. It was the intellectual dimension of Proust's novel that first attracted me. When I became an instructor of French at Indiana University, I was invited to teach some literature, and, even though I was terribly incompetent, I accepted. I had not even read all the novels I was supposed to teach. I could not talk about literature in a meaningful way. Very quickly, however, I was impressed by similarities between the Proust I knew and such novelists as Stendhal, Flaubert, Dostoyevsky, and, above all, Cervantes, the one who has remained dearest to my heart and who contributed most, I believe, to the definition of mimetic desire. This is how my first book on the novel [*Deceit, Desire and the Novel*] was born.

It was my good fortune at the time that I knew nothing of "critical theory." I did not realize that critics were supposed to look for differences, singularities, and not similarities, in the works they studied. Similarities were and are still frowned upon. They contradict the romantic fetish of originality and novelty at any price. If a writer resembles other writers too much, he is suspected of not being original enough and his reputation suffers. Similarities are out; differences are in. This has been true since the early Romantics and, nowadays, it is more true than ever, but in a slightly different form. Deconstruction is the ultimate democratization of romantic singularity. Let us all cling to difference and be "ourselves." It might even provide us with the fifteen minutes of fame that Andy Warhol has promised to each one of us. A world in which difference as difference is the ultimate intellectual fetish must be a world in which imitation and the pressure for conformity are irresistible.

As an academic institution, literary criticism is completely alien to what I really enjoy in good literature. It still operates along the lines of romantic singularity or, when it reacts against it, it does so in the manner of

Stanley Fish and the war against the literary canon, which is an even worse disaster and one, by the way, that the fetish of romantic singularity makes completely predictable and inevitable. Anti-elitist hysteria is the perfect mimetic double and twin of romantic singularity.

RA: I understand that your reading of these texts, then myths, and finally the Hebrew/Christian Scripture – which though very similar, turned out to say something very different from myth – led you back to a reconsideration of Christianity. Your writing sometimes almost seems to be in the strain of French pietism; I'm thinking, for instance, of writers in the Catholic renaissance in the 1930s France. In the introduction by Francois Mauriac to Elie Wiesel's *Night*, Mauriac tells the powerful story of meeting Wiesel soon after the end of World War II. Wiesel tells him the story of seeing a hanged child, and his anguish of wondering where God is. That child is a scapegoat figure, like every lynch victim. For the young Wiesel the child is the stumbling block to religious faith. But for Mauriac, the child is a Christ figure, the very thing that gives him hope in that hopeless situation: God is up there on the tree with the victims, he thinks. The parallels with your own thought are obvious.

RG: I find the word pietism a little misleading. In our world, scapegoating and all related subjects arouse a tremendous emotional response. This is indirectly relevant to my work, of course, but quite indirectly. The central role of scapegoating in my anthropological views is rooted not in emotion but in a certain attitude toward textual interpretation. When I became persuaded that scapegoating is the key to the genesis of mythical and cultural texts, I entered a spiritual and intellectual world very different from the one I had known until then. It became obvious to me that some problems can be solved, or are already solved, that most of us regard as completely insoluble or even meaningless. As far as I am concerned, such ideas as "textual indeterminacy," "infinite interpretation," "undecidability," and the like, while they may be true as far as Mallarmé's poems are concerned, do not apply to myth and the other great texts of traditional culture.

The interpretation of myth which I propose is either true or false. What it most closely approximates is our historical demythification or deconstruction of late medieval witch hunts and that deconstruction, too, is either true or false. The victims were real behind the texts, and either they were put to death for legitimate reasons, or they were victims of mimetic mobs on the rampage. The matter cannot be undecidable. There cannot be an infinite number of equally "interesting," or rather uninteresting, interpretations, all of them false, and so on. The interminable preciosity of contemporary criticism is completely irrelevant to my question.

This problem of interpretation leads me back to a religious view of the world, but it is alien to the religious, and especially the Catholic, literature of the last generations. I am interested in that literature, but for reasons which have little to do with my work, at least directly. I am also interested in defending the reputation of these writers. For instance, the greatest French prose writer of the twentieth is probably Claudel, who is almost never taught in French departments. Few people even dare mention him, for fear of sounding politically incorrect. The most absurd legends are being spread about Claudel which everybody dutifully repeats as if they were demonstrated truth. Behind our universal tolerance and multiculturalism an enormous amount of crude scapegoating is going on which should be denounced, and I thank you for giving me a chance to denounce it.

The Catholic literature you allude to had very little influence on me. I am rooted in the avant-garde and revolutionary tradition, against which I reacted quite strongly, to be sure, as I became older; but my roots are still there, not in the French Catholic tradition, which is a more recent interest of mine.

RA: Was there any other philosopher, historian or critic that you read who was influential or whom you admire?

RG: There were many, of course. In my first years in this country, I recall, I was still reading André Malraux on art. His work was very comparative and probably had a certain influence on my first articles, when I started publishing. He is not mentioned very often nowadays and, when I reread him, I find him luridly romantic. I was influenced by Sartre and Camus, like other people of my generation, especially by Sartre, who was the first philosopher I understood. He, too, is no longer fashionable in our world. There is something naive, no doubt, about his idea of a philosophical system. The reason for his being summarily dismissed, however, is not that he is too remote from the current philosophical temper. He is really too close for comfort, especially in his appropriation of Heidegger for unHeideggerian purposes. If you mention Sartre in certain circles, a certain embarrassed silence follows, as if you have broken some social taboo so powerful that it cannot be formulated explicitly.

Literary Theory and Myth

RA: Let's talk about your dialogue with contemporary philosophy. In his book, *Violence and Difference: Girard, Derrida and Deconstruction*, Andrew McKenna demonstrates that deconstruction has important ethical implications that Derrida shies away from, essentially, because he doesn't want ultimately to have to stop the play of meaning within texts in favor of victims or scapegoats. It seems that Derrida's refusal to do so just reifies the traditional gap between academic theory and practical social and political reality. It has even been suggested by some feminist theorists that theory – the practice of theory – might itself be violent, especially if it insists on remaining abstract. What would you say is the role of theory, and how do you see your role as a theorist?

RG: If a Rabelais shows up at the right time, he will do hilarious things with our current scholasticism and in particular with our use of the word "theory." My anticipation of this future – I am old enough to have seen several literary fashions – makes it easy to understand why I prefer not to define myself as a theorist. The word "theory" has been so fashionable in recent years that, in the near future, it will sound horribly dated and ridiculous. The next generation will wonder what impulse could so move so many people that to go on endlessly writing the most convoluted prose in a complete void of their own making, disconnected not only from the reality of their world but from the great literary texts, of which recent theory has been making a shamelessly parasitic use.

An even more serious problem with the word "theory," from my point of view, is that it implies an abandonment of the search for truth. Intellectual life in a "theoretical context" is called "play" because it is without a purpose. From my standpoint, a theorist who is securely tenured and still writes a lot of theory is an unfathomable human mystery. If I were in his or her shoes, I would prefer almost any activity, or no activity at all, to the tedium of more of this kind of theory.

On the other hand, a search for truth is necessarily violent since it may lead to some definite stance regarding what is true and what is false. A clash with people who have different conceptions becomes a distinct possibility. There is, no doubt, some violence in the life of ideas, but it seems minimal to me when compared with the violence of mimetic rivalry, of academic competitiveness, for instance. Whenever people really believe in some truth larger than the academic world, they do not dedicate themselves to the pursuit of academic success with as much ferocity as the people who believe absolutely nothing. This is what I have observed in recent years, if I am not mistaken. It seems to me that, far from making people more relaxed and generous, the current nihilism has made academic life harsher and less compassionate than before.

Mimetic rivalry hides behind ideas, of course, and many people confuse it with a war of ideas, but it is really something else. But even if people still believe in the ideas currently fashionable, they are not existentially attached to them in the manner that they were in the past. Our ideas are less and less lovable and, as a result, they are no longer loved. I am no Platonist, but when I see this, I feel I understand better, after all, why Plato glorified *Ideas* as much as he did in his own world of cultural decadence and intense sophistry.

I do not agree that ideas and beliefs are the real cause of violence. Religious beliefs, especially. It is fashionable, nowadays, to say that religion is extremely violent and the real cause of most wars. Both Hitler and Stalin were hostile to religion and they killed more people than all than all past religious wars combined. When Yugoslavia started to fall apart, there were dark hints once again that the true culprit was religion. Since then, I have not seen one single piece of evidence that religion has anything to do with the various abominations that are going on there. If we had more *genuine* religion, we would have less violence. This is what most ordinary people still believe, and, as a rule, when the ordinary people and the intellectuals do not agree, it is safer to go with ordinary people.

RA: Your ideas have often been controversial, and have praised, ignored, and attacked. In your view, what is the main misunderstanding about your work?

RG: The main misunderstanding concerns the reality of victims in mythology. Most people feel that this reality is an *a priori* decision on my part, a misguided humanitarian response to victimage in the real world, or some philosophical deficiency, some intellectual inability to fathom the subtleties of post-structuralist theory. In reality, my point of departure and my entire analysis are purely textual. I make no assumption whatever regarding textual "referent" behind myths. What I maintain is that the reality of the victims behind the text can be ascertained from inside the text, for the same interpretive reasons and with the same certainty as can be the reality of the persecuted witch behind the account of a witch trial in the fifteenth century. If you do not postulate a real scapegoat, the accused witch, nothing makes sense in the deluded account of a witch hunt. If you do, everything in the text makes sense. The interpretation of myth is not decided on this basis, and I say that it should be.

The same rule should apply, I believe, in the case of myths as in the case of historical texts, because the texts are really structured in the same fashion. If the same rules were applied, the themes of the myths would lead us to assume that there must be real victims, too, behind most myths, and everything in them would make sense. What people call "my" theory of myth is not really mine at all. It is a type of interpretation already present in our world, which we systematically apply to deluded texts of persecution. All I am really suggesting is that this type of interpretation, which, in the case of historical texts, is now quite banal and even automatic, but has not always been, should be extended to those non-historical texts we call myths.

RA: When you say the idea of a real victim isn't an *a priori* thing in your thinking, you're saying everything in a cultural text such as a myth is already a representation, in a sense. The whole "victimage mechanism" you talk about is really a symbolic system that *creates* the victim, and the victim *creates* the system. So it only makes sense to talk about a "victim" from within the system of representation already being there.

RG: That's right. But the system of representation will lead you to the *real* victim if you question it vigorously and uncompromisingly. The mythical system of representation itself, however, will also never detect the real victim as innocent; it always represents the victim as guilty. Oedipus is supposed to be a parricidal and incestuous son. The myth is lying to us and, at this time, at the end of the twentieth century, the lie is obvious.

When I first read "Plato's Pharmacy," just before *Violence and the Sacred* came out, I was absolutely sure Derrida and I were traveling on the same road. I still believe that his early work is part of an historical uncovering of scapegoating as a genetic principle. He never reached what I regard as the crucial conclusion, but some of his analyses are most powerful, especially in the case of what he calls the *supplement*. The name comes from Rousseau, but the structure behind it appears in many texts analyzed by Derrida, under a variety of names. If you examine closely the operation of the Derridian supplement you will discover that foundational myths are the most striking exemplifications of it, because they are the crudest, the most obviously illogical and the most consistent in their illogicality. At the beginning of these myths, there seems to be no need for a new origin of culture: the culture seems to be in place. In other such myths, however, the culture is still incomplete, or it is in a state of disruption. The hero is then some kind of stranger who shows up from nowhere and commits some kind of crime, or violates some law, or makes some apparently innocuous but ultimately fatal mistake; as a result, this hero, or heroine, is unanimously expelled and/or killed. Thanks to this violent expulsion, a new beginning, or a first beginning, becomes possible. The cultural law is established that did not really exist when the hero transgressed it. The system comes into existence that did not exist when the hero disrupted it. This is the pattern that Derrida calls "the supplement." It is not true that no sense can be made out of it. Like all genuine riddles, this one can be solved. In order to solve it, we must first give up post-structuralist complacency about the impotence of language. All supplemental structures are naive traces of scapegoat phenomena which are only partly rearranged from the standpoint of the total process.

The archaic sacred is the necessary transcription of the scapegoaters' delusion. The victims are transfigured into all-powerful manipulators of disorder and order, founding ancestors, or divinities. Later on, the descendants of the scapegoaters will draw spiritual sustenance from their distorted recollections of the community's ordeal. The divinized victims become models of ritual performance and countermodels of prohibition. This is how religion and culture originate.

RA: I know that you use the word "myth" in a negative fashion to describe thinking which fails to see that the "origin" is always already there, to see the logic of the supplement. Yet it's also possible to turn this term to the opposite meaning, to describe discourse which recognizes and expresses the supplement. In "Plato's Pharmacy," when Derrida shows how philosophy constitutes itself by excluding – scapegoating – writing, he also shows how Plato aligns myth (myths or stories) with writing. Myth and story are both excluded from philosophy, as poetry is excluded from the Republic. Myth is on the side of writing. Derrida seems to be using the word "myth" in a different way than you do. What he is showing is that *philosophy* is "myth," in the sense that *you* use the word "myth," that is, an ideology which excludes something in order to constitute itself, then conceals its own violence.

RG: Philosophy constitutes itself by excluding writing. But also by suddenly excluding primitive religion.

RA: Because that's part of myth in Plato, and it's part of writing.

RG: I think that philosophy excludes religion for both good and bad reasons. Good reasons in the sense that Plato is repelled by its violence. He thinks he can move away from it by expelling it ever more, which I think is the movement of culture. But there is no difference at this point between Derrida's use of the word "myth" and mine. He reads the supplemental structure in philosophical texts and I read it in myth properly speaking. The only possible conclusion (which, of course, should be supported by a great deal of textual analysis) is that philosophy is the continuation of myth by more sophisticated means. The essential means is, as shown by Derrida, the expulsion of myth and archaic religion, which have become too embarrassingly transparent as methods of scapegoating. What philosophy does by expelling myth is to discard an outmoded vehicle of scapegoating and to reinstate the same process in less violent forms which are invisible once again.

The differences between Derrida and myself are very well defined by Andrew McKenna in his most remarkable book. Under the influence of Heidegger, Derrida emphasizes the metaphysical tradition and, more generally, he stigmatizes Western civilization, but he says nothing of other cultures, thereby suggesting that they might be alien to the supplement and less prone to victimization. As a result, deconstruction is suitably anti-Western and "politically correct." If you look at myths from all over the world, however, you will see that the supplemental structure is not characteristic of European myths only. Contrary to what Dumézil believed, "Indo-European" myths are not really distinctive as myths. They are structured just like African myths, or Polynesian myths, or Amerindian myths. The supplement is not specifically metaphysical and Western, it is universally human. And Derrida's question of *écriture*, of writing, is only a sideshow. There is no reason to single out the West as the cultural villain *par excellence*. To the politically correct, of course, this is dark heresy, and for this reason, as well as a few others, I am not in *odeur de sainteté* with our academic establishment.

Culture, Mimesis, and Theology

RA: Let's take a theological angle on the concept of the victimage mechanism. I see your overall theory as in some way reconstituting the doctrine of Original Sin. It uses a new language and sophisticated concepts, but in some ways it is similar to an Augustinian worldview. In the section in *Things Hidden since the Foundation of the World* on hominization, the way human beings become differentiated from animals, I get the impression that you almost tell a Genesis story of original sin – but a fall without creation.

RG: Yes, some of my theological friends are very worried about that. But they are wrong. I do not exclude creation in the biblical sense. I am writing about culture. We must distinguish two things carefully: 1) the creation story which is the work of God alone and 2) the creation of the first culture which, in the Bible, comes after both the creation and the fall. It is the story of Cain. Both the synoptic Gospels and John talk about the foundation of the world (*katabole tou kosmou*), or the origin, the beginning (*archē*) in terms of murder. Traditionally, these texts have been read as polemical accusations against the Jews. In reality, they are a revelation, the main revelation, of what I am talking about, the "founding murder." I did not make this concept up; it really belongs to the Gospels. But I do not confuse this material with a doctrine of creation. I am not trying to do away with the beginning of Genesis. The fact that I am extremely interested in what the Gospels have to say about human culture and its murderous beginnings does not mean that I am deviously trying to displace or minimize the biblical view of creation *ex nihilo*.

Many people are mistaken in regard to my views, notably John Milbank. In his *Theology and Social Theory*, he portrays me as a man who sees chaos as the absolute beginning of all things. He does not realize that I am reading very specific passages of the Gospels. Milbank is not an insignificant thinker, but his strange combination of postmodernism and traditional Catholicism makes him particularly unfit to understand the role that the Gospels play in my work. He is the Catholic philosopher through and through, and cannot even imagine that one might question the Gospels directly rather than through the mediation of the Church fathers or Thomas Aquinas. As far as I can tell, there is not one single quotation from the Gospels in his entire book.

People see me too much as one more Christian philosopher, or maybe as an inspirational writer. I am not necessarily hostile to all the things which I do not mention in my writing. The people who complain about not finding this or that in my books are the same, as a rule, who ridicule the excessive ambition of *le système-Girard*. What they mistake for an encyclopedic appetite is the single insight that I pursue wherever I can recognize it and which is too alien to their way of thinking for them to perceive its singleness.

RA: You say you are not trying to account for everything in your work and that you are discussing certain texts and ideas specifically. The particular section of *Things Hidden* where you talk about hominization is, however, very dense, and it does very much give the impression of being an attempt at a cohesive, comprehensive theory of human origins.

RG: I wrote this text carefully, no doubt, but quickly, and the reason I wrote it is that it seemed to fit beautifully with everything else. It is part of the single insight and it was an irresistible temptation. The mimetic theory provides the perfect bridge between the one-sidedness of ethological theories, which glibly assimilate animal culture to human culture, as if the symbolic nature of the latter were an unimportant supplement, and the one-sidedness of structural anthropologists *à la* Levi-Strauss, who see human culture as if, literally, it had fallen from heaven, completely disregarding the similarities between human and animal culture.

When I wrote these pages, their theological repercussions were far from my mind, but the more I think about them now, the more I wonder if the whole theory is as irreconcilable with Christianity as is claimed by some theologians. I am talking, of course, about the Christianity of those who do not *a priori*, reject all evolutionary views. According to this hominization theory, man is a product of religious forms that are very crude, no doubt, but are religious nevertheless. This is a far cry from the usual modern view of religion as mere "superstition." Theologians should see something positive in this primacy of religion. I point this out not because I want to demonstrate logical merit of my hominization theory, but because I find it suggestive not from one but from many normally incompatible perspectives: an evolutionary perspective, an anthropological perspective, a Christian perspective. This theory, I repeat, was an "opportunistic" one, and I regard it as tentative. In some respects, it is nothing more than the mimetic theory flexing its muscles, so to speak, and the same is true of many other analyses in *Things Hidden since the Foundation of the World*. It was written as one more example of what happens when you unleash this theory in the anthropological field.

RA: So you were opening up a dialogue at that point, not giving some definitive account of human origins, which is perhaps where the theological misunderstanding comes from?

RG: Yes and no. All theories intend to be definitive accounts of what they theorize, of course, and I find this one quite attractive from my perspective, but it is not engraved in marble.

When I say that my mimetic anthropology is a series of hypotheses I truly mean it, and the so-called *"système-Girard"* which is attributed to me, even in the introduction to the French paperback edition of my books, exists primarily in the mind of those who have no first-hand experience of the dynamic force of the mimetic theory. They see my work as something static, a bunch of dogmatic propositions about the way things are. I do not recognize myself in their summations of my views. This does not mean I am not serious about my work. Just the opposite. What should be taken seriously, however, is the mimetic theory itself – its analytical power and versatility – rather than this or that particular conclusion or position, which critics tend to turn into some creed which I am supposedly trying to force down their throats. I am much less dogmatic than a certain reading of my work suggests.

RA: I remember you have a disclaimer at the beginning of *Things Hidden since the Foundation of the World*, that all the concessions to the reader are left out.

RG: That was Jean-Michel Oughourlian's idea.

RA: Let's go on with some more theological implications of your arguments. At the end of *Things Hidden*, then, you make the statement that to follow Christ means to "give up" or renounce mimetic desire, yet the hominization section implies that mimetic desire is the only kind of desire there is. There seems to be a covert suspicion, throughout the theory, of real agency. The theory of mimetic desire itself seems to entail an – again, almost Augustinian – idea of the bondage of the will. Freedom of the will is an illusion, an illusion which must be renounced. But in your thought, it's not even as if we once had real agency before the "fall," as Calvin, for instance, believed.

RG: No, that impression is not true. I believe in freedom of the will. Jesus says that scandals must happen, and he tells his disciples that they will all will be scandalized when he is arrested; but at the same time he says: happy are those to whom I will not be a scandal. So there are nevertheless a few who are not scandalized. That scandals must happen might sound like determinism, but it is not.

RA: So are you saying that mimesis, imitation and the violence it engenders, is extremely seductive and powerful like a current in a river, but it is not as if a person cannot resist it?

RG: Even if persons cannot resist it, they can convert away from it.

RA: But again, that's the idea of renunciation of the will, isn't it?

RG: The idea of renunciation has, no doubt, been overdone by the Puritans and the Jansenists, but the blanket hostility that now prevails against it is even worse. The idea that renunciation in all its forms should be renounced once and for all may well be the most flagrant nonsense any human culture has ever devised. But as to whether I am advocating "renunciation" of mimetic desire, yes and no. Not the renunciation of mimetic desire itself, because what Jesus advocates *is* mimetic desire. Imitate me, and imitate the Father through me, he says, so it's twice mimetic. Jesus seems to say that the only way to avoid violence is to imitate me, and imitate the Father. So the idea that mimetic desire itself is bad makes no sense. It is true, however, that occasionally I say "mimetic desire" when I really mean only the type of mimetic desire that generates mimetic rivalry and, in turn, is generated by it.

RA: This is an important clarification. It seems that it wouldn't make sense, in light of your theory itself, to say mimetic desire should be renounced, because mimetic desire is itself a *pharmakon* – a medicine or a poison. The claim at the end of *Things Hidden* that to "give up" or renounce mimetic desire is what we must do is, I think, particularly misleading in this regard. Perhaps mimetic desire *per se* is not to be done away with, but is to be fulfilled – transformed, "converted."

RG: A simple renunciation of desire I don't think is Christian; it's more Buddhist. Undoubtedly there are similarities between what I am saying and Buddhism. If you read the descriptions of Buddhism, they are very profound; they are very aware of mimetic desire, and of contagion, and of all the things that matter in human relations. Like all great religious writing. The thing that is unique about Christianity is that it wants to go back to the origin, to the sacrificial origin, and uncover it. Buddhism is not interested in doing this at all. And Buddhism advocates getting out of the world altogether. Christianity never does that. Christianity says, the cross will be there for you, inevitably. But that kind of renunciation is very different.

RA: What you are advocating, actually, is not renunciation but imitation of a positive model. St. Paul, too, says "imitate me". He also says, think upon these *positive* things, the fruits of the spirit: love, joy peace, and so forth. In his book *The Peace of the Present: An Unviolent Way of Life*, John S. Dunne has a short section in which he has an exchange with you over this issue of desire. His concept of "heart's desire" seems initially to be very similar to what speaking of "imitating" Christ; if the heart's desire is indeed mimetic, in other words, it would express itself in imitating Christ, or God through Christ. But Dunne doesn't talk about desire in mimetic terms. He speaks as if we have an active, positive agency to desire the good, the capacity and choice to desire non-violently.

RG: But I would say that mimetic desire, even when bad, is intrinsically good, in the sense that far from being merely imitative in a small sense, it's the opening out of oneself.

RA: Openness to others.

RG: Yes. Extreme openness. It is everything. It can be murderous, it is rivalrous; but it is also the basis of heroism, and devotion to others, and everything.

RA: And love for others and wanting to imitate them in a good sense?

RG: Yes, of course. And the fact that novelists and playwrights, and that primitive religion, are inevitably concerned with rivalry – conflictual mimetic desire, which is always in the way and is a huge problem for living together – doesn't mean it is the only thing there is. Now writers are what I would call "hypermimetic," which cannot be considered necessarily pathological. Literature shifts into hypermimeticism, and therefore writers are obsessed with bad, conflictual mimetic desire, and that's what they write about – that's what literature is about. I agree with Gide that literature is about evil. That doesn't mean evil is the whole of life. I hear this question all the time: "Is all desire mimetic?" Not in the bad, conflictual sense. Nothing is more mimetic than the desire of a child, and yet it is good. Jesus himself says it is good. Mimetic desire is also the desire for God.

RA: For those who would not *a priori* accept a religious framework, nor a concept of the "imitation of Christ" as you employ it, it might be understood also as the desire for love, for creativity, for community.

RG: Cultural imitation is a positive form of mimetic desire.

RA: In *Saints and Postmodernism: Revisioning Moral Philosophy*, Edith Wyschogrod, a contemporary moral philosopher, talks about excessive desire on behalf of the Other as the basis for ethics: desiring for the other because of the otherness of the other. Note how this would look in terms of mimetic desire. Positive mimetic desire works out to re-capitulate the Golden Rule: we desire for the other *what the other desires for her or himself*. This kind of desire is therefore neither colonialist, nor does it scapegoat.

Wyschogrod calls for a new postmodern sainthood based on this excessive desire and the genuine valuing of difference. I guess I'm wondering whether it's possible within your theory to fully account for this desire on behalf of the Other – for nonviolent, saintly desire – as an excess of desire rather than as a renunciation of desire.

RG: Your question makes sense to me, and more so these days since I no longer hesitate to talk about theology. Wherever you have that desire, I would say, that really active, positive desire for the other, there is some kind of divine grace present. This is what Christianity unquestionably tells us. If we deny this we move into some form of optimistic humanism.

RA: Divine grace is present, you would say, whether or not it is recognized as such?

RG: Whether or not it is recognized as such.

RA: It seems clear that there are movements and ideas and currents in the intellectual world which are centrally concerned exactly with such an ethical conception of desire. Some contemporary continental theory (one thinks especially of Levinas), certain strains of poststructuralist and feminist thought, are concerned with the same task you are: doing an analysis of structural violence within culture and/or constructing a new, non-violent, ethical paradigm such as that you develop in "A Non-Sacrificial Reading of the Gospel Text." Many of them, though, aren't using theological discourse because they believe all theology is sacrificial.

RG: That's right. There's an idea that theological language and concepts are inevitably sacrificial.

RA: So religion is dismissed as being part of the problem.

RG: Religion is dismissed as being, as you say, necessarily sacrificial. And the god that is dying, is dead in Nietzsche's words, is the sacrificial god. Which is not a bad thing.

Sacrifice in Culture and Christianity

RA: I'd like to ask now about your understanding of history, and how you interpret both sacrifice itself and Christianity within the movement of history. It seems as if your thought tends toward Gnosticism, in the sense that it is knowledge which eventually saves us, history is a process of coming to greater and greater knowledge of the victimage mechanism, and there is some point toward which we are progressing, at which we will be enlightened in a definitive sense.

RG: Yes, but don't forget that I say that this knowledge is very ambivalent in the way it works with people, that there are always perversions of this knowledge.

RA: So history is not a straight line, a humanistic progress toward an end goal, or something like that.

RG: No, no.

RA: And yet you do seem to have a sense of progression.

RG: I do. The nineteenth century had too much of this sense; our age has too little of it. We are a big reaction against the nineteenth century, and in many ways that's very positive. But in some ways it's excessive: all the pessimism against our own religion, against our own culture, against everything which is ours. So I think that's a problem as well.

RA: You are referring to multiculturalism, at least in some of the extreme separatist or punitive forms it takes?

RG: Yes, and that sort of thing.

RA: Because we're reacting against our own ethnocentrism, and that's a healthy impulse, but what we are doing essentially is scapegoating our own culture in the process, and that's problematic.

RG: It is the little compensation we can give to the people who have been historically scapegoated. But we are then turning around and scapegoating our own tradition. Scapegoating and betraying our own tradition has become an absolute duty, especially when it is done in the name of Christian charity, of course.

RA: That betrayal is something like what Derrida does, Andrew McKenna argues. Derrida does violence to his own ethical insights in deconstruction rather than seem to get caught up in the violence of logocentrism. So you're saying something similar about Christianity.

RG: That's right. Saying that it's "unChristian" to claim the unique truth in Christianity is like that. And what Derrida does, that's in a very French, avant-garde tradition, of being so ethical and so puritanical about ethics, that you never talk about it, or turn it into a self-destructive urge. There was a great deal of this in Sartre and then a great deal again in Foucault and post-structuralism. That is why I say that, in some essential respects, deconstruction is neoSartrian.

RA: Regarding extreme forms of multiculturalism, to scapegoat Western tradition or Christianity wholesale is simply to remain caught in the cycle of racism and violence which is supposedly being repudiated. To put it in Freudian terms, to kill the "Father" is to remain within and reaffirm the law of the Father. This is essentially what you say about the vicious cycle of scapegoating, and many feminists have had the same insight. I see your theory, however, implicitly raising some interesting questions about Scripture and its revelation in this regard. You seem to fix on The Epistle to the Hebrews as the "bad father" within the Scriptural canon, because it's "sacrificial." To be exact, in *Things Hidden since the Foundation of the World* you imply that the theology of Hebrews belongs to an earlier mode of sacrificial thinking, which has now been superseded. Of course that wouldn't be any problem from within an ordinary evolutionary way of thinking about history and revelation, it *is* a problem in terms of traditional notions of the authority of Scripture, canon, and so forth. Even more interestingly, your reading of Hebrews seems unsatisfactory from within the premises of your own theory, which stresses that one must be careful not to scapegoat even scapegoating itself. Is Hebrews then not authoritative in a certain sense? Do you in a sense "kill" this sacrificial father, scapegoating Hebrews?

RG: Well, I agree entirely with you that there are problems with my treatment of Hebrews. It's a problem of language: the "last sacrifice," even though in *Things Hidden* I say, ultimately, that the word "sacrifice" doesn't matter that much. But I say it too briefly. And I give too much importance to that word. That's one of the reasons of my misinterpreting Hebrews. I was aware of these great things in it, especially in the quotation of the Psalms.

RA: You're saying that you dismissed Hebrews too quickly.

RG: Yes, sure. I was completely wrong. And I don't know what happened to me, really, because I was pretty careful not to do that, generally.

RA: Hebrews is one of the main sources, of course, for sacrificial theology. And so it deserves careful treatment.

RG: Yes, it deserves careful treatment. And its concept of the "last sacrifice" can be very easily interpreted, made to fit, the view I propose. There is no serious problem. But in *Things Hidden*, I ask Hebrews to use the same vocabulary I do, which is just plain ridiculous.

RA: Some of the early Church fathers used the word "sacrifice" in such a way that made it clear to readers that in some sense "sacrifice" – in the sense of Hebrew propitiatory animal sacrifice – was a completely inappropriate way to talk about Christ; the same word was converted to an overtly opposite usage, theologically speaking.

RG: I like that idea very much.

RA: We'll look for further work on Hebrews, then?

RG: That's true. That's one part of *Things Hidden* that I would like to change.

RA: Let's continue then with the question of "sacrifice" as a developing and fluid concept.

RG: I say at the end of *Things Hidden* – and I think this is the right attitude to develop – that the changes in the meaning of the word "sacrifice" contain a whole history, religious history, of mankind. So when we say "sacrifice" today inside a church or religious context, we mean something which has nothing to do with primitive religion. Of course I was full of primitive religion at the time of the writing of the book, and my main theme was the difference between primitive religion and Christianity, so I reserved the word "sacrifice" completely for the primitive.

RA: So you scapegoated Hebrews within the canon of Scripture.

RG: So I scapegoated Hebrews and I scapegoated the word "sacrifice" – I assumed it should have some kind of constant meaning, which is contrary to the mainstream of my own thinking, as exemplified by my reading of the Judgment of Solomon in the book. This text is fundamental for my view of sacrifice. And there once again the question arises of the two usages of the word, two ways that we use it which are entirely different, which in that passage of *Things Hidden* I examine accurately. But then again there's my rejection, in my reading of the Judgment of Solomon, of the term "self-sacrifice," a notion which has been criticized by psychoanalysts and other thinkers. Rightly so, because it has been abused. But at the same time, there should be a valid use of it. When I wrote that book I was under the influence of the psychoanalysts, who have some kind of phobia about the word "sacrifice." So I was really trying to get rid of it. I was mostly thinking about answering certain objections to Christianity that rely on the presence of sacrificial language in the New Testament in order to deny its singularity.

RA: It makes more sense for the word "sacrifice" to have a shifting meaning that evolves over time, and actually becomes "sacrificial" in the sense of violent primitive religion, in the context of your theory as a whole. That fits in with your view of history as progressively – though maybe not in a linear way – unveiling the victimage mechanism. It also says interesting things about the relation of language to that ethical process. In your analysis of the Judgment of Solomon, the word "sacrifice" can mean two opposite things: the first sense of the word "sacrifice" is "bad," in the sense that it means scapegoating of someone else or of oneself. But the second way is "good." You point out that the woman who gives up her child in order to save it does not do so as an act of "self-sacrifice" or from any wish or duty to scapegoat herself. What she does is desire life for the other, the child; she's thinking about love, not sacrifice. So you might be able to reinterpret the traditional notion of "self-desire on behalf of the Other"; the emphasis is upon giving another life; but it's not to be understood as a call to scapegoat oneself.

RG: The idea that self-sacrifice is necessarily bad, "masochistic," is once again the dogmatic renunciation of renunciation, the modernistic moralism in reverse we are honor bound to follow even if it kills us. One of the reasons the Judgment of Solomon was enormously important to me is that it liberated me from this reverse moralism. I must confess, though, that my language has retained traces of it almost to this day, because of my own timidity, no doubt, and of my continued subservience to the myth of false liberation.

RA: We've been talking about the Bible. I'm curious about your view of the Bible as unique, and this has everything to do, by extension, with earlier remarks you have made about the reverse scapegoating of Western culture and Christianity in particular. You say that the scapegoat mechanism is revealed uniquely by the Bible, and that's basically a reconstitution of the Christian idea of special revelation. But some people who admire your work but are nonetheless critical of this claim have suggested that the mechanism is perhaps self-destructing, or that maybe that one can understand it – and the way that violence is being demythologized – in purely secular terms. Theirs would be (from within a Christian point of view) an insistence on the idea of "general" revelation.

RG: I do not believe that the mechanism is really self-destructing and that you can understand it in purely secular terms. We think we understand it because we do not believe in it as religion, but many people still believe in the Oedipus complex, which is a makeshift religion based on an unimproved Oedipus myth. It is a new twist in the belief that Oedipus is guilty, and this guilt, as I said, is the most mythical element in the myth.

In my view, the idea of a special Christian revelation is essential to Christianity. But this is not my main reason for accepting it. I accept it because I believe it to be true. Everything in my research leads to this special revelation which defines the uniqueness of Christianity. My ultimate purpose is to show that this special Christian revelation can and must be approached in rational terms, in terms of the Gospels' own critique of all human religion. All religions, including the great Eastern religions, and also Judaism and Christianity, were preceded by archaic forms of the sacred, rooted in the mimetic unanimity of a scapegoat mechanism. The special revelation of Christianity really centers on the claim that Jesus was unjustly put to death. The claim is a denial of the scapegoat's guilt, which is the basis of the scapegoat consensus by the community, the very essence of religion. This vindication of Christ extends to all victims "since the foundation of the world" and is the source of all genuine demystification in our world.

If we are already able to demystify the medieval witch hunt and not yet able to demystify the Oedipus myth, the reason is that we are in a transitional period. The special Christian revelation has penetrated deep enough to enlighten us regarding scapegoating in our own society (at least most of the time), but not deep enough until now for us to finish the job and interpret archaic religion as a more fully transfigured version of the same scapegoating. Witch trials came to an end when enough people realized that the witch hunters behaved with their presumed witches more or less in the same fashion as a previous mob had behaved with Christ. For the first time, the witch hunters were perceived as a mob on the rampage and this is still the way they are perceived today.

The demystification of scapegoating is a specifically Christian and Jewish phenomenon. It is prominently displayed in the Hebrew Bible, mostly in narrative form. When we are told, for instance, that Joseph is innocent *vis-à-vis* his brothers, that he is innocent of fornication with the Lady Potiphar, and that he is innocent of causing the drought (unlike Oedipus, who causes the plague and is guilty on every other count against him) we are being taught the biblical lesson *par excellence*: the victims at the center of myths are innocent. They were wrongly accused. The Joseph story is a subversive, demystifying re-reading of myths which must have been similar to the Oedipus myth. Job is another rebellious Oedipus who tries to confront his accusers and heroically fights his own scapegoating, the mythification of his own political downfall. You will not find a comparable text in any religious tradition, even the ones in which anti-sacrificial trends are present, the Indian Brahmanas, for instance.

What you will not find in myth and in any other religion is the relentless drive to uncover the truth of the victim, which implies an awareness of the purely mimetic nature of the scapegoat reconciliation experienced by the community. As I mentioned before, Buddhism, with all its perceptiveness, is not interested in getting back to uncover the origin of violence. This is exclusively Judaic and this is the engine behind the unique power of our world to desacralize religion. This is what people like Feuerbach, Hegel, and Marx understood, but incompletely. They thought it was the historical role of Christianity to unleash the power of a reason that is ultimately self-sufficient and independent, which is not true.

RA: What are the implications of your claim for other religions that the revelation of the victimage mechanism comes uniquely from the Christian Bible? Especially in the past, Christian missionaries, for instance, have often ended up saying other religions or cultures couldn't be saved or valued outside the special revelation of Christianity. Your claim could be construed as dangerously colonialist in just this way.

RG: No doubt it will be; it already is. But unpopular as it may be, unpleasant as it may seem, the truth Christianity claims for itself must not be eluded. But the question, I think, is to rehabilitate, up to a point, all scapegoat or sacrificial religions, wherever they are found. I think you have to face the fact that they are called "Satan" in the Gospels – but that doesn't mean they are entirely Satanic, or evil, but rather that they are limited. When Paul speaks of the "powers," he says that they are legitimate religiously, and that they can be a vehicle of the truth: in all the great religions, the Orphic traditions, you have notions of conversion which are not Christian, but are true in the sense that they are against violent mimetic desire, and have other positive religious aspects which we can recognize. The idea that other religions are "satanic" does not mean that they should be destroyed by force – there was no question of planning such destruction when Christian Scripture was written. It really means that most religions are based on a lie, which is the supposed guilt of the victim, the crimes of Oedipus.

Myth is "satanic" because it is based on Satan's power of *accusation*. "Satan," in the Bible, means first and foremost the accuser, whereas the word "Paraclete" means the lawyer for the defense, the defender of victims. In John, Jesus defines Satan as a liar and the father of liars, which means the whole human race, and not the Jews alone, because all human beings still

71

live inside systems of representation ultimately rooted in myth, in the guilt of the victim, in the denial of God's ultimate goodness. And when Paul talks about the "powers," and "Satan," it's very striking to us, because modern people tend not to believe in a literal "Satan." In fact Paul's point has nothing to do with the "good" and the "bad" angels of the tradition. He's talking about this power of accusation within religious systems.

"Satan," in the Oedipus myth, is the false accusation that makes the hero responsible for the plague. This accusation is Satan's lie. We are the mythless society, I have said, because we automatically demythify Satan's lies inside our own culture but this demythification does not yet extend to other cultures. This development will be resisted as long as possible. The day this resistance breaks down, the entire edifice of our anti-Christian, post-Enlightenment culture will collapse. Once we surrender to the pull of revelation, the uniqueness of the Gospels and of the Bible will become obvious. The true source of all demythification in our world is the Paraclete, the defender of victims, the Holy Spirit. I find it enormously significant that the name of the Spirit in the Christian religion is an ordinary Greek word that means lawyer for the defense.

I sense some hypocrisy in those Christians who do not want to acknowledge Christianity's uniqueness anymore. Let us give up all Christian truth-claims, they say, in the name of Christian charity. They do not want to offend the believers of other religions. Behind this attitude I see not so much a genuine respect for other creeds as a lack of respect for all religions, a gnawing suspicion that all are equally mythical, including Christianity. All our attitudes are really a deepening of the crisis of faith which the early twentieth century called modernism.

The "death of God" is nothing, in my view, but a misinterpretation of the tremendous desacralizing process brought about by the Christian revelation. The gods who are dying are the sacrificial gods, really, not the Christian God, who has nothing to do with them. The confusion between the two, however, is likely to continue and to become even more complete than at the present time before the true singularity of the Christian God can be acknowledged.

CHAPTER 6
"REVELATION IS DANGEROUS. IT'S THE SPIRITUAL EQUIVALENT OF NUCLEAR POWER."
Michel Treguer/1996[*]

Michel Treguer: At the beginning of our conversation, you observed that a few men of good will in positions of power would suffice to "put humanity back on the right path," convince the rich to feed the poor, and so forth. The difficulty lies in reversing mimetic desire, in putting it in the service of Good rather than Evil: many people, everyone, would have to change *at the same time*, everyone would have to become good and charitable at the same time.

René Girard: Nothing would be easier if we wanted to do it: but we don't want to. To understand human beings, their constant paradox, their innocence, their guilt, is to understand that we are all responsible for this state of things because, unlike Christ, we're not ready to die.

MT: The biblical story of Babel leaves me bewildered: the variety of languages is presented as mankind's punishment, and the bestowing of those languages as a maneuver intended to weaken human beings, a trial inflicted by Yahweh, who is jealous of the power their unity affords them.

I prefer not to go back quite so far, and to look at the variety of cultures as an originary given, a gift of God, if you like. Couldn't the message of the one God have been that he intended to love all of his children just as they were, in all their variety?

*Excerpted from *When These Things Begin* (East Lansing, MI: Michigan State University Press, 2014), 70–75, 105–11. Originally published as *Quand ces choses commenceront: Entretiens avec Michel Treguer* (Paris: Éditions Arléa, 1996). Reprinted with permission of Michigan State University Press and Éditions Arléa. Translated by Trevor Cribben-Merrill.

RG: Yes, that is indeed his message. It's not his fault if we betray him. You're forcing me to keep repeating the same thing.

MT: When the Gerasenes ask Christ to leave, to let them continue functioning in their culture, maybe they aren't wrong to do so, insofar as Christ could have unleashed more serious and more violent catastrophes than their ordinary demons.

RG: But Christ does leave; Christ doesn't stay.

MT: I wanted to hear you say it: here's an instance in which Christ himself goes away. In the end he lets them remain pagan, he lets them maintain their differences.

RG: But that's because the *hour* of Christ hasn't yet sounded for the Gerasenes. That doesn't mean that they don't need the Savior. From their treatment of the possessed man emerges an image of their collective life that seems pretty sinister to me. You're idealizing them a lot. I don't think you would exchange your fate for theirs. And why do you insist on the fact that Christianity as such has a leveling effect? By making scapegoats less and less effective, it fosters communication among worlds that are becoming less and less closed off from one another. But it's not Christianity that compels these worlds to become the same. It's our mimetic nature. Christianity isn't forcing us, the French, to imitate the worst that America has to offer and to remain indifferent to the best. It didn't invent the lust for conquest and domination.

MT: Of course, but, all the same, it made the best of the situation, it used those things to serve its own expansion.

RG: It's not Christianity that makes us into the rabid tourists that we are, intent on consuming the entire planet so as to boast upon our return of having traveled more than our friends. Tourism, too, is mimetic and a source of undifferentiation.

MT: So, despite everything, you're not immune to some form of nostalgia?

RG: I'm probably a lot more nostalgic than you think. I'm quite willing to admit that in my books I've spent too much time condemning sacrificial systems. Their purpose was to contain the unleashing of violence, and thus to replace the possibility of generalized violence with a lesser form of violence, the violence of sacrifices. I'm not glorifying what's happening now, the evolution of the world toward homogenization: but I'm saying that it has a meaning, I'm saying that mechanisms of the "scapegoat" type no longer function; I'm saying that our history has as many positive as negative aspects.

MT: Everything has meaning, even overpopulation, even AIDS?

RG: It certainly does. AIDS reminds us that the sexual taboos of the primitive world had a raison d'être. The same goes for the Decalogue, whose principles are sometimes presented as oppressive: they're rooted in human nature.

MT: You make uniformization out to be the price that has to be paid for a better world, a ticket to paradise. But there are people who are just coming out of uniformization, and for them it was a nightmare. The citizens of the Eastern European countries, who were all uniformly Soviet while their freedoms slumbered, are waking up as members of a particular group, as Russians, Ukrainians, and Armenians. For them, it's part of their newly discovered freedom.

RG: I'm not making uniformization or anything else out to be the price to pay for anything whatsoever. That's where you're wrong. There is neither any transaction nor any negotiation between religion, on the one hand, and, on the other, history and society. It's your utilitarian vision of religion that makes you see things that way. Uniformization is the search for differences, it mistakes itself for difference, because it's the source of conflicts. For example, the way in which we intellectuals seek to differentiate ourselves from one another by ceaselessly inventing pseudo-differences, revolts that are even more radical than the ones that came before, leads to avant-garde fashions that are ever more sheep-like, ever more repetitive. In a hundred years, the imperative of originality at all costs has killed creativity.

I recently asked a female Croatian student at Stanford what differentiated her from the Serbs. "Nothing!" she replied. "But, all the same, they're Orthodox and you're Catholics!" "That has no importance whatsoever!" "But what has importance then?" "Nothing! Except precisely the fact that we're the same!" The intensity of conflicts has nothing to do with the reality of differences.

People react out of fear to the obviously global nature of contemporary phenomena and that's what pushes them to latch on to local characteristics: how can the local context have any meaning in a place like America, where the average person moves every five years?

[A pause] What are you suggesting? That we dress up in traditional Provençal costumes and play wooden flutes? [*Laughter*]

MT: I'm suggesting that, at the very least, for example, we try to save the treasure of our languages, if only for pleasure's sake: speaking personally, my attachment to the Breton dialect is hardly of a political nature. But I like to think that I'm speaking the language of Tristan and Lancelot, that, better still than Béroul and Chrétien de Troyes, who only recounted their exploits, I have intimate access to the way they thought. I'll take this interior voyage over a Club Med vacation any day.

RG: Brittany is something special, but where the rest of France is concerned, regionalist authenticity is historically suspect. The regional costumes that the Americans like so much are hardly more than provincial adaptations of Parisian fashions that have been forever immobilized in the Romantic era by the modern infatuation with folklore and quaintness. What relationship is there between authentic Provence and the vacation houses that are now scattered throughout the Luberon? As for languages, I fear that French has lost the battle. The world speaks English, and, even in France, English is insinuating itself at the highest level, in research institutes and scientific periodicals.

The philosophers who are critical of modernity have shown that human rights, which were invented to put an end to various forms of oppression, have created new ones: insane asylums, prisons, and so forth—look at Michel Foucault's arguments, for example. Some intellectuals defend the idea that there is something particularly perverse about the West, which, according to them, is good at talking about freedom the better to establish its hegemony. Even if this were true, it would be impossible to prove, first of all because we're lacking points of comparison: no society before ours has taken aim at sacrificial mechanisms. So, what's revealed by all of this is the tenacity of those mechanisms. If you stamp them out here, they pop up again over there. The value of Foucault's work consists in having shown this. One day, he told me that "we shouldn't invent a philosophy of the victim." I replied: "No, not a philosophy, I agree—a religion! But it already exists!"

Foucault understood the very thing that optimistic rationalism didn't foresee: new forms of "victimization" are constantly emerging from the instruments that were intended to do away with them. It's his pessimism that separates us: unlike him, I think that historical processes have meaning and that we have to accept this, or else face utter despair. Today, after the end of ideologies, the only way to embrace this meaning is to rediscover religion. Of course, even as the victimary mechanism keeps being reborn, Christianity is always there to transform and subvert it, like a leavening agent—in the humanist rationalism of the eighteenth-century Enlightenment, for example. When Voltaire defended Jean Calas, the persecuted Protestant, he was being more Christian than the Catholic priests who were against him. His mistake was to have had too much faith in his own perfection, to imagine that the correctness of his position was due to his own genius. He couldn't see how much he owed to the past that stretched out behind him. I respect tradition, but I'm not justifying History.

MT: But you are. You are justifying it.

RG: I'm trying to show that there's meaning at precisely the point where the nihilistic temptation is strongest today. I'm saying: there's a Revelation, and people are free to do with it what they will. But it too will keep reemerging. It's stronger than them. And, as we have seen, it's even capable of putting mimetic phenomena to work on its behalf, since today everyone is competing to see who is the most "victimized." Revelation is dangerous. It's the spiritual equivalent of nuclear power.

What's most pathetic is the insipidly modernized brand of Christianity that bows down before everything that's most ephemeral in contemporary thought. Christians don't see that they have at their disposal an instrument that is incomparably superior to the whole mishmash of psychoanalysis and sociology that they conscientiously feed themselves. It's the old story of Esau sacrificing his inheritance for a plate of lentils.

All the modes of thought that once served to demolish Christianity are being discredited in turn by more "radical" versions of the same critique. There's no need to refute modern thought because, as each new trend one-ups its predecessors, it's liquidating itself at high speed. The students are becoming more and more skeptical, but, and above all in America, the people in power, the department chairs, the "chairpersons," as they say, are fervent believers. They're often former sixties' radicals who've made the transition to administrative jobs in academia, the media, and the church.

For a long time, Christians were protected from this insane downward spiral, and, when they finally dive in, you can recognize them by their naïve modernist faith. They're always one lap behind. They always choose the ships that the rats are in the midst of abandoning.

They're hoping to tap into the hordes of people who have deserted their churches. They don't understand that the last thing that can attract the masses is a Christian version of the demagogic laxity in which they're already immersed.

Today, it's thought that playing the social game, whether on the individual or the group level, is more indispensable than thinking ... it's thought that there are truths that shouldn't be spoken. In America, it's become impossible to be unapologetically Christian, white, or European without running the risk of being accused of "ethnocentrism." To which I reply that the eulogists of "multiculturalism" place themselves, to the contrary, in the purest of Western traditions. The West is the only civilization ever to have directed such criticisms against itself. The capital of the Incas had a name that I believe meant "the navel of the world." The Chinese have always flattered themselves that they are the "Middle Kingdom," and they're not the only ones. All peoples have always lived very comfortably in the most extravagant ethnocentrism, with the exception of the West, ever since Montaigne's *Essays*,[1] and even before.

The best of eighteenth-century literature is Montesquieu's "How can one be Persian?" and the whole tradition of the philosophical tale that goes along with it, which satirizes the cultural provincialism denoted today, not without pedantry, by the word "ethnocentrism." We don't have a lot to teach Voltaire on this subject, but he, on the other hand, could teach us quite a few lessons.

Since the Renaissance, Western culture has consistently been divided against itself. First we were for the Ancients and against the Moderns; then we were against civilization and for the savages; then, during the Romantic period, we were for the exotic and against the familiar, and so on. In our era many people think that they're breaking with tradition when in reality they're repeating it, but without the elegance displayed by their ancestors.

Very impressed by its role as scapegoat, the West decries itself as the worst of all societies. Could it be that we're entering an era in which the West, with respect to the rest of the planet, will play a role a bit like the one that the Jews played with respect to Christians?

* * *

Freud

RG: What I like about Freud is a certain kind of analysis, a way of writing, and of working with texts. What I don't like is his fundamental prejudice against culture and against the family: *Civilization and Its Discontents*, "the Oedipus complex." What Freud doesn't see is that social and religious institutions have an essentially protective function. They decrease the risk of conflict.

Of course, it sometimes happens that they do so in a violent way inasmuch as they limit certain forms of freedom. In truth, cultural prohibitions aren't there to prevent people from having fun, but to make vengeance impossible: to separate potential antagonists by forcing them to choose different objects, preventing mimetic rivalries.

MT: But nothing breaks those bonds and dissolves those barriers like Christianity does by liberating the individual. "You will leave your mother and father ..." You're practically taking up the defense of archaic sacrificial structures.

RG: Those are the structures that Freud talks about. Yes, I take up their defense against the idea that they are fundamentally neurotic. They're very realistic. As I already said in *Violence and the Sacred*, Freud came very close to the mimetic system, it really bothered me when I was starting to work, it cost me a lot of time, to the extent that I could see the ambiguity of my relationship to Freud. I had a tendency to think – and a lot of people think this today – that my hypothesis was nothing but bad Freud, simplified Freud.

As I kept going, I discovered the explanatory power of mimetic desire, even in specifically Freudian domains like psychopathology. The argument's elegance remains a fundamental criterion: you suddenly see that there is a single explanation for a thousand different phenomena, masochism, sadism, and so on.

MT: But can't the elegance and simplicity of the explanation also be a trap? How is it a criterion of truth? After all, maybe the world is all twisted and messy, and maybe the system's elegance is only in our minds, in our logic and language. Suppose that "simplicity" was just a "simplification"?

RG: Of course it's always possible, but when you study a complicated problem and all of a sudden a very simple hypothesis illuminates all of its facets, while less simple hypotheses flounder miserably, it's hard not to think that one has the right solution, wouldn't you agree?

If you never get your hands dirty, there's nothing more tempting than to criticize the traditional preference for the "most elegant" solution, nothing more tempting than to see it as a kind of intellectual preciosity. In reality, it's quite the contrary. When you're trying to demonstrate something, elegance means maximum efficiency at minimum cost. Concretely speaking, it's unbeatable. Those who say the opposite never grapple with real problems. Our world is succumbing to the allure of sham complexity. It establishes your reputation as a researcher, gives you a scientific air. "A mathematical model for everything – or death!" That's our motto!

But I agree that the possibly illusory nature of the most elegant demonstrations must be acknowledged. Where the human order is concerned, I think, false solutions abound, but they're often, perhaps always, due to flights of unconscious mimetic enthusiasm. The position I'm defending is, by definition, as wary as can possibly be of this danger.

MT: What do you think of the famous "death drive" introduced by Freud?

RG: It's a good example of pointless complication. In my view, the death drive exists, but it is entirely linked to mimetic rivalry. Mimetic desire makes you into the rival of your model: you fight with him over the object that he himself pointed out to you. This situation reinforces desire and increases the prestige of the obstacle as such. And the supreme obstacle, of course, is death, it's what can kill you. The death drive is the logical outcome of this mechanism. But Freud is unable to link this paradoxically narcissistic desire for a biological, inanimate state to the other phases of the process; nor even, to use his own concepts, to link it to the Oedipus complex, for example, even though he's perfectly aware of the latter's mimetic nature. He contents himself in some sense with adding an extra drive. This motley assemblage inspires awe in the credulous, but if it can be simplified, we have to simplify it.

MT: This is the question that comes to mind as I listen to you: "death drive" or "drive to murder"?

RG: [A pause] It's the same thing! And eroticism tends toward both. Just think about the symmetry of the processes at play. Take Romeo and Juliet, who are defined perfectly by Friar Lawrence: "These violent delights have violent ends" (*Romeo and Juliet*, II, vi, 9). It's always forgotten that Shakespeare starts by showing us the young Romeo madly in love with a woman who wants nothing to do with him. Shakespeare's plays always contain things that contradict in spectacular fashion the conventional – and stubbornly romantic – image that, in spite of everything, we have of them. The cult of the obstacle drives human beings from their human condition toward what is most against them, toward what hurts them the most, toward the non-human, toward the inert, toward the mineral, toward death ... toward everything that goes against love, against spirit. The *skandalon* that the Gospels speak of in relation to covetousness is the obstacle that is increasingly attractive the more it pushes you away. You want it because it rejects you. This seesawing back and forth between attraction and repulsion cannot fail to be mutually destructive and destabilizing at first, before leading to utter annihilation.

Refusing God is the same thing because God is the opposite of the *skandalon*. God died for human beings. Remaining blind to God while going for the first super model who comes along—that's what human beings do.

* * *

The Surrealists

RG: If I had been in Freud's shoes when the surrealists came to see him, I would have reacted like he did. He said: "What fanatics!"

They're really just spoiled children who set fire to the curtains knowing that daddy, mommy, and the firemen will always be there to clean up after their foolishness and to admire them. You can already sense the spirit of May '68 at its most comical in their behavior: the bourgeois parents who say "Don't forget your scarf!" to their children as they go out to play revolution ... Revolution as an article of consumption.

* * *

Marx

MT: We've already spoken a little about this, there are no doubt similarities in form if not in content between Marxist and Christian eschatology: the idea of a paradise to come.

RG: Unlike Nazism, Marxism wants of course to save victims, but it thinks that the process that makes victims is fundamentally economic. Marxism says: "Let's give up the consolations of religion, let's get down to serious business, let's talk about caloric intake and standards of living, and so on."

Once the Soviet state is created, the Marxists see first of all that the wealth is drying up and then that economic equality doesn't stop the various kinds of discrimination, which are much more deeply ingrained. Then, because they're utopians, they say: "There are traitors who are keeping the system from functioning properly"; and they look for scapegoats. In other words, the principle of discrimination is stronger than economics. It's not enough to put people on the same social level because they'll always find new ways of excluding one another. In the final analysis, the economic, biological, or racial criterion that is responsible for discrimination will never be found, because it's actually spiritual. Denying the spiritual dimension of Evil is as wrong as denying the spiritual dimension of Good.

* * *

Sartre (and Virginia Woolf)

RG: What makes Sartre seem a little ridiculous today, though it's also touching and even worthy of admiration, is his desire to have a philosophical "system." Like Descartes. I myself have been accused of building a system, but it isn't true. I'm not just saying that to seem up-to-date, I'm too old for that sort of thing.

I find the analyses of the other's role in what Sartre calls "the project" – the café waiter in *Being and Nothingness*—the analyses of bad faith, and of coquetry, to be marvelous. It's all very close to mimetic desire. He even invented a metaphysical category that he calls "for the other," "for others."

But, strangely, for him, desire belongs solely to the category of the "poursoi," "for itself." He doesn't see that the subject is torn between the Self and the Other. And yet he admires Virginia Woolf, who shows this agonizing struggle in admirable fashion, notably in *The Waves*. This is another example of the superiority of the novel over philosophy. Deep down, Sartre was very comfortably petit bourgeois, a lover of tourism, and too even-keeled to become a true genius.

* * *

The Structuralists

RG: Modern structuralism is floating in a void because it doesn't have a reality principle. It's a kind of idealism of culture. You're not supposed to speak of things, but of "referents": the real is conceived in linguistic terms, instead of bringing language back down to reality, as was done back when the real was real. This way of thinking knows nothing but difference. It cannot comprehend that the same, the insistently identical, correspond to something real.

From the structuralist point of view, there is no difference between a class of real objects and a class of monstrous objects, which in my opinion are a trace left by the disorder of mimetic crisis, without which the genesis of myth cannot occur. Structuralism studies sequences with real women and real jaguars, on the one hand, and, on the other, sequences with jaguar-women, and it puts them all on the same level.

Durkheim, at least, was able to say: "How curious, there are real differences in mythical thinking – human intelligence is beginning to function – but there are also false categories. Primitive thought is sometimes based on divisions that are similar to our own, and sometimes on totally meaningless categories." Structuralism does an admirable job of highlighting differences. But if you study the development of human thought, you have to come right out and admit that modern rationalism isn't the equivalent of myth, because it has done away with the jaguar-women. If there were dragons in the user's manuals of Toyotas and Nissans, it's unlikely that the Japanese auto industry would have succeeded in spreading its products all over the world.

* * *

After Darwin

MT: What do you think of the "creationists" who take the Bible literally?

RG: They're wrong, of course, but I don't want to speak ill of them because today they are the scapegoats of American culture. The media distorts everything they say and treats them like the lowest of the low.

MT: But if they're wrong, why not? You speak of scapegoats, but, as far as I know, nobody's putting the creationists to death, are they?

RG: They're ostracized from society. It's said that Americans can't resist peer pressure, and it's generally true. Just look at academia, that vast herd of sheep-like individualists: they think they're persecuted, but they're not. The creationists are. They're resisting peer pressure. I take my hat off to them.

MT: But what if they're absolutely wrong? For someone who places such emphasis on the truth, whatever the cost, I suddenly find you very indulgent.

RG: And what do you do with freedom of religion? In America, as elsewhere, fundamentalism results from the breakdown of an age-old compromise between religion and anti-religious humanism. And it's anti-religious humanism that is responsible for the breakdown. It espouses doctrines that start with abortion, that continue with genetic manipulation, and that tomorrow will undoubtedly lead to hyperefficient forms of euthanasia. In at most a few decades we'll have transformed man into a repugnant little pleasure-machine, forever liberated from pain and even from death, which is to say from everything that, paradoxically, encourages us to pursue any sort of noble human aim, and not only religious transcendence.

MT: So there's nothing worse than trying to avert real dangers by means of false beliefs?

RG: Mankind has never done anything else.

MT: That's no reason to continue.

RG: The fundamentalists often defend ideas that I deplore, but a remnant of spiritual health makes them foresee the horror of the warm and fuzzy concentration camp that our benevolent bureaucracies are preparing for us, and their revolt looks more respectable to me than our somnolence. In an era where everyone boasts of being a marginal dissident even as they display a stupefying mimetic docility, the fundamentalists are authentic dissidents.

I recently refused to participate in a supposedly scientific study that treats them like guinea pigs, without the researchers ever asking themselves about the role of their own academic ideology in a phenomenon that they think they're studying objectively, with complete and utter detachment.

Note

1. See, in particular, "On Cannibals," *Essays,* I, 31 (1580).

CHAPTER 7
"WHAT IS HAPPENING TODAY IS MIMETIC RIVALRY ON A GLOBAL SCALE."
Henri Tincq/2001*

Terrorism arises through an exacerbated desire for convergence and resemblance with the West. Islam provides the bond that was once found in Marxism. Its mystical relation with death renders it even more mysterious to us.

Henri Tincq: Can your theory of mimetic rivalry be applied to the present international crisis?

René Girard: The error is always in reasoning from categories of "difference." The root of all conflicts lies rather in "competition," in mimetic rivalry between persons, countries, and cultures. Competition is the desire to imitate the other in order to obtain the same thing he or she has, by violence if necessary.

Terrorism is undoubtedly connected to a world "different" than ours. But what gives rise to it is not this "difference," which distances it most from us and renders it beyond our comprehension. What gives rise to it, on the contrary, is an exacerbated desire for convergence and resemblance. Human relations are essentially relations of imitation and competition.

What is happening today is mimetic rivalry on a global scale. When I read the first documents from Bin Laden, alluding to the American bombing of Japan, I felt from the outset that this went beyond Islam to the scale of the entire planet. In the name of Islam, one finds a will to rally

*This interview originally appeared in *Le Monde* on November 11, 2001, and was republished in English by *South Central Review* 19 (Summer/Autumn 2002): 22–27. Copyright 2002 *South Central Review*; reprinted with permission of Johns Hopkins University Press. Translated by Thomas C. Hilde.

and mobilize an entire Third World of those frustrated and victimized in relation to their mimetic rivalry with the West. But the destroyed towers were occupied by as many foreigners as Americans. And given their efficiency, the sophistication of the means employed, their understanding of the United States, and their training conditions, weren't the attackers a bit American themselves? The whole situation is entirely mimetic.

H.T.: "Far from turning away from the West," you write in your latest book, "they cannot avoid imitating it, adopting its values without admitting it, and are all as consumed as we are with individual and collective success."[1] Should one understand by this that the "enemies" of the West make the United States a mimetic model of their aspirations, killing it if necessary?

Girard: This sentiment is not true of the masses, but of the leaders. We know that, in regard to personal wealth, a man like Bin Laden has nothing to envy of anyone. And how many party or faction leaders are in this intermediate situation, identical to his? Consider Mirabeau at the beginning of the French Revolution: he had one foot in one camp and one in the other, and as such lived an even more acute resentment. In the United States, some immigrants integrate easily, while others lead a torn life of permanent resentment, even if their success is resounding. This is because they are returned to their childhood, to frustrations and humiliations inherited from the past. This dimension is essential, particularly for Muslims who have proud traditions and a style of individual relations that is closer to the feudal system.

H.T.: But the Americans should have been the least surprised by what happened, since they live these relations of competition permanently.

Girard: America, in effect, embodies these mimetic relations of competition. The ideology of free enterprise makes it an absolute solution. Effective, but explosive. These relations of competition are great if one ends up the victor. But if the victors are always the same, there will be a day when the vanquished turn the tables. This mimetic conflict, when it leads to unhappy outcomes, always returns at a given moment in violent form. In this sense, Islam provides the bond once found in Marxism. Khrushchev said to the Americans, "we will bury you." This had a good-natured air about it. ... But Bin Laden is more troubling than Marxism. In Marxism we recognized a conception of material happiness, of prosperity, and an ideal of success not that far removed from that experienced in the West.

H.T.: What do you think of the fascination with sacrifice by the Islamic kamikazes? If Christianity is the sacrifice of innocent victims, would you go so far as to say that Islamism is the permission of sacrifice and Islam a sacrificial religion in which one also finds this notion of "model" or mediator of desire at the core of your mimetic theory?

Girard: Islam maintains a relationship to death that convinces me even more that this religion has nothing to do with archaic myths. It is a relation to death which is, from a certain point of view, more positive than what we see in Christianity. I am thinking of the agony of Christ: "Father, why have you forsaken me? ... Let this cup pass from me." Islam's mystical relation to death renders it even more mysterious to us. At the beginning, the Americans took the Islamist kamikazes for "cowards." But they changed their view very quickly. The mystery of their suicide deepens the mystery of their terrorist act.

Yes, Islam is a religion of sacrifice in which one also finds the theory of mimetism and model or mediator. There was already no shortage of suicide candidates when terrorism seemed a failure. So imagine what is happening now when, if I dare say this, it is a success. In the Muslim world these kamikaze terrorists obviously embody models of saintliness.

H.T.: The Church Fathers said that the martyrs of the Christian faith were also the "seed" of Christianity...

Girard: Yes, but in Christianity the martyr does not die in order to be copied. The Christian may pity him, but he does not covet his death. He even dreads it. For him, the martyr may be a model of accompaniment, but not a model to follow into the fire. It is different in Islam. One dies a martyr in order to be copied and thus to manifest a project of transformation in world politics. Applied to the twenty-first century, such a model leaves me speechless. Is it proper to Islam? We often make reference to the medieval sect of "hachachins"[2] who killed themselves after having put the infidels to death. But I am not able to comprehend this gesture, still less to analyze it. I can only make note of it.

H.T.: Would you go so far as to say that Islam's dominant figure is the warrior and that Christianity's is the innocent victim, and that this irreducible difference dooms all attempts at understanding between the two monotheisms?

Girard: What strikes me in the history of Islam is how quickly it spread. It represented the most extraordinary military conquest of all time. The barbarians blended into the societies they had conquered, but Islam remained as it was and converted two-thirds of the Mediterranean population. It is therefore not an archaic myth, as one has the tendency to believe. I would even go so far as to say that it is a reprise – rationalist from certain points of view – of what Christianity does, a sort of Protestantism before its time. There is a simple, crude, and practical aspect to the Muslim faith that has facilitated its diffusion, transforming the lives of a great number of tribal peoples by opening them to Jewish monotheism modified by Christianity. But it lacks the most important part of Christianity: the cross. Like Christianity, Islam rehabilitates the innocent victim, but it does so in a warlike way. Conversely, the cross signifies the end of violent and archaic myths.

H.T.: But aren't monotheisms bearers of a structural violence, since they were born from a notion of one unique truth, exclusive of all competing articulations?

Girard: One can always interpret monotheisms as sacrificial archaisms, but the texts do not prove that they are. It is said that the Psalms in the Bible are violent, but who else is heard in the Psalms if not the victims of the violence of myths: "strong bulls of Ba'shan surround me; they open wide their mouths at me"? The Psalms are like a magnificent fur coat on the outside, which, once turned inside out, expose a bloody skin. They are characteristic of the violence that weighs on humankind and the recourse that man finds in God.

Our intellectual fashions only want to see violence in texts, but from where does the threat really come? Today we live in a dangerous world where all mass movements are violent. The crowds were already violent in the Psalms. They were in the story of Job. They demanded of Job that he recognize the guilty: they put him through a real Moscow trial of the Stalinist era.[3] A prophetic trial. Isn't it that of Christ, adulated by the masses, then rejected at the moment of the Passion? These stories announce the cross, the death of the innocent victim, and ultimately the victory over all sacrificial myths of antiquity.

Is it so different in Islam? The stories also contain powerful prophetic intuitions regarding the relation between the masses, myths, victims, and sacrifice. In the Muslim tradition, the ram sacrificed to Abel is the same as that which was sent by God to Abraham in order to save his son. Since Abel sacrifices rams, he does not kill his brother. Since Cain does not sacrifice animals, he kills his brother. In other words, a sacrificial animal prevents the murder of a brother or a son. This is to say that it provides an outlet for violence. There are thus intuitions for Mohammed that are at the level of some of the great Jewish prophets. But there is also on his part an antagonism toward and desire for separation from Judaism and Christianity that could render our interpretation negative.

H.T.: In your last book, you insist on Western self-criticism, always present at the side of ethnocentrism. "We other Westerners," you write, "are always simultaneously ourselves and our own enemy." Does this self-critique remain after the destruction of the Towers?

Girard: It remains and it is legitimate for rethinking the future, for correcting, for example, the idea of Locke or Adam Smith that competition is always good and generous. This idea is absurd, and we have known it for a long time. It is surprising that after the blatant failure of Marxism the ideology of free enterprise still doesn't show itself any more capable of defending its own case. The announcement of the "end of history" because this ideology prevailed over collectivism is obviously a lie. In the Western countries the salary gap is increasing considerably and we are going to see explosive reactions. And I am not talking about the Third World. What we still need in the post 9/11 era is a more reasonable, renewed ideology of liberalism and progress.

Notes

1. *Je vois Satan tomber comme l'éclair* (Paris: Grasset, 1999). Published in English as *I See Satan Fall Like Lightning* (Maryknoll, CA: Orbis, 2001). – ED.

2. *Hachachin* were eleventh-century narcotic-using assassins controlled by Hassan Sabbah.

3. Girard's discussion of the Book of Job is found in *Job: The Victim of His People* (Stanford, CA: Stanford University Press, 1987).

CHAPTER 8
HOW SHOULD MIMETIC THEORY BE APPLIED?
Maria Stella Barberi/2001*

Maria Stella Barberi: As someone who is not unaware of the risk that a model will become a rival, what advice do you have for those who take mimetic theory itself as a model?

René Girard: I myself am very mimetic. Since I'm polemical, I'm mimetic. I recognize that I'm polemical, and in my writing I need a kind of bait, a lure. Often it's the desire to retaliate that spurs me on, that makes me want to write. But this isn't very effective as a means of vengeance.

MSB: It may be effective as a means of motivation.

RG: As a means of motivation, you're right. Besides, all this is always mimetic, always.

MSB: And so your advice would be –

RG: To refrain.

MSB: And to renounce mimetic theory if one isn't mimetic enough?

RG: Yes, if one isn't at least a little mimetic. And yet why should I be giving advice in the first place? I have no business telling people what to do or what to believe. But if you ask me what mimeticism is, I will tell you: it's pride, anger; it's envy, jealousy – these are the cardinal sins. It's lust as well. Human sexuality is very important, because it's a permanent impulse, not something episodic or intermittent. There are no tranquil interludes in human life. Rivalry is what sustains desire. One finds the like of this among

*From René Girard, *The One by Whom Scandal Comes* (East Lansing, MI: Michigan State University Press, 2014). Originally published as *Celui par qui le scandale arrive* (Paris: Desclée de Brouwer, 2001). Copyright Desclée de Brouwer, and reprinted with permission. Translated by M. B. DeBevoise.

other animals. Take monkeys, for example, which are quite vicious and highly sexed in their own way. The mimetic analysis of sexuality contradicts Freud.

MSB: In setting an agenda for scientific research, what would you recommend?

RG: It remains to elaborate a properly mimetic method. This is exactly why authors such as Dawkins interest me, because they have developed an original and extremely suggestive method, one that is distinct from the method of history or of sociology; nor is it the method of zoology. But even assuming that a properly mimetic method could be worked out, I wouldn't dare go so far as to tell people what to do with it.

MSB: Not even tell them what *not* to do with mimetic theory?

RG: One mustn't think in terms of grand concepts – concepts devoid of human feeling. Everyone knows this, but it's hard to put into practice. The truth of the matter is that most people aren't really interested in mimetic theory. They are interested in the social ramifications, the moral implications. This is perfectly legitimate. But my interests are essentially intellectual, there's no doubt about that. Early on, people thought that I had a taste for violence. When I began to look at Shakespeare they urged me to write about *Titus Andronicus*, one of the early tragedies and especially horrifying in its violence. Its popularity was a sign of the appalling taste of the period – everyone said to me, you've got to check this out, it's really terrific. They also thought I was a great fan of violent films. Most people today, I think, realize I'm a non-violent person. No doubt with age they've come to see that what they used to think isn't true. What caused me to turn my attention to violence was the hope of succeeding where nineteenth-century anthropology failed, namely, in explaining the origins of religion, of myths and rites. All of which, of course, was meant to prepare the way for Christianity.

CHAPTER 9
SHAKESPEARE: MIMESIS AND DESIRE
Robert Pogue Harrison/2005*

Robert Harrison's interview with René Girard originally aired on the Stanford radio station KZSU on September 17, 2005, and shows the French thinker "at ease" with a friend, as they discuss mimetic desire and its appearance in Western literature. It is the first of a two-part series, both included in this volume.

— ED

Robert Harrison: The founding adage of western philosophy is "know thyself." That's not an easy proposition. To know yourself means, above all, to know your desire. Desires lurk at the heart of our behavior, determine our motivations, organize our social relations, and inform our politics, religions, ideologies, and conflicts. Yet nothing is more mysterious, elusive, or perverse than human desire.

Our government invests billions of dollars in scientific research every year so we might better understand the world of nature, so that we might continue our pursuit of knowledge, yet commits only a tiny fraction of that to advancing the cause of self-knowledge. Most of our major problems today are as old as the world itself. The problem of reciprocal violence, for example. You would think we would want to understand its mechanisms, its psychology, and its tendencies to spiral out of control. Instead, we keep on perpetuating its cycles much the way our ancestors have done for centuries, and even millennia. Nor are we any closer to knowing the deeper layers of our conflicting and conflict-generating desires than they were.

René, your work has an enormous reach. It branches out into various areas and disciplines – literary criticism, anthropology, religious studies, and so forth. Today, I'd like to focus on what I take to be the foundational

---

*From the *Entitled Opinions* radio show. Reprinted with permission of Robert Pogue Harrison. The interview transcript was published by *Standpoint* (December 2018/January 2019).

concept of all your thinking, namely mimetic desire. Can you tell our listeners exactly what you mean by that term, mimetic desire?

René Girard: Mimetic desire is when our choice is not determined by the object itself, as we normally believe, but by another person. We imitate the other person, and this is what "mimetic" means. For example: why have all the girls been baring their navels for the last five years? Obviously, they didn't all decide by themselves that it would be nice to show one's navel – or that maybe that one's navel is too warm, and one must do something about it.

We'll see the mimetic nature of that desire the day that fashion collapses. Suddenly, it will be a very old-fashioned to show one's navel and no one will show it anymore. And it will all happen because of other people – just as now, it is because of other people that they show it.

Harrison: But how far do you want to go in saying that desire – by its very nature, and in human beings – is fundamentally mimetic?

Girard: Maybe one can start from this question: what is the difference between need, appetite, and desire? Need is an appetite all animals have. We know very well that if we are alone in the Sahara Desert and we are thirsty, we don't need a model to want to drink. It's a need that we have to satisfy. But most of our desires in a civilized society are not like that.

Think of vanity, or snobbery. What is snobbery? In snobbery, you desire something not because you really had an appetite for it, but because you think you look smarter, you look more fashionable, if you imitate the man who desires that object, or who also pretends to desire it.

Harrison: Well, let me read one quote, a few lines from one of your essays from the volume *To Double Business Bound*, where you say that mimetic desire "precedes the appearance of its object and survives … the disappearance of its object. … Mimesis cannot spread without becoming reciprocal." And then, the important sentence for me: "Desires attract, ape, and bind one another, creating antagonistic relationships that both parties seek to define in terms of difference."[1]

So let's ask about the young women who are baring their navels: There doesn't seem to be an element of antagonism in this kind of fashion-based mimetic imitation of others. However, in your theory, it's very important that you hold to the fact that antagonism is almost the inevitable result of mimetic desire when it becomes rivalrous.

Girard: Perhaps the best example would be the plays of Shakespeare, in which you have two male friends. They always desire the same thing. They've lived together. They have the same dreams, the same meals. And they even say to each other, if you don't want what I want, you're not my friend. But suddenly, one of them falls in love with a girl. And as soon as the other one falls in love with a girl – the same girl, because of his friend – antagonism is going to start.

There are two types of objects. The objects we can share, because they are abundant – soft drinks, and so forth. And there are the objects we cannot share or do not want to share, which is the case for the love of a girlfriend. We do not want to share that, especially with our best friend.

These characters are very insecure. As soon as they desire a girl, they are trying to get their friend to desire the same girl.

Harrison: This is a crucial point. Because it's one thing to compete over a scarce object. Two men compete over one woman, or two women over one man. But I take it you are suggesting that it's much more complex than that?

Girard: Much more complex.

Harrison: It's not just two men desiring the same object, it's that their desire is promiscuous, one with the other. Their rivalry sets up a kind of desire for the rival, no?

Girard: Yes. It's very obvious. For instance, in the *Two Gentlemen of Verona*, as soon as one of the two boys is in love with a girl, his friend is inevitably drawn into the game.

Harrison: Now why is that?

Girard: Because if his friend does not love his girlfriend, he's not sure he made the right choice. Therefore, he too is mediated. And this type of friendship is something that obsesses Shakespeare and other writers.

Harrison: In Francesca's speech in Canto V of Dante's *Inferno*, she recounts how she and Paolo were reading the romance of Lancelot one afternoon. When they get to the part where Lancelot kisses Guinevere, Paolo and Francesca put the book down and kiss one another.

Girard: Paolo and Francesca are in-laws. Francesca is married to the brother of Paolo. They have absolutely no previous idea of making love to each other. No thought of it. But when they read this, they are suddenly inspired by the book to do the same thing. That's why Dante, obviously, views the book as, in a way, the devil who incites that: "*Galeotto fu 'l libro e chi lo scrisse.*" The book was their Galeotto.

Harrison: Galehaut was the go-between the adulterous lovers in the Lancelot story.

Girard: Galehaut is the traitor, the one who suggested to the boyfriend that he should make love. The theme of the go-between is extremely important in Shakespeare, too. Pandarus, you know. So the go-between is, in a way, a man who plays with the mimetic desire of others. And the men of the theater set up some kind of story by inciting mimetic desire and watching the results, which are usually drama – a drama of jealousy, of envy, of conflict.

Harrison: Literature first led you to see the structure of mimetic desires. Your first book, *Deceit, Desire, and the Novel,* is when you first laid out this theory.

Girard: Yes.

Harrison: So what role does literature play for you in your thinking about the structures and mechanisms of mimetic desire? You have undertaken a massive probing of European fiction, beginning with Cervantes and going all the way up to Camus. Literature clearly has a revelatory function.

Girard: Yes, but it was more the contact between literature and my own experience. I was in my early twenties, then, and of course I was interested in girlfriends. Suddenly I realized that I was just like most heroes of novels – like Proust, you know. One girlfriend wanted me to marry her, and I didn't want to do that. So I would move away from her when she demanded some commitment on my part. But as soon as I had moved away and she had accepted that and left, I was drawn back to her again by the very fact, in a way, that she denied herself to me.

I realized suddenly that she was both object and mediator for me, some kind of model. You see? She influenced my desire by denying it. All these negative games are always present in desire. Even the people who know least about desire are aware that the denial of the object increases the desire. The denial of the object is very much linked to the presence of the third person who might steal the object from you. Absence is a form of mediation.

Harrison: So when you turned the literature, you found, in European fiction, a variety of representations of this very common syndrome.

Girard: There are two types of writers. There are what I call romantic writers. The romantic writers believe in the genuineness and spontaneity of desire. They believe that their choice of the object is dictated only by who they are and so on. But the more interesting writers are the ones who realize the role that a third person has in our desires, and play with it in order to obtain their results.

Harrison: Who would be these writers in your opinion?

Girard: In the European novel, the first great example is Cervantes. Why does Don Quixote want to become a knight errant in a world where there are no more knights errant? He's exactly like Francesca. He reads novels of chivalry. And it is because he reads novels of chivalry that he wants to become a great hero. He imitates Amadis of Gaul, who is a purely fictional character, of course. The result is that he gets beaten black-and-blue on all the highways of Spain. But he's very happy because he thinks he's the great disciple of Amadis, and he's going to re-establish knight-errantry, which had disappeared for centuries.

Harrison: So literature not only reveals these mechanisms of mimetic desire, but it also proposes models of imitation for readers. Of course, this is something we see everywhere, not only in readers of literature but obviously moviegoers, television-watchers. It's undeniable that we live in a culture where we're steeped in models of imitation that come to us through the entertainment industry and other media.

Girard: That's right. And of course, the more recent media are more powerful than the old ones. Today, we try to get children to read books and not watch television. But in the old days, books were really fascinating because they played the role of television today. They were a temptation *per se*. When you try to convince students that they should read them *against* their mimetic impulse, of course, you more or less tell them that they hold no interest for them. That they are not going to get any incitement for their desire there. That's probably why it's so hard to teach literature today.

Harrison: So for authors like Stendhal, Flaubert – I mean, obviously, Emma Bovary is like a Francesca in...

Girard: That's true.

Harrison: Emma is a modern-day version of Francesca. She was nourished on the cheap romantic fiction of her day. I call it cheap – let's say it was popular romantic fiction, which provided her with her models of emulation.

Of course there's much more to it than that. In *Deceit, Desire and the Novel*, you describe a whole typology of emotions, especially what we might call negative emotions: hatred, jealousy, envy, resentment...

Girard: Which are all linked to pride, of course. Because if you have a mimetic rivalry, your vanity is involved and you want to win at all cost. The main fight, anyway, is between two young men to seduce a woman. They spend quite a bit of time on it, especially in Latin culture. I think one of the reasons Anglo-Saxon culture is – what should I say? – more economically dynamic is because not so much energy is deviated into that sort of mimetic desire, which plays such an enormous role in the Italian little town, or in southern France, or in Spain.

Harrison: That raises a question that I'll ask you in a provocative spirit. What you're describing is correct and accurate when it comes to a culture like France, which has had a long aristocratic tradition, typically highly committed to forms of snobbery, vanity. And also in other Latin cultures, as you were mentioning. But if it doesn't apply equally well to Anglo-Saxon cultures, let alone non-Western cultures, to what extent can you make a claim of universality?

Girard: We can claim universality. Of course, in these novels sexual desire plays a great role. But mimetic desire is very important in the world of "entrepreneurs" – as you say in English, although it's already a French word. The most mimetic institution of all is a capitalistic institution: the stock market. You desire stock not because it is objectively desirable. You know nothing about it, but you desire stuff exclusively because other people desire it. And if other people desire it, its value goes up and up and up. Therefore, in a way, mimetic desire is an absolute monarch.

The analysts of the market have not yet discovered that. When they tell you psychology is getting into the market, they mean that the mimetic wave that makes stocks rise is getting out of bounds. It has no more relationship to reality than that. The stock market is always threatened with a mimetic wave of such importance and such a lack of objectivity.

Inevitably, there will be a collapse, which is also lacking in objectivity. Just as a fashionable woman in Balzac, when she's abandoned by a lover, may be abandoned by all potential lovers at the same time. It's a total disaster for her. She becomes like a stock that has lost its value.

The error of Marx was to believe that the economic aspect is more fundamental than the other ones. The error of Freud was to believe that the sexual aspect was fundamental. Each one of them limits mimetic desire to one sector, one aspect of human activity, which is regarded as the only important one, the key to everything. But mimetic desire reveals the relationship between Freud and Marx.

Harrison: Whereas I take it, your theory of mimetic desire is not a psychological theory. It's not based on psychological premises.

Girard: No, because it's based on human relations.

Harrison: And on external structures that determine those relations over and above the individual psyche.

Girard: Yes.

Harrison: Your mimetic theory, from what I understand, is not limited exclusively to human beings. There is a basis for it in the animal world.

Girard: Sure. In the animal world, you have what they call dominance patterns. How are they established? The males fighting for the females. And the males are so eager to fight for the females that sometimes, when the females disappear, they continue fighting just because they are mimetically aroused. The fight becomes more important than the object.

But they will never kill each other, whereas human beings invented vengeance. Vengeance is the ultimate form of mimetic rivalry, because each act of vengeance is the exact imitation of the preceding one. If you study vengeance, you'll realize how mimetic imitation is all over the place in all manifestations of desire. In human beings, it's pushed to such an extreme that it can result in death. Vengeance cannot be limited.

Harrison: That's why I asked in my opening remarks about why can't we have an institution devoted strictly to the study of vengeance, for example, and work out its logic – reciprocal violence, these kinds of things. We are far from overcoming the behavior that has characterized human history throughout the centuries.

But let's move on to another emotion, which is closely linked, obviously, to hatred, vengeance, and jealousy, namely envy. I think envy is a highly underestimated emotion in the human relations. How do you see the role of envy?

Girard: I see it the same way. Today envy is the emotion which plays the greatest role in our society, where everything is directed towards money. Therefore you envy the people who have more than you have. You cannot talk about your envy. I think the reason we talk so much about sex is that we don't dare talk about envy. The real repression is the repression of envy.

And of course, envy is mimetic. You cannot help imitating your model. If you want money very badly, you're going to enter the same business as the man who is your model. More likely than not, you will be destroyed by strength. So when people talk about masochism and so forth, they are still talking about mimetic desire. They are talking about how we move always to the greatest strength in the direction of the desire we envy most. We do so because that power is greater than ours – and it's probably going to defeat us again. So there will be what Freud calls repetition in psychological life, which is linked to the fact that we're obsessed with has defeated us the first time. Our victorious rival in lovemaking becomes a permanent model. So novelists like Dostoevsky and Cervantes will show you characters who literally asked their rival to choose for them the girl they should love.

Harrison: In the Middle Ages, envy was often depicted iconographically as a woman blindfolded. And I think it probably has to do with a false etymology of *invidia* as not having sight. Do you see a blindness at the heart of envy in this regard –

Girard: Yes.

Harrison: – or is there a blind spot in our own failure to recognize envy as one of the most dominant passions of our own society?

Girard: Yes, it's so difficult to acknowledge because it involves your whole being. In a way, envy is a denial of your own being and accepting the fact that you prefer the being of your rival. This is so hateful to you that it awakens a desire for murder, for the murder of that other you envy. You cannot repress that envy.

Harrison: Sometimes murder, but you could say also, in other cases, admiration.

Girard: It's the same thing. [*Laughter.*]

Harrison: We hope they have different outcomes. I wonder if the advertising industry knows what you're saying. It knows the lesson of envy very, very well.

Girard: I think they know it very well. Advertising doesn't try to demonstrate to you that the object it is selling is the best from an objective point of view. They're always trying to prove to you that this object is desired and possessed by the people you would like to be. Therefore, Coca-Cola is drunk on a very beautiful beach, in the marvelous sun, with a bunch of suntanned people who are always between the ages of 16 and 22, who are everything you would like to be, who obviously wear very few clothes, but very expensive ones, because they have the most shapely bodies. Everything you might envy.

There is something *sacramental* about this. Religion is always mixed up in these things. If you consume Coca-Cola, maybe if you consume a lot of it, you will become a little bit like these people you would like to be. It's a kind of Eucharist that will turn you into the person you really admire.

Harrison: Let's talk about your book on Shakespeare, *A Theater of Envy*. Why this title for your Shakespeare book – *A Theater of Envy*?

Girard: It comes from a very specific text from an early Shakespeare poem, "The Rape of Lucrece." It is a story of all the male population in Rome, who are in a camp because they are fighting a war. In the evening, they talk about their wives. And one of them, Callatine – Collatinus, in Latin – describes his wife in such glowing ways that Tarquin, the son of the king, leaves on his horse during the night, goes to Rome, and rapes the woman.

In the original story by Livy, he sees the woman first. In other words, he falls in love with her. He realizes, sees, or thinks she's as beautiful as her husband described her. Shakespeare suppressed that part. He rapes the woman sight unseen. He's aroused only by the words of her husband. So in other words, Shakespeare emphasizes the paradoxical aspect of mimetic desire. The role of what I call the mediator, who is the husband. That's the reason why most critics regard "The Rape of Lucretia" as a mad poem. I think they dislike it because it tries to show to them what's really important for Shakespeare – "that envy of so rich a thing." This line is essential.

Harrison: But it would seem to lack plausibility unless one understands mimetic desire the way you do. Because the idea of going to rape a woman sight unseen would seem not to follow rules of verisimilitude.

Girard: Up to a point, it does not follow the rules verisimilitude. But Shakespeare, in a way, exaggerates in order to show you the truth, in order to make it more visible.

Harrison: One of the claims of your book – and this has irked some critics, one has to admit – is that Shakespeare understood the truth about mimetic desire. He was the one literary author among the whole canon who really understood it thoroughly and theoretically. He had such mastery with regard to the mimetic phenomenon that he was able to imbue it in all of his plays and to give us a corpus of works which becomes a vast theater of mimetic desire, present everywhere.

As the commentator on Shakespeare, you claim him as your great predecessor in the discovery of mimetic desire. One has to say that it's not the first time someone has claimed the authority of Shakespeare on behalf of a theory. We know how Freud used him.

Girard: Sure.

Harrison: But you really see him primarily as the poet of mimetic desire. Is that correct?

Girard: I see him primarily as the poet of mimetic desire. If you take a play like *A Midsummer Night's Dream*, you would observe that two men always tend to be in love with the same girl. They suddenly change because of the love-juice which is put into their eyes, and they both fall in love with the other girl. And then they become rivals.

The theme of the fairies, which is greatly emphasized by most people who represent Shakespeare on the stage, should be understood as the way human beings in archaic societies fail to recognize mimetic desire. Myth and stories of that type are always excuses in order to explain through miraculous means the bad consequences of mimetic desire.

Harrison: And you think Shakespeare understood that explicitly?

Girard: I think so. "O, Hell! To choose love by another's eyes," is one of the essential lines of that play. In other words, hell is really when you choose love by another's eyes, and you are inevitably drawn into a conflict of jealousy and a problem with your friend, which is the story. *Midsummer Night's Dream* is nothing else.

Harrison: You claim in your book that mimetic behavior is much more present in the comedies than the tragedies, or at least it's present in such a way that it's much more obvious.

Girard: Much more obvious because you can have all sorts of arrangements. I mentioned before the *Two Gentlemen of Verona*. In the first plays of Shakespeare, you have only one pair of lovers. Two boys were in love with the same girl. After that, you have two pairs, and the two pairs are entangled with each other. It's like a ballet. If you look at the shape of a ballet, of the movement, you can assume that a form of mimetic rivalry is behind it, too. Ultimately, we are moving towards a type of art in which gestures and words are all in a way symmetrically arranged because of mimetic rivalry.

The more mimetic rivalry you have with someone, the more different you feel from that person. In reality, however, you always do the same thing, you always act in the same way, and in that way the differences collapse. As the differences collapse, the characters become literally doubles of each other. They act in the same way. They speak the same way. And they have a feeling that they are imitated by the other who is making fun of them. But this imitation, in fact, is compulsive. This is Hermia and Helena in *A Midsummer Night's Dream*.

Harrison: Let's take a test case of Hamlet. In literary criticism, Hamlet is considered to be maybe one of the first modern examples of consciousness that is at odds with itself. It's an internalized self, which speaks to itself, and seems to be alienated from society. He would seem to be exactly the kind of character who is free from the promiscuous circulation of desire around him. He withdraws within himself. And this is the birth of the romantic sort of inward melancholic –

Girard: During much of the play, in fact, he is. And that's why he cannot do what society requires of him, which is revenge. He sees the similarity between his father and his uncle. They are both murderers. They hate each other, but they are mimetic characters.

Harrison: And he sees the futility –

Girard: He sees the futility.

Harrison: – of the law of revenge.

Girard: That's right.

Harrison: And then what happens? In what way can we say that Hamlet ends up becoming a victim of that very phenomenon?

Girard: Well, there is another plot inside the plot, which is really the whole story of Polonius killed by Hamlet. And then Laertes, who is the son of Polonius, and in many ways he is the anti-Hamlet. He's willing and ready to commit the vengeance Hamlet is unable to commit. He's ready to mourn his sister in a very powerful, emotional way. And when Hamlet sees this, he says "the bravery of his grief did put me into a towering passion" – a towering rage.

This means that out of an imitation of Laertes, he will become able to kill Laertes and start the vengeance process which he could not start before – because Laertes is closer to him. It's very different, but Laertes becomes a model of the mimetic desire which he feels unconsciously. An imitation finally resolves the tension and the inability to act.

In a way, the inability to act in our world is an awareness of the stupidity of mimetic desire and how equivalent things are to each other. The more you act, the more you get into these mimetic situations, which are circular.

Harrison: Would that be the essence of the tragedy?

Girard: This is Shakespeare. Most tragic writers are not that modern. Shakespeare, in the way I interpret him at least. I don't claim total truth, you know. Shakespeare is enormously modern. What he says is that it's very difficult to keep a revenge tragedy going on for three, four, five hours. To do so, we must have a hero who is unable to get revenge. A hero who does not believe in the situation. He does not believe in the virtue of his mother. He does not believe in the difference between his uncle and his father. He does not believe in anything he should believe.

And he's surprised when he sees an actor who is capable of shedding real tears for the queen of Troy, Hecuba. The actor should know it's not true. But for Hecuba, he thinks, that actor can shed tears, and he cannot shed them in his real family life. The theater scene is very important in that sense.

Harrison: "What's Hecuba to him or he to Hecuba."

Girard: Yes. What's Hecuba to him?

Harrison: I think what is tragic is that even when one understand the madness of reciprocal violence, in the forms of vengeance and the perpetuation of those cycles, one is still not be able to resist falling into their –

Girard: Pattern.

Harrison: – their pattern again. That gives a deep level of pessimism to a play like *Hamlet*. As I was saying at the beginning of the program, even if we were to create institutions of self-knowledge to study things like vengeance, reciprocal violence, and so forth: Why is it that human behavior is so resistant to adapting itself to what the mind knows?

Girard: But in many instances, it actually isn't. Many people pull back from mimetic situations, just as Hamlet does. And in a way, is not modern wisdom very much this? We don't analyze a mimetic situation completely, but we are aware that we are in a situation that is totally classical, which is present all over the world in thousands of examples of every minute, every second. And we pull back from it because we don't want to repeat something we know too well is going to end in exactly the same fashion as all previous examples.

Harrison: One more case from Shakespeare: *Romeo and Juliet*. That is a play where two lovers seem to have a completely unmediated relationship, one to the other. What do you make of *Romeo and Juliet* in terms of mimetic desire?

Girard: Well, I really believe that in that case Shakespeare wrote a romantic play. In other words, Romeo and Juliet do not play tricks on each other. They are really in love. Their love is completely true. So most people always quote *Romeo and Juliet* as the play that contradicts my thesis. But at the same time, Shakespeare gives you many clues. The reason Romeo and Juliet fall in love with each other is that they shouldn't. They are separated by the blood feud. They belong to the two different tribes that are constantly fighting.

So if you look at the language of *Romeo and Juliet*, what is the language of love, of mimetic desire in Shakespeare? It's the oxymoron. I love-hate this girl. Love and hate are always together. And people don't realize that the reason for the oxymoron is that love and hate are always mixed.

In the case of Romeo and Juliet, they are not mixed. But Romeo and Juliet can use the language of hatred and violence because they are on both sides of the blood feud. "I loved my beloved enemy" is the fundamental expression of love in the sixteenth, seventeenth centuries. And in *Romeo and Juliet*, the word "enemy" really means he's a Capulet or a Montague. You see, therefore, you can suppress mimetic desire but it is there, underneath in the language, because you have the blood feud that brings you the violence you need in order to have convincing passion.

Harrison: Right. I remember Zeffirelli had a film version of *Romeo and Juliet* where he wanted to end the play with the great romantic myth of love, so the two lovers are there on the stage in the final scene alone. In Shakespeare's version, however, there is a dead body on the stage with them, namely Paris, whom Romeo has slain.

Girard: And it's a hindrance.

Harrison: Yes. It's certainly a reminder of violence...

Girard: When Juliet does not wake up at the right second she's supposed to wake up, the stupid Romeo kills himself. Then, when finally Juliet wakes up, she can see that he's dead and she kills herself. Now at just about the same time as *Romeo and Juliet*, Shakespeare wrote a satire of that ending saying, "Look at these fools who believe in their true love and have a true tragedy, whereas, in fact, these lovers are the victims of a stupid misunderstanding."

In the story of Pyramus and Thisbe in *A Midsummer Night's Dream*, the same thing happens: They are supposed to be separated by their parents. They give each other an appointment. And when Pyramus shows up in the forest, he finds a lion there, chewing the scarf of Thisbe, and he kills himself. Two minutes later, Thisbe comes back, finding Pyramus dead. She kills herself. And of course, it's a parody of *Romeo and Juliet*.

Harrison: I have to tell our listeners that I've known René a long time. And I can ask him about any text in the history of literature, and I will be thoroughly convinced that mimetic desire is absolutely everywhere. And that the theory is finally unfalsifiable. This is an issue. Now hold on.

As Karl Popper said, in order for a theory to be true, there has to be certain conditions under which it's falsifiable. So let me ask you: under what conditions do you think your theory of mimetic desire is falsifiable?

Girard: In *Romeo and Juliet*, Shakespeare himself is showing you that if you do away with mimetic desire, you have to use other props that will create a tragedy. You can write a comedy. Comedy is a more honest genre, I fear, than tragedy. But to have a tragedy, you must underhandedly bring in something like the blood feud, which is ready-made violence. It's been going on for generations, and so you have the son of one tribe make love to the girl of the other tribe.

Look at the balcony scene between Romeo and Juliet. They are very young people. She's about thirteen. It's supposed to be the greatest love scene in Shakespeare. But what do they talk about? They talk about the henchmen of the family who are down there in the bushes trying to kill Romeo. In the balcony scene, there is no language of love. They cannot say much to each other, but they can talk a lot about the henchmen of the two families that are going to kill Romeo. That's what Juliet is worried about. They don't have much to say because Juliet has already accepted making love to Romeo, and Romeo is about to do it.

Harrison: I promised I wouldn't do this, but I think I have to ask. We've been talking about literature and mimetic desire within individuals, in relations between individuals. But blood feuds, vengeance, reciprocal violence, these are also geopolitical realities in the world we live in. Do you see any sort of pulling back from the endless repetition of the old cycles? Or do you see a danger of falling into a vortex in which we never really get beyond cycles of reciprocal violence, politically speaking?

Girard: I think we are free. It's a question of understanding and of will. Human beings are so passionate that they always get caught in the old traps. We ourselves do, you know. We are committed to what we do. We want to succeed. And we always succeed at the expense of someone. And therefore, I really think we are moving more and more towards more and more violence because of rivalry.

I've talked a lot about literature, but recently, I read a book which is very informative for me: Clausewitz's *On War*. Clausewitz calls war a chameleon. He says it's an escalation to the extremes, and he says in order to win, you have to imitate your enemy constantly. And if you start reading Clausewitz carefully, you can see it works exactly like a mimetic novel. It doesn't matter which side wins. Clausewitz does not teach you how to win, but he constantly shows you the mimetic nature of war.

He was a Prussian, and he said, in order to beat the French, you must have a popular war. You must draft everybody. So here we see the move towards total war. And he sees very well, too, that the technical side of war, the power of the artillery, for instance, is a mimetic game. If you have a big gun, I must have a bigger gun than you have. So in other words, he shows us the move towards total war and total mimetic conflict.

Harrison: If they were to listen to you, what would you propose to politicians in order to try to avoid falling into this syndrome?

Girard: It's a complicated question because my vision fundamentally is religious. I believe in non-violence, and I believe that the knowledge of violence can teach you to reject violence. It will assure you that we are always getting into a game, which is exactly like the previous ones, which is going to be a constant repetition.

Harrison: Yes, but Hamlet already saw that. It didn't save him.

Girard: Ah. But Shakespeare had to bring in Laertes. And if Laertes had been another Hamlet, there would have been no end to the play. It would have been the end of tragedy. But when Shakespeare wrote *Hamlet*, what he said is, "I'm tired of tragedy." And he's really very close to the end of tragedy. After that, he moves to the romances. And in the romances, we have a bunch of characters who repent of their violence, their mimetic desire for vengeance – like Leontes in *The Winter's Tale*. Leontes becomes aware that he's been a wild man, totally mad, by suspecting his wife of being unfaithful with his friend.

Harrison: René, we've only really scratched the surface. After your first book, *Deceit, Desire and the Novel*, you extended your thought into an anthropological realm. You went on to write books like *Violence and the Sacred* and *Things Hidden Since the Foundation of the World*, where you come up with essentially what amounts to an anthropogenic theory of human culture based on scapegoat rituals and sacrifice and the violent origins of religion.

Next time you're on this program, we're going to go from here to the sacrifice and scapegoating.

Girard: I'm sure it will be just as pleasant as today.

Harrison: Oh, it will be. So please stay tuned for a second installment of *Entitled Opinions*. You won't want to miss it.

Note

1. "Delirium as System," *To Double Business Bound* (Baltimore: Johns Hopkins University Press, 1978), 91.

CHAPTER 10
WHY DO WE FIGHT? HOW DO
WE STOP?
Robert Pogue Harrison/2005*

Robert Harrison's interview with his friend and colleague René Girard originally aired on the Stanford radio station KZSU on October 4, 2005. Together, the two review Girard's theories about violence, rituals, sacrifice, and scapegoating. This is the final interview in a two-part series, both included in this volume.

—ED

Robert Harrison: By any measure, René Girard is one of the giants of twentieth-century thought. His career took a remarkable and unconventional turn after his first book, *Deceit, Desire, and the Novel* (1961), when he turned to hitherto unexplored territories in religious studies and in anthropology. He was a literary scholar who, through the study of fiction, stumbled upon an insight into mimetic desire that he then subsequently brought into these other anthropological spheres. In his intensive study of ancient myth and primitive religions, he began to plumb the depths of how mimetic desire becomes an organizing principle of societies as a whole.

René, welcome to the show.

René Girard: It is a pleasure to be here.

Harrison: Let's begin with your concept of religion. For you, religion is not a collection of beliefs or creeds, nor explanations of the world and the mystery of the cosmos; rather, it's a set of practices, first and foremost. Do I get that right?

*From the *Entitled Opinions* radio show. Reprinted with permission of Robert Pogue Harrison. Excerpts from the interview transcript were published in *Neue Zürcher Zeitung* on March 9, 2019. Published as "René Girard: Warum kämpfen wir? Und wie können wir aufhören?"

Girard: Yes. And these practices are called "ritual." Ritual is understood by all archaic people as something indispensable to the survival and well-being of the community. The original type of ritual is the killing of a victim by a priest in the presence of the entire community.

Harrison: This is the cornerstone of your theory of the foundation of ritual. It entails the scapegoating of a victim by a collective. Can you say how you went from mimetic desire to your theory that the so-called "scapegoat mechanism" lies at the origins of human societies?

Girard: Mimetic desire, when it spreads, spreads violence with itself, conflict among people, rivalry, because it means that people all desire the same thing. Now, how far can that go?

There are signs that communities—archaic communities, but even modern communities, all communities—are subject to disturbances that tend to spread to the entire community contagiously, through a form of mimetic desire. If you have two people who desire the same thing, you will soon have three, when you have three, they contaminate the rest of the community faster and faster. The differences that separate them collapse. And therefore you go toward what I call a mimetic crisis, the moment when everybody at the same time is fighting over something. Even if that object disappears, they will go on fighting, because they will become obsessed with each other. And as that conflict grows, it threatens to destroy the whole community.

What happens to end that sort of crisis? My answer to this is that one particular victim seems to more and more people to be responsible for the whole trouble. In other words, the mimetic contagion moves from desire to a specific victim.

When this happens, everybody becomes hostile to that victim. Ultimately, that victim is going to be ... the only technical term that exists in English is "lynching."

The lynching of a victim, of a single victim, causes the community to be reconciled against that victim. Therefore that victim is hated as being responsible for the trouble. But immediately after, if the trouble ends there, that victim will be worshipped as the one who resolved that conflict. In my view, the main characteristic of archaic or even ancient gods is that they are both bad and good. That duality is extremely important – a sign that behind that victim is the "scapegoat" of that community. In other words, the victim universally chosen, is not in fact responsible for anything, but is chosen by the mimetic contagion and, therefore, is perceived, first, as guilty and then as a savior, a god.

Harrison: How does a natural disaster, like a plague, unleash this mimetic contagion among a community?

Girard: We have lots of descriptions, ancient and modern. If you read descriptions of plagues in the Middle Ages and the Renaissance, you will see that many people understand that scapegoat phenomena are connected with this phenomenon. Of course, as long as the real plague is going on, a scapegoat is not going to solve the problem.

Harrison: Right.

Girard: But the problem that it *will* solve is the total disunion, the disruption of the community, which is caused by the mimetic belief of everybody that someone else is responsible.

Harrison: So you believe that whatever creeds or beliefs a religion sponsors or gives rise to occur after a literal lynching or scapegoating, which is the true, hidden foundation for archaic religions. You hold this as a universal.

Girard: Because what is universally observed is that sacrifice is the main religious institution of all archaic religion. We have never found a religion without sacrifice.

What is sacrifice? Sacrifice is not what I just described. What I just described, the actual scapegoat phenomenon, is the foundation of sacrifice. When a community is reconciled by a scapegoat, it's very happy at first. But it very quickly discovers that rivalries reappear. And then, what is it going to do? It's going to remember that that single victim ended the fighting, brought back the peace. So what a community is doing – what all communities do – is to pick a victim and kill that victim in the way that this first victim was killed, only this time ritualistically and not hysterically.

Harrison: So this is what gives rise to ritualized sacrifice?

Girard: That's right. What amazes anthropologists about the ritualization of violence is that sacrifices are usually preceded by a free fall, in which the entire community has been disrupted. They don't understand why, in order to stop disruption, you should go into a greater disruption. But what you do is to imitate the whole process of crisis and resolution, and that is what ritual is. And indeed, it works.

Harrison: It works in terms of restoring order to a community that has...

Girard: Of restoring order. The order which was created by the original scapegoat.

Harrison: What evidence do you rely on to argue that, prior to the institution of ritual, there was lynching or a...

Girard: Ritual and myth. If you look at myth seriously, you will see stories about some kind of scoundrel who disrupts a community, who is punished by the entire community and, after that, turns out to be a god. This is the misunderstanding of the process which creates the community.

Harrison: Where is the misunderstanding? In the stories that are told about it?

Girard: No, in the fact that people believe that the victim is really guilty. What is characteristic of sacrificial societies is that they believe that the god is, as much as a good god, a bad god who can and does disrupt the community in order to punish the community, and then save it through his own action.

Harrison: There's a distinction now between myth and ritual. Ritual is a set of practices that you just described. Myth is the recounting in another mode of events that have their foundation in ritual. Your theory of myth suggests that myths, archaic myths above all, reveal the mechanisms you're talking about on the one hand, but camouflage them on the other.

Girard: They don't reveal it. Because if they had revealed it, we would know about it.

Harrison: But they must reveal it, at least to the extent that you're able to deduce the existence of these mechanisms through your reading of myth.

Girard: The more myths you take as examples, the more you realize that they always say the same thing. In Greece, the most revealing system of accumulation of myths is in the Dionysiac cycle. Because in the cycle, you have a lynching each time.

What is amazing is not that I noticed this – but rather that no one noticed it before. We have a religious system entirely based on a bunch of myths, at the center of which there is a lynching. The lynching becomes the most important factor – that should be taken into account by the interpreters and never was. A society is very reluctant to think that something fundamental in human beings leads to violence. Indeed, that's what these myths demonstrate: that societies have a tendency to go wrong when you have more and more mimetic rivalry.

That's why all rules in societies are an effort to prevent mimetic rivalry. If you look at primitive communities, for instance, why do they have such complicated marriage rules? In order to prevent men who would fight over the same women from gathering on these women and desiring them together. Brother incest is always forbidden because it would lead to a battle between these brothers.

Harrison: I'd like to get clear about myth. Is it because you begin with a theory about the foundations of ritual that you're able to read the myths the way you read them, or is it by reading the myths that you come to the conclusion that the scapegoat mechanism is always hidden behind the stories that were –

Girard: Inevitably, it's a little bit of both. The discovery of prehistorical remnants of animals was very riveting, thanks to the Darwinian theory. You have to have a theory in order to verify it, and you have to have the verification also. It's a dual process.

Harrison: How did you come to your theory in the first place?

Girard: I was reading the findings of the British anthropologists in the English colonies. You find that religious phenomena are the same everywhere and theories, in a way, have not recognized this. They are the same everywhere, and they use the same vocabulary. But they have to repeat the same thing about phenomena which repeat themselves constantly. But there is no way to theorize them. I'm absolutely convinced that there must be a correct theory of these facts.

Harrison: I like the idea that there's a correct theory of certain facts. But let me read something that you said in an interview you gave with *Diacritics* in 1978: "It is true that many interpretations and variations of the same mythical text are possible but they are all false and one interpretation alone is true, the one which reveals the structuring power of the persecutors' standpoint, to which all the others remain blind."

Would you say in retrospect that you overstated the case?

Girard: The case is overstated if the evidence that goes with it is not mentioned, which is the case now. You have to see the evidence.[1]

To have a scapegoat phenomenon in a text, no scapegoat must be mentioned, because people must believe in the guilt of the victim. The god who is a scapegoat is both very bad and very good. How can you make sense out of that continuously without something like the scapegoat phenomenon? How could not the sacrificial crisis, in which everybody is against everybody else, ultimately be solvable through this principle of the single scapegoat?

Mimetic desire spreads around in diverse ways until it gets all people fighting. The only way to solve this type of conflict is through a single victim. And a single victim is possible because, at that point, everybody is doing the same thing.

I could reply with a question, "Do you believe there are scapegoats in our society?"

If there are scapegoats in our society, it's obvious that, in an archaic society, these scapegoats would have been victims, would have been killed.

Harrison: But let's take a commonsensical reading of mythology – for example, Ovid's *Metamorphoses*. It is a compendium of all sorts of different kinds of myths –

Girard: Yes, but it's a compendium without the end. Ovid is doing something very literary and very different from a myth.

He's collecting myths for their picturesqueness. He's very popular with us precisely because he takes the teeth out of them and turns them into stories. So thanks to people like Ovid, we think that myths are nothing *but* stories.

Harrison: So the myths that you have in mind are which ones exactly? Are they archaic myths, the oldest ones?

Girard: Well, sure. We don't have too many myths from these really archaic societies because it was very difficult for nineteenth-century Westerners to get the natives to tell their myths in an intelligible way. But some people were extremely gifted at that, and we have enough myths to understand that they are scapegoat stories. They are all misunderstood scapegoat stories.

Harrison: Let's take one myth. The Oedipus myth was huge for Freud. He built a whole theory of the unconscious on it. You have your own reading of that myth. It is the perfect mimetic crisis situation that you were describing earlier. There's a plague...

Girard: There's a plague going on and it is described in the tragedy. There was probably also a sacred kingship, in which the king was a god. Therefore, he had to be guilty like a god. He had to commit incest and parricide. He had to commit all sorts of crimes. We saw with our own eyes, at the beginning of colonization, that there were sacred kingships in Africa which were just like the Oedipus myth. When they appointed the king, they had him commit incest with his sister or his mother, and he was told he had to do it to scare his own people into believing that he was both a dangerous man and a savior, for the reasons that mythical heroes are.

Harrison: Well, here one gets a sense of how you bring a very special hermeneutic to bear on the ancient texts and the archaic myths that we're dealing with. From what you say, they are distortions of some originary event. They have power to reveal what's at work. Archaic societies were founded on this connection between violence and the sacred...I'm using the title of your book here, *Violence and the Sacred* (1972), in which you see violence as the necessary form of the sacred in ancient societies. However, they come together in a way that, actually, enables societies to survive these crises.

Girard: That's right –

Harrison: Societies survived their mimetic crises by committing measured, ritualized acts of violence, which saved the collective from cannibalizing itself.

Girard: And there's proof that it works. Even someone as intelligent and as modern as Aristotle thought that the tragic hero who was killed at the end was fundamentally guilty. In other words, *hamartia* indicates mythical guilt – which no one has ever identified, really. It is the guilt of Oedipus.

Harrison: So let's take this concept of *hamartia*, or guilt, connected with myth and move our discussion now to the Hebrew Bible. You understand the Hebrew Bible as the beginning of a demystification of myth and the violent origins of the sacred.

Girard: The fundamental text in the Jewish Bible, from that point of view, is the much later part of Isaiah that is called the "Second Isaiah." It has the famous songs of the "Suffering Servant." The "Suffering Servant" is a very good prophet, but very weak. He's described as the type of person who is always unpopular in a society, the one that people turn against without reason. Finally, he's killed by the whole people in a kind of lynching which has been seen as a model for the Christian Passion. Other people will say, rightly, that it's not a model – but it *is* the same process. It is the overturning of mythology, the discovery of what mythology is about, for the first time in mythical text, instead of being treated like a myth – in other words, being read by people who don't understand that the victim is innocent, and therefore represent the victim as guilty.

That victim is represented as hated by the whole people and, nevertheless, killed by people who make a mistake. Just as in the Gospels, when Jesus says, "Forgive them, O Lord, for they know not what they do," we have to take these words literally. They are not words of pity, words of being nice, to these poor, befuddled people, and so forth. They are the actual revelation of the thing. These people really believe the scapegoats are guilty.

Peter, too, when he talks to the crowd in Jerusalem, says, "You are not as guilty as now you're going to think. Before, you felt you were innocent because your victim was guilty. Now, you're going to think you are guilty." This happens all the time.

You must change your behavior. You must no longer get together against the victims the way you have done in the past. We are entering a new world in which this type of truth will be visible. It'll be a much more difficult world, but it'll be much better.

Harrison: We'll talk about the Christian Scriptures shortly. First, two stories from the Hebrew Bible. The sacrifice of Isaac...

Girard: There, we're going back much earlier than the "Suffering Servant," of course.

Harrison: I'd like you to talk a little bit about that, as well as the story of Joseph.

Girard: What is interesting in the Bible is that we are always moving towards less violence, less archaic stuff. The beginning of the Bible is very archaic, and the background is one of child sacrifice, unquestionably.

Child sacrifice is still around when Abraham hears the call. My reading is not at all like Kierkegaard, who thinks that God is playing some kind of trick on the father in order to test his obedience. That's an incredibly modern reading, which has *no* relationship to the archaic text. We know now that human sacrifice – the sacrifice of the first-born, especially – was much more widespread. There was quite a bit in North and South America, too, by the way.

It's a very important phenomenon, and we see it in the case of Isaac. It's a fantastic thing. It's the only text in the world that documents the shift from human sacrifice of the first-born to animal sacrifice. Isaac is finally replaced, and this is presented as a divine action. The whole movement of the Bible is toward that, to reveal the guilt of sacrifice and replace it either with a lesser victim or with no victim at all.

Harrison: Can an animal play the role of a scapegoat?

Girard: An animal, to a certain extent, can play the role of a scapegoat. We can still see in our world the employee who goes to his job and who is mistreated by his boss, and is so afraid of losing his job that he will do nothing. But when he gets back home, if he's really mad, he will kick the dog. If he is even more mad, he will slap his child. And if he's really insanely mad, he will hurt his wife. And the sacrificial instinct is so visible in us that as we say this it makes us laugh, in a way. But it's a kind of sinister laugh. The sacrificial hierarchies of the archaic world are present in our psychology. And they are, of course, the reactions to anger.

Harrison: So you think we can fall back at any moment into these kind of archaic forms of behavior?

Girard: We still have quite a bit of them. Even when you break a plate, you are really going back to sacrifice.

Harrison: What about the story of Joseph in the Bible?

Girard: This is one of the most magnificent stories because Joseph is a scapegoat.

The story of Joseph is fascinating. There are so many brothers that it's like a community. Twelve brothers, and one of them is hated by all the others. You must not try to explain that hatred. It's enough to say, "His father likes him because he's better, because he's more intelligent than his brothers, because he dominates them." So they all get together in order to get rid of him. They try to kill him. But finally, one of the twelve, Judah, who is a little more humane than his brothers, says, "Let's sell him into slavery," and so they send him to Egypt. And in Egypt, pretty much the same thing happens to him.

Because he's so full of talent – he's a bright, young Jewish boy who becomes very powerful in the household where he is sent as a slave, which is the household of Potiphar, who is a great civil servant of Pharaoh. And one fine day, because he's handsome and nice, the lady Potiphar, the wife of Potiphar, tries to make love to him, and she fails because he's completely faithful to his master. But when she denounces him as having tried to make love to her, he's sent to jail. Therefore, he becomes a scapegoat a second time. And there, he's saved by the fact that – like Oedipus, in a way – he's a kind of prophet. He can foretell the future. He has two dreams in which he reveals that there will be a great famine. And therefore, Pharaoh appoints him as the prime minister of Egypt. And during the seven years in which there is a lot of food, he stores that food.

During the famine, people come from all over the Middle East for relief. Among those who show up are his brothers. Joseph recognizes them. But they don't recognize him because he's dressed like an Egyptian. He is an incredibly powerful man. And he puts them to a scapegoat test. He says he wants to keep the youngest brother, the last one, the one who is equivalent to him, who is named Benjamin, and he slanders Benjamin. He says that Benjamin has stolen his cup. And then, finally, what happens: Judah, who had already more or less saved Joseph, says, "I cannot stand it. I'm going to stand in the place of my brother. You keep me, and you let Benjamin go. Because if Benjamin doesn't go back, our old father, Jacob, will die." Joseph is so touched that he forgives all his brothers.

In that story, you have the whole movement of the Bible toward the revelation of the scapegoat, and the giving of oneself as a scapegoat in order to reveal the truth, to the abolition of the scapegoat system. It's one of the most beautiful stories ever written and in which the whole spirit of Judaism and Christianity is present. That's why, from a technical viewpoint, the Christians say, "It's a perfect prophecy of the death of Jesus."

Harrison: René, I want to move to the modern era. But before that, a word or two about the role of the Christian Scriptures in your thinking. Is it fair to say that you read the Christian Scriptures as, not just a halfway revelation, but a *full* revelation of the scapegoat mechanism of ancient religions? And that through the lynching, scapegoating of Jesus, you have finally the open revelation of the violent origins of antecedent religions?

Girard: Let me give an example. Just before his Passion, Jesus asks the people with him, "Why don't you explain to me this sentence?" The sentence is in Psalm 118: "The stone that the builders rejected has become the keystone." Now, tell me that the scapegoat is not the foundation of society – because that sentence is obviously about that. The people who listened to Jesus never answered his question. Theologians are lost in all sorts of Greek stuff, and they've never answered this question since.

Or ask a theologian why, in the Gospel of John, Caiaphas says, "It is better that one man dies and the whole people be saved." This is regarded as a prophetic line. Why, if the scapegoat is not important to human culture and religion? The Bible is full of things like that. The great parables, the parable of the murderous winemakers, for instance, is nothing but that. The master of the vineyard always sends messengers to them, and they kill them and say, "After we kill them, we'll be the masters of our own world. We'll be our own foundation."

Harrison: In Orthodox Christian theology, the sacrifice of Christ on the cross is perceived to have redemptive value. I take it, for you, it's not so much a redemption that takes place on the cross, but rather a revelation of what you call "the scandal," the *skandalon*. How do you answer theologians who say, "Well, where is the salvational aspect?"

Girard: Let them tell me where the salvation is. I believe it just as they do, but they have not yet explained it. And what you're talking about is really the theory of Saint Anselm, you know, in the twelfth century.

Harrison: Saint Paul, as well.

Girard: I know. But Saint Paul never does it in the same way. As a matter of fact, if you look at the church, the church has plenty of darkness. But there is no official theory of redemption, of how the cross works. So you're allowed to make guesses and try to understand it. But of course, I say what can be understood from the human side of it.

You see what I mean? But I don't deal with theology. I deal with the anthropology of religion.

Harrison: Yes, exactly.

Girard: And I think that the fault of both theologians and anthropologists is that they haven't seen that they are talking about the same thing in different languages.

Harrison: A huge jump forward. Friedrich Nietzsche in the nineteenth century marks a huge shift in Western culture, especially with the war that he waged against Christianity for example in his book *The Antichrist*. His denunciation of Christianity as a slave religion is based on a psychology of resentment and frustration. You have worked a lot on Nietzsche, and you have a very interesting relationship to him because for you, he's not just wrong or mad in his insights. He saw a lot that you think is important.

Girard: That's right. He's so wrong that, in some ways, he's right.

Harrison: And what was he wrong about, principally?

Girard: Now that we have the complete works of Nietzsche, thanks to the Italian publisher Colli and Montinari, we have this text: "Dionysus and Jesus, same death, same collective death."

But Christianity does not accept sacrifice, doesn't want anyone to die, whereas Dionysus accepts it. Therefore, Dionysus is life. What Nietzsche would say, if he were really honest, is "Dionysus *is* the crowd I'm talking about. Dionysus is the lynching of that crowd, which makes it the religion of the slaves, par excellence." We know very well that, in a way, it's a destruction of the most ancient social system that revived or invented Dionysus. Dionysus *is*, par excellence, the religion of the crowd.

Nietzsche inverted that, because he hated Christianity so much. But that hatred was so close to profound love that he's always talking about the right subjects. Very often, he's inverting a solution, which is completely obvious. Today there are very few people who are Christian. Christianity has never been the religion of the elite, as much as it is today.

Especially, in Europe, there are very few people who dare be for Christianity. And Christianity is, in a way, the religion of the people who reject the lynch mob that, ultimately, Nietzsche accepts and glorifies.

Harrison: When he collapsed in Turin, he wrote a number of brilliantly lucid, but mad, letters, some of them he signed "Dionysus." Others he signed, "The Crucified."

Girard: I think that's very important. It has to be analyzed in detail. But I think it's finally the collapse of his system. Because instead, he's been trying to build up that difference in favor of Dionysus. And now, at the end, it collapses completely, and both have become equivalent. But Nietzsche cannot stand that and, literally, falls into the hands of the living god – which is a very dangerous fate, as the Jews well knew.

But deep down, I feel Nietzsche is saved because he thinks beyond his lucid thoughts. And the moment he does that is precisely when he can swing either way. In other words, his whole world collapses. One could say that the entire effort of his life was to demonstrate the superiority of Dionysus over Christ. And at that moment, he collapses.

Harrison: In 1966, another German thinker, Heidegger, gave an interview to the German weekly magazine, *Der Spiegel*, where he was asked about his politics and his view of modern technology and so-called modern nihilism, the forces of nihilism. That's a word that's also dear to you, as well – although, you understand it in a very different way than Heidegger did. The interviewers, at a certain point, ask him: "Well, what can the philosophers do in order to offset nihilism or do something about the destructive forces of technology, and to rehumanize politics and the world, and so forth?" And Heidegger answers that there's nothing that the philosophers can do, there's nothing anyone can do. "Only a god –"

Girard: Only a god.

Harrison: "– can save us."

Girard: And what, precisely, the modern world is *not* going to produce is a new god. What Heidegger asserts, in a way, is that the great succession of archaic gods was not destroyed by Judaism and Christianity. In other words, was not revealed as the lie that it is. If it were not revealed, indeed, there could be new archaic gods. That's what Heidegger was talking about. If there cannot be any archaic gods, that means we are deprived of sacrifices. It means we are threatened, if we continue to be as violent as we are, by the destruction of the world.

Harrison: For you, that's a good thing?

Girard: It's not a question of a good thing. But the Christian and Jewish documents always contain apocalyptic material which is not about the destruction of the world by God, as the fundamentalists believe, but the destruction of the world by human beings themselves. If you read the great apocalyptic chapters of the Gospels, which are much more important than the Apocalypse of John, you will see that we're in a world that always becomes more and more violent, that finally destroys itself. It's not the responsibility of God, as we hear today. These texts should be revived. It is a great fault of the churches that they don't talk about them.

Harrison: Two questions, then. Heidegger says, "Only a god can save us." Your answer is that only we can save ourselves?

Girard: Only we can save ourselves. I'm much more of a humanist than he is.

Harrison: And what prescriptions do you offer for this sort of self-help, so that we can come to our own rescue?

Girard: The one that is at the foundation of the Gospel, which is non-retaliation, which is peace. If you don't have sacrifices to return peace to you, you have to do it by yourself, and we know what the recipe is. It's a very difficult one. It's non-retaliation. It's the rules defined by the three synoptic Gospels as the rules of the Kingdom of God.

Harrison: The other aspect of Heidegger's dictum, "Only a god can save us," is that we live in a world which is completely desacralized, and that some dimension of the holy would be brought forth by such a god.

Girard: Yes.

Harrison: So do you think that human beings would be comfortable enough within themselves in a world without sacrality?

Girard: No, no. But...

Harrison: ...with no dimension of the holy?

Girard: ...wait a minute, because...

Harrison: And can one have the sacred without violence?

Girard: Well, I prefer not to use the word "sacred." My answer to your question is, yes. And this real "divineness," this real holiness will come out of desacralization itself. The sacralization for which Heidegger is asking is a return to the archaic, and he knows that himself. Therefore, he knows fully that it's impossible. The modern is not bad, as Heidegger thinks. The modern is made bad by the badness of men. But in itself, it is a good thing. It is a good development. It is more intelligence to man, more humaneness – because in spite of all the bad aspects of the world, it is also true that our world is the best we have ever known in many ways. Therefore, it's *this* world which must be saved. And it can be saved, as you just said, only by human beings getting along together.

Harrison: Well, that's easy to say, but when –

Girard: Oh, I don't say, "It's easy to do." Probably, it's not going to happen.

Harrison: What sort of recipes would you put forward?

Girard: There cannot be any recipe. There cannot be any recipe because this is the reason why the Gospels begin with the Kingdom of God, the offer of the Kingdom of God, and the attempt to convince human beings that they should refrain from retaliation.

Harrison: Is the Christian Gospel essential to your notion of human beings being able to come to their own rescue? Or can one arrive at the same result independently of that particular body of texts?

Girard: That body of text includes the Jewish Bible and the prophets, and the Christian Gospels, which are truly indispensable. What we need is to complete the theological reading with an anthropological reading that would make it intelligible on the human plane. It's very difficult because people are not interested in it, because people are trying to fight it back. In my view, that is the real unconscious, the real defense mechanisms – the rejection of an awareness of our own violence. Especially, in terms of national and international intercourse, of course, where the other nation is always available for insults and vilification and scapegoating.

This is true in all countries still today. This is probably the most essential thing. And the experience of international life today shows this to us absolutely marvelously. When I'm in France today, I have to treat Iraq as if it were the fault of every American. When I'm in America today, I have to treat every Frenchman as if he were a traitor to America.

Harrison: Do you see the Enlightenment as growing out of the traditions that we've been talking about?

Girard: Yes, of course. It's a complex question. In the Enlightenment, people understand many things about Christianity that are not specifically religious, but are just good human relations. They are convinced that they will be able to establish this relationship simply because human beings are "good," human beings have "goodwill." And that is the reason we don't read anthropology as it really is today. Because we believe that the Enlightenment, the discovery of the goodness of man, must take place *against* religion, which has been an obstacle to it. In reality, it's the action of religion which made it possible to reach the Enlightenment. Therefore, this action seems unnecessary. And indeed, it is, in a way, unnecessary. We understand today that sacrifice is crazy. To have substitute victims? We can't believe in them.

Therefore, the Enlightenment says, "Human beings don't need that. Human beings are good. And let them be good. And religion is really the obstacle of that goodness." And they see something quite real. But they see it wrongly because they don't understand history, and they don't understand that they have reached that point, in a way, because the action of sacrifice has made them very slowly better. And they should, indeed, get rid of sacrifice, but not in a spirit of anti-religion. They have a huge illusion about their own goodness.

Harrison: But if it's the case that we have to come to our own rescue, that human beings are the perpetrators of the social and existential woes that befall us, then the Enlightenment, in many ways, was a call to this sort of self-responsibility, was it not?

Girard: Yes. And this is good. There is no doubt that Voltaire was right when he said that during the persecution of Jean Calas that he was more Christian than his Christian opponents. There is no denying that. And indeed, all the churches have reached that point. We must be very careful of is not to think in terms of open-and-shut categories. History is a very difficult discipline.

CHAPTER 11
"WAR IS EVERYWHERE."
Elisabeth Lévy/2007*

Le Point: You have found in Clausewitz's work some surprising resonances with your own. Just as his thinking is indissolubly linked, if not to the direct experience, at least to the concrete observation of the Napoleonic wars, were you influenced by the Second World War, which took place when you were an adolescent?

René Girard: That is undeniable. My awareness of events, of history, of politics, grew with the totalitarian threat. I was born at the end of 1923 and was ten years old when Hitler came to power. A child could understand well enough that the rise of Hitlerism put France in danger of being invaded. My father was very perceptive, and he was a great reader of the press; he was a French Radical-Socialist[1] – not an activist, but an intellectual with an interest in current events, exactly what I became myself. He immediately saw that we were witnessing the return of Germany and also that it was impossible to hold it back, that we could not reenact Verdun. Later, he recognized, even before the autumn of 1941, that things were starting to go wrong for the Germans and that Moscow and Leningrad might well hold out.

Le Point: Do you mean that, even while events were unfolding, you were conscious of History as you lived through it?

René Girard: Of course! I remember very clearly the remilitarization of the Rhineland in 1935. If the French had gone into Germany, they could have changed the course of events: the Germans were incapable of putting up the least resistance. But Albert Sarraut [the prime minister] and the French government would have been pegged as the bastards who kept the world from going back to normal. They lacked the moral force to do more. Sarraut took a lot of flak later for his passivity. But he was in an inextricable

*From *Le Point*, October 18, 2007. Reprinted with permission of *Le Point*. Copyright *Le Point*, 2007, Elisabeth Lévy. Translated by Mark R. Anspach.

situation. In any case, this turn of events left me with the certainty that we were "trapped like rats," to quote Céline's leitmotiv in *Journey to the End of the Night*.

Le Point: After that, did you suffer directly from the Occupation?

René Girard: As long as I stayed in Avignon, it was not too hard to bear. I left for a preparatory school in Lyon, where my brother was studying medicine. My family came from a bourgeoisie on the wane so I suffered from social inferiority compared to my classmates from the Lyonnaise elite. By the end of the first week, I had had enough and returned home. I should explain that I had already passed my baccalaureate by taking correspondence courses because, having been a terribly unruly pupil, I had been thrown out of high school. I therefore studied at home for the entrance exam at the École des Chartes, the school my father had attended. I was accepted in 1942 and found myself in Paris, in a hotel that was heated for 15 minutes a day. Fortunately, after spending a year there, friends of mine got me into the boarding house at 104 Rue de Vaugirard, an institution run by the Marist Brothers where François Mitterrand had lived. Thanks to my clandestine radio receiver, I was the first to tell my friends of the Normandy landings in 1944.[2]

Le Point: In any case, the question of violence is at the heart of your work and of your theory of mimetic desire. But up until now, you have been more interested in myth and literature than in military strategy. What brought you to Clausewitz?

René Girard: As it happens, I came upon him in an English edition marked up by a US Air Force pilot. And the correspondence with my work jumped out at me. Here is a nineteenth century thinker who does not have a reputation as a literary figure even though I discovered that he is a marvelous writer. There's a whiff of the devil about him, a sort of sinister aura. The Germans don't want anything to do with him. But everyone admits that Clausewitz is serious stuff! My theory of mimetic desire was much criticized as being based solely on literature, which was a way to undermine its credibility.

Le Point: In any era, literature has something to do with truth. That is the meaning of Aragon's phrase "lying true." And that is also the thesis of your "Romantic Lie and Novelistic Truth,"[3] which sparked controversy in the Sixties...

René Girard: For me, literature is much more powerful than the human sciences of the Sixties that have completely faded away by now. And, in its essence, Clausewitz's work is a military version of the "Romantic lie." In his first chapter, he suggests, without expressly saying so, that war has not ceased since the beginning of history, and therefore that human history is the story of an inexorable "escalation to extremes" as reciprocity engenders ever increasing vengeance. But he hastens to hide the terrifying side of his theory by asserting that absolute war never occurs. In reality, Clausewitz secretly fears a return to gentlemanly "Lace Wars" once Napoleon is gone. His passion for Napoleon combines fierce hatred and prodigious love: it is difficult to find a better example of mimetic rivalry.

Le Point: He has a presentiment of what we call total war, where the fight is no longer between armies but entire societies…

René Girard: Yes, absolute war calls for the infinite mobilization that Peter Sloterdijk has analyzed very well. Raymond Aron's reading of Clausewitz tries to save political science. Everyone knows the phrase "war is the pursuit of politics by other means." In truth, for him, war and politics are equivalent. Which means that politics does not exist.

Le Point: For you, mimetic rivalry is the very engine of History. What makes you think that today it is racing out of control?

René Girard: The world wars marked one stage in the escalation to extremes. September 11, 2001, was the beginning of a new phase. Contemporary terrorism still needs to be theorized. We do not yet understand what makes a terrorist ready to die in order to kill Americans, Israelis, or Iraqis. The novelty with respect to Western heroism is the willingness to suffer and die for the sole purpose of imposing suffering and death on the other. Americans have made the mistake of "declaring war" on al-Qaeda when we are not even certain if al-Qaeda exists as such. The era of wars is over: henceforth, war is everywhere. We have entered the era of universal acting out. There is no intelligent politics anymore. We are close to the end.

Le Point: Is the Apocalypse coming tomorrow?

René Girard: Of course not, but in today's world, many things do correspond to the atmosphere of the great apocalyptic texts of the New Testament, especially Matthew and Mark. One finds there the principal mimetic phenomenon, which is the struggle of doubles: city against city, province against province… It is always the doubles who fight and their brawling makes no sense since the same thing prevails on either side. In these conditions, I see no more important task than to constantly summon the realism of revelation and of the apocalyptic texts. But even the Church never refers to them any more. When I was little, the Sundays that followed Pentecost were apocalyptic Sundays, and that is what the sermons were about. Preaching on that theme ceased in 1946: after the Bomb, it had become too hot a topic.

Le Point: But then, does humanity still have a choice or is it already too late?

René Girard: We are threatened with death. The Judeo-Christian message is that if we do not reconcile with one another, there are no longer sacrificial victims to save our skin. The kingdom of God offers reconciliation or nothing. Unfortunately, we are making the second choice out of ignorance and laziness. The only solution is to refuse all violence, all reprisals. I'm not at all sure of being capable of that myself, but the Gospels tell us it is the only way. The tragedy is that we always choose the short term. We are all in the position of Louis XV: "After me, the deluge."

Notes

1. Translator's note: Despite their name, the French Radical-Socialists were not radical leftists but centrist social democrats with a strong anticlerical streak. Albert Sarraut, the French premier cited by Girard in the next paragraph, was a Radical-Socialist.

2. Translator's note: The French text refers erroneously to the landings of "August 6, 1944." The Normandy invasion began on June 6, 1944.

3. Translator's note: The original title in French of the book translated as *Deceit, Desire, and the Novel.*

CHAPTER 12
"I HAVE ALWAYS TRIED TO THINK INSIDE AN EVOLUTIONARY FRAMEWORK."

Pierpaolo Antonello and João Cezar de Castro Rocha/2007*

"Here, then, I had at last got a theory by which to work."

(*Charles Darwin*, Autobiography)

[Y]ou said that whenever an appetite becomes a desire it is affected by a model. Desire is completely socially constructed. However, it seems that in your general theory there is no scope for basic needs.

Let me draw a fundamental distinction: an appetite doesn't imply imitation. When someone is being choked, there is a great appetite for breathing and there isn't imitation in it because breathing is physiological. One doesn't imitate anyone when one walks for miles in a desert in order to find some water. Nonetheless, in our modern world, it is different because there are social and cultural models of fashionable eating and drinking, and any form of appetite is mediated by behavioral models, and, paradoxically, the more we do it, the more we think we are exercising "personal," "individual" preference which are only our own ...

The more cruel and wild a society is, the more violence is rooted in pure need. One must never exclude the possibility of violence that has nothing to do with mimetic desire but simply with scarcity. However, even at the level of basic needs, when rivalry begins and is related to an object, any kind of object, there's no doubt that it will soon become impregnated with mimesis. In these cases, there is always some social mediation at play. Marxists are convinced that certain sentiments are specifically social, since they appear in one specific social class. For them, mimetic

---

*Excerpted from René Girard, *Evolution and Conversion: Dialogues on the Origins of Culture* (London: Continuum, 2007), 74–78, 81–87, 96–100, 234–38. Reprinted with permission of Continuum.

desire is a form of aristocratic distinction, a kind of luxury. I would simply answer: of course it is! Before modern times, only the aristocrats could afford it. The theory of chivalry, for instance, is a way of glorifying mimetic desire, and Cervantes understood this perfectly. Don Quixote is a *hidalgo*, meaning "son of someone," a man of leisure, an aristocrat. There's also no doubt that in a world of dire need, the average man has only needs and appetites. If you look at the medieval genre of the *fabliau*, it deals chiefly with physical appetites, and the struggles or fighting which occur are connected with the piece of bread which the disputants don't have. So the Marxists are partly right: if the mimetic theory denied the objectivity of certain struggles it would be false; it would be no more than a denial of existence and its basic needs. It is no less true that mimeticism, especially among those who have a knack of it, can flourish in the most extreme misery. Witness, for instance, the snobbery of Marmeladov's wife in *Crime and Punishment*.

That is why you did not accept Lucien Scubla's reading of your work, according to which "mimetic rivalry is the only source of human violence."[1]
I agree about the essential part, although this formula undervalues objective needs and appetites too much. As I just said, basic appetites can trigger conflicts, but it is also true that the conflicts once triggered easily become trapped in a mimetic mechanism. One might say that any violent process that has any duration, any temporality, is bound to become mimetic. Nowadays there is a growing concern about "the act of violence," meaning the random act of violence, like being robbed or mugged or raped, that could happen to anybody in the "harmonic life" of a big city. That is what people are most worried about in contemporary affluent societies. It is a violence that is totally divorced from any relational context. Therefore, it has neither antecedents nor followers. Nonetheless, specialists on violence show that haphazard aggression isn't the main cause of violence. Violent behavior mostly occurs among people who know each other, who have known each other for a long time.[2] Violence has a mostly mimetic history, as in those sad cases of domestic violence. That is the most common type of crime, much more than violence between strangers. Being mugged in the street isn't directly mimetic in the sense of a relationship between the victim and the mugger, although behind random aggression there are mimetic relationships in the mugger's personal history, or in his relationship with society at large, which remain invisible but could nonetheless be discovered and explored.

We should also emphasize, however, that mimesis does not only engender disruptive effects through acquisitive mimesis, but it also allows for cultural transmission.

That is true. In the past I have mainly emphasized the rivalrous and conflictual mimesis.[3] I did so because I discovered the mimetic mechanism through the analysis of novels, where the representation of conflictual relations is essential. Thus, in my work, the "bad" mimesis is always dominant, but the "good" one is of course even more important. There would be no human mind, no education, no transmission of culture without mimesis. However, I do believe that the "bad" mimesis needs to be emphasized because its reality remains overlooked, and it has been always neglected or mistaken for non-mimetic behavior, and even denied by most observers. The intense capacity of humans to imitate is what forces them to become what they are, but this capacity carries a high price, with the explosion of conflicts related to acquisitive mimesis. Imitation channels not only knowledge but also violence.

A strong emphasis on positive mimesis is given in theories such as the one proposed by Richard Dawkins. His theory of memes, as a minimal unity of cultural transmission, would be a case in point.[4]

Dawkins has no awareness of mimetic rivalry, mimetic crisis, scapegoating and other figures uncovered by mimetic theory. However, I think that, in general, and from my perspective, biological or neurocognitive theories of mimesis are more advanced than literary ones.

Scientists aren't afraid of developing theories and concepts which are the most relevant to the human mind and social behavior, like imitation and mimetism, for instance, but which remain totally alien to most literary scholars and students of social sciences. Traditionally, literary studies have been grounded in the idea of interdividuality, on the notion of the uniqueness of a given author. Therefore, literary criticism tends to deny mimetic desire. The denial of mimetic desire and the prevalence of individualism are one and the same thing. Because the more mimetic desire one has, the more one has to be individualistic in order to deny it.

Are you suggesting that the institutionalization of literary studies helps to conceal the mechanism of mimetic desire?

Yes, absolutely. This is exactly what Sandor Goodhart affirms in *Sacrificing Commentary*.[5] According to him, the real function of criticism is to bring literature back to conventional individualism, refusing and masking mimetic desire. Literary criticism has a social function which is always bringing literature back to the social norm, rather than emphasizing the gulf between the vision of a great writer and the vision of that norm. Literary criticism should help to uncover the mimetic nature of desire instead of concealing it through its engagement with concepts such as originality and novelty, constantly advocated in an incantatory and empty fashion.

Returning to the definition of mimesis: wouldn't your approach be clearer if you distinguished "cultural mimesis" from "acquisitive mimesis"?[6]
I don't think so. This expression would entail that cultural imitation does not involve any form of rivalry, which is not true because we could compete over cultural objects as well. Maybe we could say that mimesis has a double-bind structure, since it isn't necessarily acquisitive, in the sense of being conflictual, but also cultural. However, I fear that there is the tendency to reduce mimesis to mimicry, while only the most superficial and harmless aspects of it are stressed. That is why I have emphasized the violent side of mimesis.

* * *

Méconnaissance

To underscore the structural continuity of the social phenomena we have been discussing – in spite of the obvious historical differences they present – we could say that as much as mimetic desire isn't a modern invention, the scapegoat mechanism is not only visible in primitive rituals or ancient societies, but is also present in the modern world.
It's true, and to see how the scapegoat mechanism works in modern societies, it is necessary once more to start with mimetic desire. The paradox of mimetic desire is that it seems solidly fixed on its object, stubbornly determined to have that object and no other object, whereas in reality it very quickly shows itself to be completely opportunistic. When mimetic desire tends to become opportunistic, the people affected by it focus, paradoxically, on substitute models, substitute antagonists. The age of scandals, in which we live, is a displacement of desire of this kind. A massive collective scandal corresponds to the *skandalon* of the two biblical "neighbors" multiplied several times. Let me repeat that *skandalon* in the Gospels means *mimetic* rivalry, therefore it is that empty ambition, that

ridiculous reciprocal antagonism and resentment that everybody feels for each other, for the simple reason that our desires are sometimes frustrated. When a small-scale *skandalon* becomes opportunistic, it tends to join the biggest scandal spread by the mass media, taking comfort from the fact that its indignation is shared by many people. That is, mimesis, instead of moving just in the direction of our neighbor, our specific mimetic rival, tends to become "lateral," and this is a sign of growing crisis, of growing contagion. The biggest scandal is always devouring the smaller ones, until there is only one scandal, only one victim, and that is when the scapegoat mechanism resurfaces. The growing resentment that people feel for one another because of the increased size of the mimetic rivals conflates into a bigger resentment toward a random element of society, such as the Jews during Nazism in Germany, the Dreyfus affair in late nineteenth-century France, the immigrants from Africa in present-day Europe, the Muslims in the recent terrorist events. A magnificent literary example of this phenomenon can be found in Shakespeare's *Julius Caesar*, in the mimetic recruiting of the conspirators against Caesar.[7] One of them, Ligario, is very sick, "a feeble tongue," but at the idea of killing Caesar he revives and his floating resentment starts to focus on Caesar. He then forgets everything because now he has Caesar as the fixed point of his hatred. What progress! Nine-tenths of politics unfortunately remembers exactly that. What people call the partisan spirit is nothing but choosing the same scapegoat as everybody else. However, because of the Christian revelation of the fundamental innocence of the scapegoat victims and the arbitrariness of the accusation against them, this polarization of hatred is soon revealed as such, and the final resolution of unanimity fails. Since I have already touched upon Christianity, let me briefly clarify my contention regarding the special place occupied by it in the history of mimetic mechanism (although most of my readers probably know about it).

In a nutshell: before the advent of Judaism and Christianity, in one way or the other, the scapegoat mechanism was accepted and justified, on the basis that it remained unknown. It brought peace back to the community at the height of the chaotic mimetic crisis. All archaic religions grounded their rituals precisely around the re-enactment of the founding murder. In other words, they considered the scapegoat to be *guilty* of the eruption of the mimetic crisis. By contrast, Christianity, in the figure of Jesus, denounced the scapegoat mechanism for what it actually is: the murder of an innocent victim, killed in order to pacify a riotous community. That's the moment in which the mimetic mechanism is fully revealed.

This brings us back to the concept of méconnaissance, *which is central to the mimetic theory. You said that the "sacrificial process requires a certain degree of misunderstanding." If the scapegoat mechanism is to bring about social cohesion, then the innocence of the victim must be concealed in a way that allows the entire community to unite in the belief as to the victim's guilt. And you have remarked that as soon as the actors understand the mimetic mechanism, knowing how it works, it collapses and fails to reconcile the community. However, according to Henri Atlan, this fundamental proposition is never posited as a problem. Rather, it is presented as self-evident.[8]*

The issue here is that I did not place enough emphasis on the unconscious character of the scapegoat mechanism. This is a very simple issue and, at the same time, a crucial point of my theory. Let's take, for instance, the Dreyfus affair. If you are against Dreyfus, you firmly believe Dreyfus is guilty. Imagine that you are a Frenchman in 1894, worried about the army and concerned about the Germans. If suddenly you become convinced that Dreyfus is innocent, this would destroy the spiritual comfort, the righteous anger, you derive from the belief that Dreyfus is guilty. That is all I mean here! It isn't the same to be against Dreyfus as to be for him. I feel that Atlan, even though he is very astute, misunderstands what I have said. Most of the theologians who have reviewed *Things Hidden* also misunderstand this issue. There were even critics who said that if there was such a thing as a scapegoat religion, it must be Christianity, since the Gospels explicitly refer to this phenomenon! My answer is very simple: precisely because Jesus is explicitly represented as a scapegoat, Christianity, as a religion, cannot be founded on scapegoating, rather it is a denunciation of it. The reason should be obvious – if you believe the scapegoat is guilty, you are not going to name it as being "my scapegoat." If France scapegoats Dreyfus, no one will recognize that Dreyfus *is* a scapegoat. Everybody will only repeat that he *is* guilty. If you recognize the innocence of the victim, you are not going to be able to use violence so easily against that victim, and Christianity is precisely a way of saying, with maximum emphasis, that the victim is innocent. After all, the victim is the Son of God. This is the key role of the *méconnaissance* in the process – it allows one to have the illusion that one is justly accusing someone who is *really* guilty and, therefore, *deserves* to be punished. In order to have a scapegoat, one must fail to perceive the truth, and therefore one cannot represent the victim as a *scapegoat*, but rather as a righteous victim, which is what mythology does. The parricide and incest of Oedipus are supposed to be real, let's not forget. To scapegoat someone is to be unaware of what you are doing.

In Shakespeare's Julius Caesar *there is a remarkable speech by Brutus in which this principle is twice made explicit: "Let's be sacrificers but not butchers, Caius"; "We shall be call'd purgers, not murderers."*[9] *How do you interpret that?*

Brutus exalts the difference between the legitimate violence of sacrifice and the illegitimate violence of civil war, but he and his co-conspirators ultimately cannot make themselves credible as sacrificers. Brutus knows what he is doing, and he knows that to do it well he should claim that it is not a murder. In my own vocabulary, he unmasks the necessary *méconnaissance*, which accompanies the killing of a scapegoat. Brutus says we must do this in such a clear fashion that it will appear as different from murder as possible. This is an incredible text with a most powerful insight. The principle is that the right hand shouldn't know what the left hand is doing. And that shows an understanding of sacrifice in Shakespeare which is extremely powerful and far superior to that of modern anthropology.

Why did you opt for the term méconnaissance *rather than the more common "unconscious"?*[10]

Because, in the reader's mind, the word "unconscious" would have the Freudian connotation. I used *méconnaissance* because there is no doubt that one must define the scapegoat mechanism as a form of misrecognition of its injustice, without ignoring who has been killed. Now, I think that the unconscious nature of sacrificial violence is revealed in the New Testament, particularly in Luke: "Father, forgive them, for *they do not know what they are doing*" (Luke 23.34). That sentence has to be taken literally, and the proof of it is a parallel statement in the Acts of the Apostles. Peter, addressing the crowd who had been present at the crucifixion, says "you acted in ignorance" (Acts 3.17).[11] The word "ignorance" is really the Greek word for "not knowing." But in our contemporary language one has to say "unconscious." However, I do not want to say *the* unconscious with the definite article because it implies a form of ontological essentialism that I distrust. However, there is definitely a lack of consciousness in scapegoating, and this lack of consciousness is as essential as the unconscious in Freud. However, it isn't the same thing and it is collective rather than individual.

Could you then clarify your criticism of Freud's concept of the unconscious?

What I'm against is the idea that there is *an* unconscious, as a separate mental entity. There isn't anything wrong with the idea of something being unconscious, but the idea of *the* unconscious as a kind of "black box," has been proved misleading. As I just said, I should have placed more emphasis on the unconscious nature of the scapegoat mechanism, but I refuse to lock it up into an unconscious that has a life of its own, in the style of Freud.

In Freud, the unconscious also has a collective structure, but it is indeed basically composed of individual experiences. Regarding interdividual psychology, the méconnaissance *seems also to prevent the recognition of the mimetic nature of desire. Do you think that the more mimetic one is, the stronger the* méconnaissance *will be?*
I will answer with a paradox. The more you are mimetic, the stronger is your *méconnaissance* and also the possibilities of understanding it. Suddenly you can realize that the nature of your own desire is strictly imitative. I believe all great writers of mimetic desire are hyper-mimetic. As I tried to show in my books, Proust and Dostoevsky, for instance, are extraordinary examples of this. In their novels, there is a radical break between the mediocrity of their early works, which are attempts at self-justification, and the greatness of their later works, which all represent the *fall* of the self, in the sense of Camus's last book, *La Chute*. I think *La Chute* is a book about the bad faith of modern writers, who condemn the entire creation in order to justify themselves and build a fortress of illusory moral superiority.

* * *

"How completely man must have personified the deity."

(Charles Darwin, Notebooks*)*

Missing Links

According to Michel Serres, your work puts forward a Darwinian theory of culture because it "proposes a dynamic, shows an evolution, and gives a universal explanation of culture."[12] Is this actually your aim?
Why not? I think that Darwin is too naïve in his conception of religion, I believe there is something extremely powerful and admirable in his way of arguing, but I have always been fascinated by the way he thinks. This is the reason why there is a Darwinian perspective in the process of hominization as I present it in *Things Hidden*. I feel a strong kinship with his way of arguing *"one long argument from the beginning to the end."*[13] The theory of natural selection seems to me quite powerfully sacrificial.

After all, Darwin, in resorting to Malthus's theory of population, stresses the importance of death just as much as the importance of survival. In some sense it is representing nature as a super-sacrificial machine.[14] Any great scientific discovery that represents a paradigm and a gestalt shift is strongly determined by the larger cultural context in which this discovery developed. I think that the discovery of natural selection is marked by the time in which it was conceived. It is part of the modern discovery of sacrifice as the foundation not only of human culture but also the natural order.

In order to explain the emergence of the symbolic sphere, in Things Hidden *you outlined a theory of hominization and the origin of culture within a naturalistic framework, mainly blending ethnographic accounts with anthropological theories. This crucial aspect of the evolution of human culture has been underexplored in your theory ever since.*

I simply didn't have the opportunity to return to it. I am also only partially equipped to articulate my theory with a specific scientific vocabulary, but I have always tried to think inside an evolutionary framework. The compatibility between theism and evolution is not an issue for me, and the whole debate between Darwinists and creationists (or advocates of intelligent design) is simply *passé* and not very interesting from my point of view. One of the central points of the mimetic theory which could contribute a good deal to the debate, if we take it seriously, is that religion is the mother of culture. In the process of the emergence of cultural elements, one also needs to stress that there is no absolute beginning. The process is extremely complex and progressive.

According to the philosopher Elliot Sober: "biologists interested in culture are often struck by the absence of viable general theories in the social sciences. All of biology is united by the theory of biological evolution. Perhaps progress in the social sciences is impeded because there is no general theory of cultural evolution.[15]

Mimetic theory is, among other things, the origin of the great cultural institutions starting from sacrificial ritual, which is fully coherent with a Darwinian framework. There is a set of hypotheses in this work that are strongly compatible with a mimetic framework and support its claims. I agree with the idea expressed by the sociobiologist E. O. Wilson. Although he believes that religion is pure fancy, he claims that it cannot be totally useless, because it has an intrinsic adaptive value; otherwise it would have been discarded as an irrelevant cultural construct.[16] This is exactly what I am suggesting when I claim that religion protects men and societies from mimetic escalation. Religion has an adaptive value. But this is not enough: it is also the source of hominization, of the differentiation between animals and human beings, because, as I explained in *Things Hidden*, through sacrifice it creates culture and institutions.

What turns many philosophers away from my theory is indeed this very point: that the creation of culture is engendered by religion through the victimary mechanism, which is in fact contingent and mechanistic. However, scientists object that this passage is purely philosophical, because it is too complex (and too hypothetical) to be proved. This is the paradoxical nature of the dialogues I found myself involved with: philosophers hardly believe in "facts"; scientists are often not interested in moving from the physical to the symbolic ground.

There is a quite contradictory attitude in the way in which evolutionary theorists handle cultural transmission. Although they are used to working with wide temporal scales, in order to account for the evolution of species, they often fall into a sort of temporal perspective when they discuss human culture, and the transmission and evolution of cultural traits. There is an unquestioned presupposition, which is linked to human agency: they seem to adopt a sort of "methodological individualism." As soon as they start discussing human culture, they seem to assume that the modern individual is the prototype of the primitive human being that produces and transmits culture. This implicit assumption is as harmful as the opposite one, like Lévy-Bruhl's "primitive mentality." Durkheim states that the autonomy of social facts cannot be simply explained by individual psychology. The emergence of culture is one of those facts.

With reference to the evolution of culture, it might be argued that it develops through Lamarckian patterns, rather than through a Darwinian framework. It is true that culture and symbolism are essentially transmitted through repetition and reinforcement. But is this truly Lamarckian? Nonetheless, it is at the level of the *social group* that one has to resort to Darwinian selection. This is purely conjectural and hypothetical, as it will be impossible to find absolute proof for this, and that is why the idea of group selection has been strongly criticized in the field, although it seems that it is now back in question.[17] However, we can surely perform a conjectural exercise. Based on presuppositions of the mimetic theory, one can argue that many groups and societies perished and were destroyed by lethal infighting, by the explosion of mimetic rivalry being unable to find any form of resolution. The scapegoat mechanism provided a fundamental contribution to the *fitness* of the group. This is the reason why such a practice is found throughout the world. This is the result of a form of systemic selection, which lasted thousands of years. It was the scapegoat mechanism, and subsequently religion, which provided that fundamental instrument of protection against the natural intraspecific violence that any group of hominids is bound to trigger at some point for purely ethological reasons. That is the liminal stage of cultural evolution, in which it makes no sense to talk about the autonomy of the individual. The group itself mediates everything.

In this sense, a hypothesis like Richard Dawkins's selfish gene is purely abstract when it comes to explaining social interactions, as it mainly resorts to game theory to show that animal altruism is possible – as if social interactions and then culture could be reduced to a purely economic explanation! To extend his theory to the cultural sphere, he then had to invent the even more problematic notion of the meme, the minimal cultural unit (which, by the way, seems quite similar to Tarde's ideas as expressed in The Laws of Imitation).

In doing so, he poses a radical break between animal and human, as he never provides an explanation for the emergence of culture. Memes, in his account, seem to emerge out of nothing, while the selective force, which should discriminate between the memes that will be retained and the ones that will be discarded, remains unexplored (or is it purely contingent).[18] Dawkins's theory of imitation seems to me quite deficient overall. He proposes a theory for imitative transmission of culture which also never accounts for the negative effects of imitation.

* * *

"Believing as I do that man in the distant future will be a far more perfect creature than he now is, it is an intolerable thought that he and all other sentient beings are doomed to complete annihilation after such long-continued slow progress."

(*Charles Darwin,* Autobiography)

The Apocalyptic Feeling

In one of the conversations you had with Gianni Vattimo, he hinted that you are not concerned with elaborating a theory of modernity and postmodernity, and

that you seem not to take into account all possible interpretive implications of your theory in relation to the contemporary world.[19] *How do you respond to that?*
First of all, I have to say that I am a theorist of mythology: I am not a moralist, or a religious thinker. I can answer questions on these themes, but they are not my main concern. However, there is a sort of outline of a theory of modernity at the end of *I See Satan* that is purely apocalyptic.[20] For me, any understanding of the contemporary world is mediated by the reading of Matthew 24. The most important part is the sentence "where the corpse lies, the vultures shall gather" (Matthew 24.28) because it seems to be a decomposition of the mimetic mechanism. The mechanism is visible, but it doesn't work. In John's Gospel there are apocalyptic elements as well: since Jesus triggers disagreement among the Jews, the rejection of him becomes more and more violent (John 8.31-59).

The apocalyptic feelings of the early Christians were not pure fantasy. These texts should be discussed: they are just as relevant today as they were at the time of their writing, and I find it disconcerting that many churches have stopped preaching on them. This started around the time the nuclear bomb was invented and used, when they decided to do away with the fear which was spreading in the world. We have these fundamental texts about our collective, yet we refuse to discuss them. Jefferson, following Darwin, couldn't conceive of the extinction of a national species. Marx, being an Aristotelian, believed in the eternity of the world. The experience of our own times, however – with their ruthless and unbounded use of violence – gives you the feeling that there is no time left, which was what the first Christians inevitably felt: "the time is short", Paul writes to the Corinthians (1 Corinthians 7.29). The apocalyptic feeling is the consciousness that the scapegoat business has run its course, that therefore nothing more can happen. What else could happen after the Christian revelation? And at the same time, what might happen to our world if the precarious order of false transcendence imposed by the scapegoat mechanism ceases to function? Any great Christian experience is apocalyptic because what one realizes is that after the decomposition of the sacrificial order there is nothing standing between ourselves and our possible destruction. How this will materialize I don't really know.

Derrida speaks of a general "apocalyptic tone in philosophy" in recent years, as he writes that the eschatological themes, starting in the 1950s, have been our "daily bread" ever since.[21] *Is your theory part of this trend?*
No, I don't belong to that school of thought.[22] However, I must say that, on the historical level, after the Second World War, something has happened

to the principle of the victim: it has become infinitely more widespread. As I said in *I See Satan*,[23] I believe that the most plausible philosophical interpretation of the Holocaust, from my viewpoint, is that it was an attempt to divorce the West from its dedication to saving victims. Of course, the same attempt was already present during the First World War and, above all, in the recurrent anti-Semitism from the Middle Ages onwards. Nonetheless, the explicit character of the Nazi Holocaust is unparalleled. It supposed that the principle of the victim could be buried under *so many* victims that everybody would see that it was not true. The attempt failed.

We have experienced various forms of totalitarianism that openly denied Christian principles. There has been the totalitarianism of the Left, which tried to outflank Christianity; and there has been totalitarianism of the Right, like Nazism, which found Christianity too soft on victims. This kind of totalitarianism is not only alive but it also has a great future. There will probably be some thinkers in the future who will reformulate this principle in a politically correct fashion, in more virulent forms, which will be more anti-Christian, albeit in an ultra-Christian caricature. When I say more Christian and more anti-Christian, I imply the future of the Anti-Christ.[24] The Anti-Christ is nothing but that: it is the ideology that attempts to outchristianize Christianity, that imitates Christianity in a spirit of rivalry.

Is it the Nietzschean program against Christianity?
It's the combination of the two positions. You can foresee the shape of what the Anti-Christ is going to be in the future: a super-victimary machine that will keep on sacrificing in the name of the victim.

Francis Fukuyama, in his controversial and much-criticized pamphlet The End of History, *wrote that we have reached the "end point of mankind's ideological evolution." However, he hints that man may be willing at some point "to drag the world back to history with all its wars, injustice, and revolution."*[25]
The idea of the end of history as the end of ideologies is simply misleading. Ideologies are not violent *per se*, rather it is man who is violent. Ideologies provide the grand narrative which covers up our victimary tendency. They are the mythical happy endings to our histories of persecutions. If you look carefully, you will see that the conclusion of myths is always positive and optimistic. There is always a cultural restoration after the crisis and the scapegoat resolution. The scapegoat provides the systemic closure which allows the social group to function once again, to run its course once more

and to remain blind to its systemic closure (the belief that the ones they are scapegoating are actually guilty). After the Christian revelation this is no longer possible. The system cannot be pulled back by any form of pharmacological resolution, and the virus of mimetic violence can spread freely. This is the reason why Jesus says: "Do not suppose that I have come to bring peace to the earth. I did not come to bring peace, but a sword" (Matthew 10.34). The Cross has destroyed once and for all the cathartic power of the scapegoat mechanism. Consequently, the Gospel does not provide a happy ending to our history. It simply shows us two options (which is exactly what ideologies never provide, freedom of choice): either we imitate Christ, giving up all our mimetic violence, or we run the risk of self-destruction. The apocalyptic feeling is based on that risk.

In an interview in Le Monde *on the recent terrorist events, you said that "ce qui se joue aujourd'hui est une rivalité mimétique à l'échelle planétaire" (What is being played out today is mimetic rivalry on a planetary scale).*[26] *What did you mean by this?*

The error is always to reason within categories of "difference" when the root of all conflicts is rather "competition," mimetic rivalry between persons, countries, cultures. Competition is the desire to imitate the other in order to obtain the same thing he or she has, by violence if need be. No doubt terrorism is bound to a world "different" from ours, but what gives rise to terrorism does not lie in that "difference" that removes it further from us and makes it inconceivable to us. On the contrary, it lies in the desire for convergence and resemblance. Human relations are essentially relations of imitation, of rivalry. What is experienced now is a form of mimetic rivalry on a planetary scale. When I read the first documents of Bin Laden and verified his allusions to the American bombing of Japan, I felt at first that I was in a dimension that transcends Islam, a dimension of the entire planet. Under the label of Islam we find a will to rally and mobilize an entire third world of those frustrated and of victims in their relation of mimetic rivalry with the West. But the towers destroyed had as many foreigners as Americans. But their effectiveness, the sophistication of the means they employed, the knowledge that they had of the United States and their training, were not the authors of the attack at least partly American? Here we are in the middle of mimetic contagion.

Far from turning away from the West, they cannot avoid imitating it and adopting its values, even if they don't avow it, and they are also consumed like us by the desire for individual and collective success. This sentiment is not true of the masses but of the ruling classes. At the level of personal fortune a man like Bin Laden has no need to envy anyone. And there have been many party or faction leaders in this situation. For instance, Mirabeau, at the beginning of the French Revolution, had one foot in one camp and one foot in the other, and what did he do but live out his resentment in even more bitter fashion.

Notes

1. Lucien Scubla, "Contribution à la théorie du sacrifice," in M. Deguy and J.-P. Dupuy (eds.), *René Girard et le problème du mal* (Paris: Grasset, 1982), 105.

2. A recent report from the World Health Organization on violent death in 80 different countries, explains that half of them are caused by suicide, while the majority of homicides are committed within the family. Only one fifth of violent deaths every year are caused by war. See *World Report on Violence and Health* (Geneva: World Health Organization, 2002).

3. See René Girard, *Things Hidden since the Foundation of the World* (Stanford, CA: Stanford University Press, 1978), 15–19.

4. Richard Dawkins, *The Selfish Gene* (Oxford and New York: Oxford University Press, 1976).

5. Sandor Goodhart, *Sacrificing Commentary: Reading the End of Literature* (Baltimore, MD: Johns Hopkins University Press, 1996).

6. In a different context, Leonardo Buff addresses a similar issue:

   "I still think that the other pole of mimetic desire should be more emphasized. I'm referring to the desire that brings goodness into history. On the one hand, there is a mimetic mechanism that produces victims and creates a historical culture grounded on victims. On the other hand, and at the same time, there is an inclusive desire, which looks for a 'solidarity' mimeticism, committed to making historically possible the production of goodness and life. (In H. Assmann [ed.], *René Girard com teólogos da libertação, Um diálogo sobre ídolos e sacrifícios* [Petrópolis: Editora Vozes, 1991], 56–57).

7. See *Julius Caesar,* II, I. See also René Girard, *A Theater of Envy: William Shakespeare* (Oxford and New York: Oxford University Press, 1991), 308–9.

8. Henri Atlan, "Violence fondatrice et référent divin," in Paul Dumouchel (ed.), *Violence et vérité. Autour de René Girard* (Paris: Grasset, 1985), 434–50.

9. William Shakespeare, *Julius Caesar,* II, i ll. 166, 180. For an analysis of that passage, see René Girard, "Let's be Sacrificers but not Butchers, Caius. Sacrifice in Julius Caesar," in Girard, *A Theater of Envy,* 210–19.

10. This concept has been developed by Jean-Pierre Dupuy in "Totalisation et méconnaissance," in Dumouchel (ed.), *Violence et vérité. Autour de Rene Girard* (Paris: Grasset, 1985), 110–35.

11. Cf. R. Girard, *I See Satan Fall Like Lightning* (Maryknoll, MD: Orbis Books, 2001), 126–27. Some early manuscripts do not have Luke's sentence.

12. M. Serres, *Atlas* (Paris: Julliard, 1994), 219–20.

13. *The Autobiography of Darwin and Selected Letters*, ed. Francis Darwin (New York: Dover, 1958), 55. See also Ernst Mayr, *One Long Argument: Charles Darwin and the Genesis of Modern Evolutionary Thought* (London: Allen Lane/Penguin, 1991).

14. The same notion was stressed by Stanley E. Hyman, which sees *The Origin of Species* as a dionysiac "tragic ritual," connected to the notion of *agone* and *sparagmos*; see S. E. Hyman, *The Tangled Bank: Darwin, Marx, Frazer and Freud as Imaginative Writers* (New York: Atheneum, 1962), 26–33.

15. E. Sober, "Models of Cultural Evolution," in E. Sober (ed.), *Conceptual Issues in Evolutionary Biology* (Cambridge, MA: MIT Press, 1994), 486.

16. Religions are like other human institutions in that they evolve in directions that enhance the welfare of the practitioners. Because this demographic benefit must accrue to the group as a whole, it can be gained partly by altruism and partly by exploitation, with certain sectors profiting at the expense of others. Alternatively, the benefit can arise as the sum of the generally increased fitnesses of all the members. (Edward O. Wilson, *On Human Nature* [Cambridge: Harvard University Press, 1978], 175).

    See also E. O. Wilson, *Sociobiology: The New Synthesis* (Cambridge, MA: Belknap Press/Harvard University Press, 1975), 559–64.

17. For a critique of the idea of group selection, see G. C. Williams, *Adaptation and Natural Selection: A Critique of Some Current Evolutionary Thought* (Princeton, NJ: Princeton University Press, 1966). For a recent reassessment, see E. Sober and D. S. Wilson's Introduction to *Unto Others. The Evolution and Psychology of Unselfish Behavior* (Cambridge: Harvard University Press, 1998), 1–13.

18. Susan Blackmore speaks of a *meme machine,* which works as a pure mindless algorithm. See *The Meme Machine* (Oxford: Oxford University Press, 1999).

19. At the COV&R Conference 2001 in Antwerp, Belgium, June 2: *The Place of Girard's Mimetic Theory in the History of Philosophy*. See R. Girard and G. Vattimo, *Verità o fede debole? Dialogo su cristianesimo e relativismo*, ed. P. Antonello (Massa: Tarnseuropa, 2006).

20. Girard, *I See Satan,* 182–87.

21. Jacques Derrida, *Specters of Marx,* trans. Peggy Kamuf (New York and London: Routledge, 1994), 15.

22. Derrida singles out the "canon of modern apocalypse (end of History, end of Men, end of Philosophy, Hegel, Marx, Nietzsche, Heidegger …)," ibid.

23. Girard, *I See Satan,* 170–71.

24. The term "Anti-Christ" is present in two of St. John's letters: 1 John 2.18-19: "Dear children, this is the last hour; and as you have heard that the antichrist is coming, even now many antichrists have come. This is how we know it is the last hour"; and 2 John 7: "Many deceivers, who do not acknowledge Jesus Christ as coming in the flesh, have gone out into the world. Any such person is the deceiver and the antichrist." See also 1 John 4.3.

25. F. Fukuyama, *The End of History and the Last Man* (London: Hamish Hamilton, 1992), 312.

26. Henri Tincq's interview is included in this volume. – ED.

CHAPTER 13
THE *J'ACCUSE* OF RENÉ GIRARD:
THE AUDACIOUS IDEAS OF A GREAT THINKER
Giulio Meotti/2007*

Despite his 84 years, René Girard has lost nothing of the fiber of a radical thinker. He is working on a new paper on Karl von Clausewitz. The author of such masterpieces of contemporary thought as *Violence and the Sacred* and *The Scapegoat* was elected to the forty "immortals" of the Académie Française. Together with Claude Levi-Strauss, René Girard is the greatest living anthropologist. In this interview with *Il Foglio*, Girard returns to what he defined as "the great anthropological question of our time."

He begins by asking: "Can there be a realistic anthropology prior to deconstruction? In other words: is it permitted and still possible to put forward a universal truth about mankind? Contemporary anthropology, structuralist and postmodern, denies this access to the truth. Current thought is 'the castration of meaning.' Such attempts to discuss mankind are dangerous."

This is the origin, according to Girard, of the "skandalon," of religion in the epoch of neo-secularization. "Since the enlightenment, religion has been understood as pure nonsense. Auguste Comte had a rigorous theory on the origin of the truth, and his nineteenth-century intellectualism recalls much that is in vogue today. As he said, there are three phases: the religious, which is the most childish; the philosophical; and finally the scientific, the closest to the truth. Today in public discourse one aims to define the 'untruth' of religion as something necessary for the survival of the human species. No one asks what the function of religion may be, one speaks only of faith: as in 'I have faith.' But then what? The revolutionary theory of Charles Darwin hoped to have demonstrated the uselessness of a 15,000-year-old ancient institution like religion. This is attempted today in

*From *Il Foglio*, March 20, 2007. Reprinted with permission of *Il Foglio*. Translated by Francis R. Hittinger IV.

the form of genetic chaos articulated by Neo-Darwinism. Take the scientist Richard Dawkins, for example, an extremely hostile thinker who sees religion as something criminal."

Religion has a function that goes beyond faith and the veracity of the monotheistic gift: "The prohibition of human sacrifices. The modern world has decided that it is the prohibition that is nonsense. Religion has returned to being understood as the costume of the noble savage, a primitive state of ignorance under the stars. On the contrary, religion is necessary to suppress violence. Man is a species unique in the world: the only one that threatens its own survival through violence. Animals, experiencing sexual jealousy, do not kill each other. Human beings do. Animals do not know vendetta, the destruction of the sacrificial victim linked to the mimetic nature of the applauding multitudes."

Today the only accepted definition of violence as pure aggression. "Thus one wants to render it innocent. But human violence is desire and imitation. Post-modernism does not manage to talk about violence: it puts it between parentheses and simply ignores its origin. And with it ignores the most important truth: that reality is somewhere accessible."

René Girard comes from French radicalism. "I've stuffed my head with the clownish jokes, the mediocre simplicity, and the stupidity of the avant-garde. I know full well how much the postmodern negation of reality can lead to the discrediting of the moral question of man. The avant-garde that was once relegated to the artistic arena now extends to the scientific one, which reasons about the origin of man. In a certain sense, science has become a new mythology, man who creates life. So, I welcomed with great relief the definition of Joseph Ratzinger of 'biological reductionism,' the new form of deconstruction, the biological myth. I situate myself also in the distinction of the ex-cardinal [Ratzinger], between science and scientism."

The only big difference between man and animal species is the religious dimension. "This is the essence of human existence, it is the origin of the prohibition of sacrifices and of violence. Where religion has dissolved, a process of decay begins. Micro-eugenics is the new form of human sacrifice. We no longer protect life from violence, instead we crush life with violence, to try to appropriate for ourselves the mystery of life for our own benefit. But we will go wrong. Eugenics is the apex of a type of thought begun two centuries ago and it constitutes the gravest danger for the human species. Mankind is the species that can always destroy itself. For this reason it created religion."

Today there are three areas that endanger man: the nuclear threat, terrorism, and genetic manipulation. "The twentieth century was the century of classic nihilism. The twenty-first will be the century of seductive nihilism. C. S. Lewis was right when he spoke of the 'abolition of man.' Michel Foucault added that the abolition of man is becoming a philosophical concept. Today one cannot speak of man anymore. When Friedrich Nietzsche announced the death of God, in reality he was announcing the death of man. Eugenics is the denial of human rationality. If man is considered as mere and raw material belonging in a laboratory, a malleable and manipulable object, one may proceed to do anything to him. One ends with destroying the fundamental rationality of the human being. Man cannot be reorganized."

According to Girard, today we are losing sight also of another anthropological function: marriage. "A pre-Christian institution valued by Christianity. Marriage is the indispensable organization of life, linked to the human wish for immortality. In creating a family, it is as if man were pursuing the imitation of eternal life. There have been places and civilizations that tolerated homosexuality, but no society has put it on the same juridical plane as the family. We have a man and a woman, that is, always a polarity. In the most recent American elections of 2006, the true victory was that of natural marriage in the referendums."

The Metaphysical Boredom of Europe

Europe is immersed in what the Arabist of the Sorbonne Rémi Brague calls metaphysical boredom. "It is a beautiful expression, even as it seems to me that the superiority of the Christian message becomes every day more visible. The more it is assailed, the greater the truth of Christianity sparkles. As the refutation of mythology, Christianity shines in the moment when our world is filling up with new sacrificial mythologies.

"I have always understood the skandalon of Christian revelation in a radical way. In Christianity, instead of assuming the point of view of the crowd, it takes that of the innocent victim. It deals with a reversal of the archaic pattern. And the exhaustion of violence."

Girard speaks of our obsession with sexuality. "In the Gospels, there is nothing sexual and this fact has been completely romanticized by contemporary gnostics. Gnosticism has always excluded categories of persons and turned them into enemies. Christianity is the complete opposite of mythology and gnosticism. Today a form of neo-paganism is emerging. The greatest error of postmodern philosophy is to have thought that it could freely transform man into a machine of pleasure. That devolves to dehumanization, beginning with the false desire to prolong life by sacrificing greater goods."

Postmodern philosophy is based on the assumption that history is finished. "From that we have a culture torn from its primitive form and put exclusively into the context of the present. Here also originates the hatred for a strong culture that affirms a universal truth. Today it is believed that sexuality is the solution to everything; rather, it is the problem, its origin. We are continually enticed by a seductive ideology of fascination. Deconstruction does not see sexuality as something that lies within the scope of human folly. Accordingly, our madness lies in wanting to make sexuality banal, making it something frivolous. I hope that Christians do not follow this direction. Violence and sexuality are inseparable. And this is because it deals with the most beautiful and vile thing that we have."

A divorce between humanity and syntax, reality and language is underway. "We are losing every contact between language and the limits of being. Today we believe only in language. We love fairy tales more than in any other epoch. Christianity is a linguistic truth, *logos*. Thomas Aquinas was the great promulgator of this linguistic rationalism. The great success of Anglo-American Christianity, and thus of the United States, is indebted to extraordinary translations of the Bible. In Catholicism today there is altogether too much sociology. The church is too often compromised with the allures of the times and modernism. In a certain sense, the problems began with the Second Vatican Council, but go back to the preceding loss of Christian eschatology. The Church has not reflected enough on this transformation. How can we justify the total elimination of eschatology even in the liturgy?"

Girard repeats that humanity has never been as in much danger as it is today. "It is the great lesson of the formulation of Karol Wojtyla: 'Culture of death.' It is his most beautiful linguistic intuition. And it makes a match with the other definition of Joseph Ratzinger of the dictatorship of relativism. The nihilism of our time calls itself deconstruction, in America also called 'deconstruction theory.' Nihilism is transformed into a respectable philosophical theory. It all becomes frivolous, a play on words, a joke. We have begun with the deconstruction of language and we have ended with the deconstruction of the human being in the laboratory."

Together with the lack of respect for human life, the deconstruction of the body is the other challenge of which Girard speaks. "It is proposed by the same people that on the one hand want to infinitely prolong life and on the other tell us that the world is overpopulated."

The literary critic George Steiner writes that even atheism is metaphysical. "Certainly, Steiner always has wonderful ideas. G. K. Chesterton said that the modern world is full of crazed Christian ideas. The Enlightenment, too, therefore was a product of Christianity. Take a figure like Voltaire, an example of a naughty Enlightenment figure who contributed to the de-Christianization of France. Nevertheless, Voltaire always defended the victims and was a great Christian, even without knowing it. For this reason I say that the nefarious interpreters of Christian doctrine are worse than the outsiders. Christianity continues to suggest to us a fascinating and persuasive explanation of human evil. But we are losing the apocalyptic dimension of Christianity. People will realize that no society can survive without religion. Christian romanticism forgot that this religion above all defused sacrificial violence. Today Christianity is much more realistic than the optimism of science that creates man only to kill him. The apocalypse is not the anger of God, but the madness of man upon himself. The apocalypse is not behind us, but in front of us. The apocalypse was not written for God, but for man. The Christian fundamentalists at present in America are apocalyptic in a mistaken sense; they think that God will punish man, not that man will punish himself. Today we need to have an apocalyptic view so as not to forget this violence originating in man."

Islam lacks something important, the cross. The speech of Ratzinger at Regensburg, according to Girard, was decisive. "The challenge of Ratzinger launched against relativism is of benefit not only for Catholics, but for secularists. And I hope that Ratzinger may be a hope for Europe. He is a pope very similar but also very different from John Paul II. Wojtyla was unstoppable, he always wanted to be seen and heard. Benedict XVI wants instead to reconcile people; he is a very great teacher of reflection and modesty. The Christian religion, the greatest revolution in human history, uniquely reminds us of the correct use of reason. It is a challenge that plays on the concept of guilt. For a long time Europe decided that the Germans had to be the scapegoat. It was impossible, too, merely to compare Nazism and Communism. Once the death of God was declared, along with the possibility for the Enlightenment to have any religious meaning, it was necessary to erect an 'anti-God,' an anti-divinity, Communism. I agree with Ernst Nolte's argument about the affinity between Nazism and Communism. Every totalitarian regime began with the suppression of religious freedom. Today this anti-Genesis lives again in a part of science."

This is the sense of the definition of Henri de Lubac's 'Atheistic humanism.' "I was honored by his friendship. When I had been accused of not being a Christian, de Lubac told me that everything that I was writing was right and there wasn't anything heretical in it. The great demographic crisis of Europe is one of the various signs of this paralysis. The ideology of our time is hostility to life as such. Modern culture deems that mythology, old and new, is in favor of life, while religion is against it. It is the exact opposite. The new Dionysianism has a violent and mortal face. Thomas Mann was one of the first to understand it. Today a type of existential nausea rules, which is the heir of the romantic spleen."

We are such ethnocentrists that we think that only others are in the right when they assert of the superiority of their religions. "Islam maintains a relation with death that convinces me of the extraneousness of this religion to the ancient myths. The mystical relation of Islam with death makes it more mysterious. Islam is a religion of sacrifice. The Christian, however, does not die to be imitated. We have to remember the words of Christ to Paul: 'Why do you persecute me?' In Christianity, which destroys every mythology, there is a constant dialectic between the victim and the persecutor; in Islam this does not exist. Islam eliminates the problem of the victim. In this sense, there has always been a conflict between Christianity and Islam. In Islam the most important thing is missing: a cross. Like Christianity, Islam rehabilitates the innocent victim, but it does so in a militant way. The cross, on the contrary, puts an end to violent and archaic myths. The cross is the symbol of the inversion of violence, the resistance to lynching. Today the cross is opposed to the Dionysian sacrifice of the new myths. Christianity, in contrast with Islam, has prohibited sacrifice."

René Girard has always chosen not to say agreeable and easy things. "I have been, even here in America, very ostracized. Today I couldn't care less what others think of me. We don't have to surrender ourselves to fascination, there is so much to learn from the past. I reread often the story of Joseph in the Old Testament because it is the most beautiful exemplification of Christianity. I have been married since 1951, I have nine grandchildren and three children. My wife is Protestant, and she has never converted to Catholicism."

Then, one of the many seraphic laughs of this serious and upright man. "I have a son in business, a painter daughter, and a lawyer son. What I love about America is its great paradox, to have within itself the most efficacious protections against the worst aspects of itself – protections that Europe ignores. Here I have known true independence. I am surrounded by life. Nevertheless, I can't help but think that this is the time of silence, a pregnant silence of meanings."

CHAPTER 14
A PASSION BORN OF RIVALRY
Mark R. Anspach and Laurence Tacou/2008*

Mark Anspach: René Girard, could you begin by telling us something about the origin of the text published here? What led you to reflect upon a subject like anorexia?

René Girard: My interest in the subject goes all the way back to my childhood. There were cases of anorexia – not very severe but real enough – in my own family, in particular a young cousin whom I talk about in the text. Consequently, when I read Claude Vigée's book *Les artistes de la faim* (1960), it brought back memories. Later, when I decided to write on the subject myself, I took that book as my starting point, since I knew Vigée.

M.A.: How did you get to know him?

R.G.: When he was teaching in America, at Brandeis, I was a young professor at Bryn Mawr, not so far away. We must have become acquainted at a meeting of the Modern Language Association. He was the first friend I made in academia. We looked each other up in France, as well, and we continued to exchange our respective books. There was a great bond of sympathy between us. He was an Alsatian Jew who had immigrated to the United States as I had. He was the colleague to whom I felt the closest.

M.A.: Were there any theoretical affinities between you?

R.G.: Not really, but at that time I was less of a monomaniac! Still, when I wrote my text on anorexia, it was the contagious, mimetic side of the phenomenon that caught my attention. Vigée hadn't made any forays into contemporary sociology, but in the 1990s, there was an acute consciousness of the problem in American society. There were even lawsuits brought

*From *Anorexia* (East Lansing, MI: Michigan State University Press, 2013), 45–75. Initially published as *Anorexie et désir mimétique* (Paris: Éditions de L'Herne, 2008). The interview was published in English as "Conversation with René Girard." Reprinted with permission of Michigan State University Press and Éditions de L'Herne. Translated by Mark R. Anspach.

against women's fashion media or designers of *haute couture*. I did a lot of research on the subject. And I also had a kind of informant on campus, a male student who had a good understanding of mimetic theory. He shared with me his observations about other boys at Stanford, about the pressure that worked in favor of anorexia ...

M.A.: What form did this pressure take? Did young people talk about their weight? Make comparisons?

R.G.: They made comparisons without even having to talk about it; they knew this preoccupation existed and dominated many aspects of student culture at the time.

Laurence Tacou: Anorexia has always been a feminine scourge. Was it really anorexia afflicting boys this time, or were they simply going on a diet to avoid becoming fat?

R.G.: These things are very difficult to distinguish. It's true there has never been this kind of dieting among boys in the past. For that reason, many of these students considered this new development to be a masculine extension of the anorexic phenomenon, interpreted as an urge to be thin. It is something very visual, tied to the gaze of the Other. Of course, my informant was well-versed in the theory, so he wasn't a totally impartial witness.

M.A.: Did he go on a diet himself?

R.G.: He told me that he was in danger of doing so, but his awareness of the collective and social character of the problem held him back. He didn't want to cave in to the pressure; he felt victimized by a social phenomenon that was out of his control.

M.A.: It sounds as if he found a remedy of sorts in mimetic theory itself ...

R.G.: In his case, the knowledge he had of it was a help to him.

L.T.: Yet the traditional norms of masculine fashion never glorified the image of the skinny fellow. On the contrary, a man was supposed to be virile; even young ephebes were not thin and frail as a rule; whereas, with girls, there is this image of the anemic young woman, pale ...

R.G.: Emaciated ... The truth is that I did not persevere in my study of the phenomenon, and I don't know to what extent it has progressed among boys. My old informant from Stanford has gone off to teach in a Wisconsin high school. He told me he has observed the same tendencies at work in that school, but without giving many details.

M.A.: In fact, it seems there has been a radical change in the type of physique considered desirable among male models. Tan and muscular young men have found themselves shunted aside in favor of pale and skinny boys. The *New York Times* devoted an article to the subject in 2008. The most sought-after models of the moment were not simply thin, but downright emaciated, with spindly arms and concave chests. According to the *Times*, this new trend began around the year 2000 with clothes produced by the stylist Hedi Slimane for Dior Homme.[1] In an advertising campaign for Dior, one could see a male model with a body mass index of 18, which is just short of anorexia.[2]

L.T.: It does look like there is growing undifferentiation between men and women.

R.G.: The difference between the sexes counts for less and less.

M.A.: The new male models are unabashedly effeminate. Some of the boys in these photos are so delicate and sylphlike, so blissfully lacking in strength and vigor, that they appear incapable of undertaking the slightest effort or least bit of work, suggesting that someone else would have to look after their needs. The maintenance of idle creatures unfit for gainful employment is another form of conspicuous consumption described by Thorstein Veblen in *The Theory of the Leisure Class* (1899). In Veblen's time, and up until quite recently, it was the man who went about with a decorative woman on his arm, a trophy wife. Now there is a turnabout, with actresses or female singers showing off their trophy husbands.

R.G.: You mean [Nicolas] Sarkozy is Carla Bruni's trophy husband? (*Laughter.*) She is a more important personage than he is!

M.A.: She is surely more important in their own eyes ... But all the same, she is quite thin. It's no coincidence that she is a model. Speaking of which, she has been appearing in an advertising campaign for a car where she says something like, "Oh, this is just the first thing I found in the garage." ... It's a good example of what you call the strategy of indifference.

R.G.: Like the new pair of blue jeans that is made to look worn and faded before it is sold. There is nothing worse than letting others see that you want to impress them. The same idea is already present in Shakespeare. Take the example of Beatrice and Benedick in *Much Ado About Nothing*. The first to tell the other "I love you" will lose. It reminds me of those bicycle races where it pays not to take the lead too early.

M.A.: By letting the other guy get in front, you give yourself a model to emulate while at the same time not letting him see you. The objective is to win without sticking your neck out and making your desire visible. The same strategy underpins minimalist literature, where authors hide their desire to impress behind a mask of indifference. Displaying indifference is itself a way to impress, a putative proof of superiority. I am thinking of the studied neutrality of the narration in *The Stranger*, which you analyze as a stylistic trick through which a young, still unknown Albert Camus concealed his desire to win readers.[3]

L.T.: There was a time when one was supposed to display indifference toward food. Polite ladies would eat something at home before going out to dinner, in order not to look gluttonous. Now there is an American television series, *Desperate Housewives*, in which five women – every one of them thin as a rail – spend their time baking and eating cakes ... Anorexia is out of favor; you still have to be skinny but not stop eating.

R.G.: Bulimia operates on the same principle. Bulimia is a very American, very practical solution to the problem. One can eat, stuff oneself, then get rid of the food. It's the height of technical progress.

L.T.: But how does one explain the appeal of the ultra-thin woman – for example Kate Moss, this very famous model who is considered extremely beautiful and sexy despite having hollow cheeks and a rather cadaverous appearance?

R.G.: This phenomenon struck me for the first time in a department store one day. On the torso of a mannequin wearing a swimsuit, I noticed that all the ribs were showing. The effect was quite sinister, but it was intentional, which gives one pause. That was about fifteen years ago. What's strange is that these fashions seem to go on forever; they must therefore have a deeper significance. Change is often thought to be the essence of fashion, yet here there is no change; things have been moving in the same direction for more than a hundred years. I believe I cite the wife of the last emperor of Austria, Sissi, and Eugénie, the wife of Napoleon III, who measured each other's waists when they met at some international get-together.

L.T.: At the same time, the criteria of beauty have continued to evolve. For example, Marilyn Monroe and Ava Gardner were not at all tall and willowy. They were rather petite and on the plump side, yet they were considered great beauties.

R.G.: In fact, that is undoubtedly the physical type men prefer. But women's fashion has become an exclusively feminine affair, an arena for rivalries among women, where there is not necessarily any place for the man.

L.T.: What do you think about "fashion victims," these women who are completely wrapped up in a mad obsession with fashion and cannot imagine any other mode of existence?

R.G.: Like all obsessive desires – the desire for wealth, the desire for power – it is a passion born of rivalry. These women want to be admired by others. They want to be at the center of the world, and they will go to extraordinary lengths to outdo everyone else. But it is more than an individual quirk; the existence of fashion victims is no doubt the sign of a social crisis. It is a sign of the times. Is there any evidence for something similar in the past? No examples come to mind ...

L.T.: Whatever examples we might find, it was never a mass phenomenon. In the past, fashion was reserved for the elite; today, it reaches the whole population.

R.G.: The phenomenon has been completely democratized. In the era of Sissi and Eugénie, it concerned the highest social classes. It would no doubt have been possible to observe class distinctions based on women's weight. The average weight of women from the social elite would have been lower. The glorification of the very thin woman as an aesthetic ideal begins with Art Nouveau. But before about 1920, this tendency to slimness is limited to the aristocracy; then the phenomenon spreads as it descends the social ladder. "*Avoir la ligne*" [to have a slim figure] is an expression that was already in use when I was a small child, but not at the bottom of the ladder. Today, all that has been democratized, leaving aside those who are out of the race because they really refuse to participate in it.

M.A.: Poor women are out of the race because they cannot eat right and become obese.

R.G.: In the United States, poor women are fatter than others because they eat fattening food and also because they do not stint themselves. The two factors converge.

M.A.: According to recent statistics, more than half the adults in the world – and almost two thirds of the men – are overweight or obese.[4] People seem to be either too fat or too thin. Curiously, it is those in the middle or "normal" range who are in short supply.

R.G.: That may be an exaggeration, but compared to the past, it is certainly the trend.

L.T.: There is even a tendency to be too thin and too fat all at once, if you think about silicone-enlarged breasts, plumped-up lips . . .

M.A.: Women are being pulled in opposite directions by two contradictory ideals, slenderness and voluptuousness. They cannot conform to both simultaneously.

R.G.: It makes one think of the bodies of certain insects that are separated into segments joined by a thread at the abdomen. There is something insect-like in such a physique.

M.A.: One sees giant insects in science fiction movies; they are a kind of *monster*. Isn't the appearance of monsters a characteristic symptom of a crisis of undifferentiation? American cinema has been crawling with monsters since at least the 1950s. The new development is the advent of female stars with monstrous physiques.

L.T.: How should we interpret this body mania that is reaching such extremes? Women today seem to be completely obsessed with their bodies.

R.G.: It's linked to the contemporary aesthetic that makes the individual the be-all and end-all, excluding social values of any kind, especially religious ones. It is the principal manifestation of this phenomenon.

M.A.: Do you mean to say that amidst a generalized absence of values, of models of what to do with one's life, people fall back on their bodies? Has the body become the last bastion of the self?

R.G.: I think so. Our society is completely materialistic; it is very difficult to find new values.

L.T.: Not only is there a lack of values, there is also a lack of *rituals*. Isn't anorexia among adolescents tied to the fact that we live in societies that are entirely "de-ritualized," where there is no longer any recognized passage to adulthood? Young people impose on themselves a kind of initiation rite, obviously copied from a model. They want to surpass their limits by fasting. In the old days there was religion: ritual fasts, Lent, things that hardly exist anymore now. For adolescent girls, isn't there a desire for purity that manifests itself in these fasts?

R.G.: Given my preoccupations, I put the emphasis on rivalry. But all of the elements you mention exist, of course; they may be present to begin with or can quite easily be superimposed. The people involved may very well not see their rivalrous motives and be dominated by them without perceiving them. The strange thing is that medieval convents were much more aware of the danger than we are in the modern world. Handbooks of asceticism took it into account. In the Middle Ages, there was competitive fasting among persons who wanted to earn a reputation as ascetics. There was a positive goal, a veritable ambition to attain dominance, analogous but not identical to modern anorexia, which is linked to the gaze, to the universe of photography. Before, it was a will to power that expressed itself in the desire to be more ascetic than one's neighbor, to be more capable of resisting hunger. With anorexics, hunger is totally dominated; it seems to me to be something that is more centered on the Self. The Other still plays a vital role, but that role is in some way mediated by many external factors. In a convent, where two sisters are in a struggle for dominance, the Other intervenes in a way that is simpler and more direct.

M.A.: A convent is not an ordinary place. It is a milieu characterized by a significant degree of undifferentiation. The nuns dress in identical fashion while veiling their hair and body; they follow the same daily routine. They are committed to living together day after day inside the same closed space. If they wanted to gain distinction within such a constrictive framework, competing for ascetic status would be one of the only ways to do so.

R.G.: That's right, the point of departure is different, but the tendency to rivalry is always the heart of the matter. And once rivalry is unleashed, there are no longer any limits.

M.A.: At first sight, modern society has little in common with a convent, but paradoxical resemblances may exist between the two. In a convent or monastery, everyone is the same sex; in our society, the difference between the sexes is fading, which in a sense comes out to the same thing. The difference between generations is also fading, with adults striving to "stay young" while young people precociously adopt "adult" behaviors. The most basic anthropological categories are in crisis. Doesn't such a context of growing undifferentiation facilitate the explosion of rivalries for objects as frivolous as thinness – rivalries that no cultural guardrail is able to contain, given the decline of traditional religious rituals invoked by Laurence Tacou?

R.G.: The modern world abolishes religion, but it produces new rites that are much more onerous and formidable than those of the past – rites that hark back to archaic religious forms in a manner still to be defined.

M.A.: Ordeals that test the body, such as the quest for extreme leanness, but also piercings, tattoos ... ?

R.G.: Yes, but the essential is always the Other – an Other who is anyone at all, the incarnation of an impregnable totality, present everywhere and nowhere – that one stubbornly hopes to seduce. It is the Other as insurmountable obstacle. That quickly becomes submission to a purely metaphysical imperative. If you do not have a real religion, you end up with a more dreadful one ...

M.A.: One of the great prophets of the dreadful religion that springs up after religion is Franz Kafka, whose *Hunger Artist* you discuss in your text. Kafka made a revealing comparison between Balzac and himself: "Balzac had a walking-stick on which was inscribed the motto: *I crush every obstacle*; my own personal motto is: *Every obstacle crushes me.*"

R.G.: That testifies clearly to a change of eras. Balzac could still express the conquering attitude of naïve modernism. But once we get to Kafka, things become more twisted; people begin to tell themselves that a crushable obstacle can't be an obstacle worthy of the name. For Kafka, the last obstacle that remains is precisely that Other who is everywhere and nowhere. It is the omnipresent and anonymous mimetic model.

L.T.: There is something that bothers me slightly in this idea of an omnipresent mimetic model. In the last analysis, you always succeed in finding mimetic models everywhere. Doesn't that risk becoming a weakness as much as a strength of your approach? Is there really no limit to the applicability of the mimetic theory?

R.G.: Mimetic theory does not apply to all human relations, but even in relationships with those who are closest to us, we must be conscious of the mechanisms it describes. In reality, it is the era in which we live that is like a caricature. Since we all participate in this exaggeration, it becomes paradoxically more difficult to detect than the normality of the past. That is the paradox of my thesis. It may be overstated, but I believe it to be true; and if I persist, it is because I also believe that the truth, today, has lost all verisimilitude.

L.T.: Do you think that some people don't like to hear about mimetic theory because it shines a harsh light on things that are ultimately too intimate?

R.G.: Most people are perfectly capable of seeing the mimetic theory as a mere social satire that does not implicate them personally. Those with enough sense of humor manage to say, "Yes, I indulge in some of these behaviors; it can happen that I, too, act out of pure imitation." Often, fashions have no meaning; people simply imitate them without reflecting on their significance. The individual becomes a vehicle for a significance that eludes him.

L.T.: What about you? Do you think you are susceptible to current fashions or trendy ideas?

R.G.: I think that as one gets older, one becomes less so. But certainly I was once. If I hadn't been susceptible myself, I would not have understood the phenomenon. It takes a kind of personal conversion, an acceptance of humiliation, to say to oneself: "I was terribly mimetic on such an occasion; I will try to be less so."

M.A.: In an autobiographical text published in the *Cahier de l'Herne* devoted to you, you describe having suffered in your youth from a particularly acute "mimetic sickness," which manifested itself by a sort of literary snobbery in reverse.[5]

R.G.: In ordinary snobbery, the kind described by Proust, one is drawn exclusively to works singled out for attention by prestigious models. My case was still more severe because I was allergic to reading anything suggested by someone else. The most extreme form of mimetic malady is an intransigent anti-mimetic attitude because, although one must not be a slave to other people's opinions, it is impossible to shut oneself off from everything that comes from others. The imitation of positive models is inevitable and even indispensable to creativity. By systematically rejecting any external model, one runs the risk of intellectual sterility.

L.T.: Aren't you afraid that the mimetic theory itself could end up being rejected if it becomes *too* fashionable and gains so much popularity as to provoke a backlash?

R.G.: In the short run, such fluctuations of opinion as a result of opposing trends are always possible. But in the long run, I believe that a theory will prove lasting if it has a strong footing in reality – I am an unqualified realist in this sense. The mimetic understanding of reality is still at a very early stage. A time will come when all this will seem obvious. There will be a shift from a refusal to see the phenomenon to seeing it everywhere ... But nothing is certain, of course.

M.A.: A moment ago, Laurence Tacou asked whether there are any limits to the mimetic interpretation. I would like to raise the same question in the specific context of eating disorders. Many observers recognize the pernicious influence of cultural models that promote an ideal of extreme thinness, but this influence affects all women, while anorexia in the strict sense – the kind that undermines health and can lead to death – remains quite rare. Why, then, does the most severe pathology strike only some women and not the rest? Gérard Apfeldorfer, a psychiatric expert on eating disorders interviewed by the French daily *Libération*, asserts: "Anorexia is not a choice, it's a mental illness. There are psychological predispositions, familial antecedents. In its most widespread form, this disease reflects a narcissistic disorder, not an effort to imitate fashion models."[6]

R.G.: I am against this type of explanation in terms of conventional psychology. I do not believe in the existence of narcissism as defined by Freud. We are all self-centered and other-dependent in the same measure; the two go together. We all compare ourselves to others, we all are prone to mimetic rivalry, but not everyone carries this tendency to the point of pathology. Why does anorexia strike some women more than the rest? Individuals are more or less rivalrous; this is just as true where thinness is concerned as in other areas. Anorexic women want to be the champions in their category. It's the same in the world of finance. The only difference is that the desire to be richer than others is not seen as pathological. By contrast, the desire to be thinner, if taken too far, has devastating physical effects that are visible in the body. But once a girl is anorexic and has undertaken to compete in this arena, it is difficult for her to give up before attaining victory – that would mean renouncing the championship. The final result is tragic in the most extreme cases, but that should not make us lose sight of the fact that the obsession with thinness characterizes our entire culture; it is not something that distinguishes these young women from everyone else.

M.A.: In her classic study of eating disorders, Hilde Bruch lists some common features in her own clinical observations about fifty-one anorexic patients and their families. She notes among other things that the patients' fathers were "enormously preoccupied with outer appearances in the physical sense of the word, admiring fitness and beauty."[7]

R.G.: And, therefore, thinness! The fathers are important here as representatives of the society at large; they are vectors of transmission for the surrounding culture. When Freud talks about the father and mother, their status remains ambiguous. It is never clear whether parents are important for biological reasons, or because they dominate the life of the child from the start. Freud remains equivocal on this point.

M.A.: In fact, Hilde Bruch adds that the preoccupation of the patients' fathers with physical appearance, as well as their desire to see their children "succeed," are doubtless traits shared by many upper-middle-class families, even if these same traits may be found in a more pronounced form in the families of anorexics.

R.G.: Anorexia is a phenomenon that appears in an era in which the family is breaking down. To try at all costs to find an explanation for it in the patients' families is to stay locked into a schema that is less and less relevant.

M.A.: A leading Italian authority on anorexia, Mara Selvini Palazzoli, the founder of the Milan school of family therapy, made an observation about the families of anorexics that should interest you all the same. According to her, the patients' parents are caught up in a rivalry to occupy the position of the sacrificial victim ...[8]

R.G.: Psychologists may turn out to be right here or there, in individual cases. But to use these to deny the social nature of a phenomenon that has been growing on all sides for the past 150 years – in my view, that is just a way to hide from ourselves what has become the norm in our society.

M.A.: All right, let's get away from the question of families and return one last time to a consideration of the social context. I have already emphasized the fact that the exacerbation of the anorexic phenomenon has occurred in a context of increasing undifferentiation, of undifferentiation between the sexes and between generations. One could speak of a crisis of differences and perhaps even of a "sacrificial crisis" in your sense, meaning a crisis that cannot be resolved by resorting to ritual sacrifices and which, therefore, lends itself to spontaneous, untamed outbreaks of victimage. At the end of your text you compare the images of "gesticulating cadavers" in fashion magazines to the *danses macabres* and *memento mori* of the Middle Ages. I wonder whether we should not interpret in victimary terms the appeal of cadaverous-looking models like Kate Moss.

L.T.: In reality, this is a recurrent phenomenon that seems to be associated with adolescence. Something analogous could be witnessed with the "living dead" in the Romantic era; it was the height of chic to be at the point of death.

M.A.: More recently, the term "heroin chic" was applied to waifish models with dark circles under the eyes and a junkie's blank stare. Not only does Kate Moss have an emaciated appearance, she is also known for her drug use. When images of her snorting cocaine circulated, the immediate reaction was negative, with advertising campaigns cancelled. But ultimately, the episode gave her career a boost (no pun intended). It would be easy to cite more examples: Britney Spears, Amy Winehouse ... Of course, there is nothing new about this; all self-respecting youth idols must flirt with self-destruction in order to burnish their image as doomed divinities, but my impression is that the whole process is turning into a caricature of itself.

R.G.: As in the case of thinness, there is a mimetic escalation. The need to commit ever bigger transgressions leads to behaviors that, if they are imitated, prove incompatible with organized society. Social life gets out of whack.

M.A.: The first victims of such societal breakdown are the individuals who follow these mimetic fashions to the point of making the supreme sacrifice. I am thinking of young models who collapse on the catwalks, like the 22-year-old Uruguayan woman who died at a fashion show in Spain on August 2, 2006. It is said that she had gone without eating for two weeks, after spending months on a regimen of nothing but lettuce and Diet Coke.[9] These are "fashion victims" in the most literal sense of the term. They give their lives to realize an ideal promoted by the community.

R.G.: It's a little like the suicide-terrorist, for those who support his actions – a kind of martyr.

L.T.: Martyrs to fashion, as it were . . .

M.A.: The comparison might seem bold, but I don't think it is off the mark. It even works both ways because in certain countries, in certain environments – and whatever the religious or political motivations may be – suicide-terrorism has clearly become a fashion craze. Fads are not a uniquely Western phenomenon. It would be a mistake to underestimate the role they play in other cultures. No human society is immune to the power of imitation. In Iraq, for example, after the fall of Saddam Hussein, there was a great vogue for religious extremism that seems already to be abating somewhat. According to a government official in Baghdad, Iraqis embraced religious fervor just as if they had "wanted to put on a new, stylish outfit."[10] In short, suicide-terrorists are martyrs to fashion, too. There are martyrs to fashion everywhere, but it is easier for us to see martyrdom in other cultures and fashion than in our own.

R.G.: We don't see the martyrdom in our own culture when we look at certain sinister images displayed in fashion magazines, images in which a healthy society would perceive the lineaments of death. It really is something that remains unconscious.

M.A.: What about the young women, fashion models or not, who actually do die while trying to conform to these images? If, in going all out to fulfill an ideal promoted by the community, they are led into martyrdom, can we describe them as sacrificial victims? That is the last question I would like to ask you.: Should we see this as a sacrifice in the sense of your anthropological theory?

R.G.: The imperative for which these women allow themselves to die of hunger comes from the whole society. It is a unanimous imperative. From that point of view, it is indeed organized like a sacrifice. And the fact that it is unconscious demonstrates, rather alarmingly, that there is a kind of return to the archaic in our culture.

Notes

1. Guy Trebay, "The Vanishing Point," *New York Times*, February 7, 2008.

2. Paola De Carolis, "Viso pallido, corpo emaciato: I ragazzi 'taglia zero,'" *Corriere della Sera,* February 11, 2008.

3. René Girard, "Camus's Stranger Retried," in *"To Double Business Bound"*: *Essays on Literature, Mimesis, and Anthropology* (Baltimore: Johns Hopkins, 1978), 9–35. Stefano Tomelleri, who compares this article to Girard's text on eating disorders, sees in Meursault's conspicuous solipsism and the anorexic's competitive self-destruction two complementary expressions of contemporary nihilism; see Tomelleri's introduction to a collection of essays by Girard published in Italy, *Il risentimento* (Milan: Raffaello Cortina, 1999), 14–16.

4. B. Balkau, et al., "A Study of Waist Circumference, Cardiovascular Disease, and Diabetes Mellitus in 168,000 Primary Care Patients in 63 Countries," *Circulation* 116 (October 2007): 1942–51.

5. René Girard, "Souvenirs d'un jeune Français aux Etats-Unis," in M. R. Anspach (ed.), *Cahier Girard* (Paris: Éditions de l'Herne, 2008), 30.

6. Quoted by Cécile Daumas, "Le corps du délit," *Libération*, September 29, 2006.

7. Hilde Bruch, *Eating Disorders: Obesity, Anorexia Nervosa, and the Person Within* (London: Routledge & Kegan Paul, 1974), 82.

8. Mara Selvini Palazzoli, *L'anoressia mentale: Dalla terapia individuale alla terapia familiare,* revised edition (Milan: Raffaello Cortina, 2006), 220.

9. Daumas, "Le corps du délit."

10. Sabrina Tavemise, "Young Iraqis Are Losing Their Faith in Religion," *New York Times,* March 3, 2008.

CHAPTER 15
APOCALYPTIC THINKING AFTER 9/11[1]
*Robert Doran /2008**

Robert Doran: Shortly after the attacks of September 11, 2001, you participated in an interview with the French news daily *Le Monde*, in which you stated that "what is occurring today is a mimetic rivalry on a planetary scale."[2] This observation now appears truer than ever. All evidence points to a continuation and intensification of mimetic conflict: wars in Afghanistan and Iraq; transit bombings in Madrid and London; even the car burnings in the Paris suburbs are not unrelated. How do you see the events of 9/11 in retrospect?

René Girard: I think that your statement is right. And I would like to begin by making a few comments on that very point. It seemed impossible at the time, but I think that many people have forgotten 9/11—not completely forgotten, but they have reduced it to some kind of unspoken norm. When I did that interview with *Le Monde*, everyone agreed that it was a most unusual, new, and incomparable event. And now I think that many people wouldn't agree with that statement. Unfortunately, in the United States, because of the war in Iraq, the attitude towards 9/11 has been affected by ideology. It has become "conservative" and "alarmist" to emphasize 9/11. Those who want to put an immediate end to the war in Iraq tend to minimize it. Now, I don't want to say that they are wrong in wanting to end the war in Iraq, but they should be very careful and consider the situation in its entirety before they deemphasize 9/11. Today this tendency is very general, because the events that you are talking about – which have taken place after 9/11 and which are in some way vaguely reminiscent of this

*From *SubStance* (Volume 37, Number 1, 2008), 20–32. Copyright 2008 Johns Hopkins University Press and SubStance, Inc. Reprinted with permission of Johns Hopkins University Press. First published as "Apocalyptic Thinking after 9/11: An Interview with René Girard." Translated by Trevor Cribben-Merrill.

event – have been incomparably less powerful, striking, and so forth. And therefore there is a whole problem of interpretation: what is 9/11?

RD: You yourself see 9/11 as a kind of rupture, a seminal event?

RG: Yes, I see it as a seminal event, and it is fundamentally wrong to minimize it today. The normal desire to be optimistic, to not see the uniqueness of our time from the point of view of violence, is the desire to grab any straw to make our time appear as the mere continuation of the violence of the twentieth century. I personally think that it represents a new dimension, a new world dimension. What communism was trying to do, to have a truly global war, has happened, and it is real now. To minimize 9/11 is to try to avoid thinking the way I do about the importance of this new dimension.

RD: You just made reference to the Cold War. How would you compare the two threats to the West?

RG: The two are similar in that they represent a revolutionary threat, a global threat. But the current threat goes beyond even politics, since there is a religious aspect. Therefore the idea that there could be a more total conflict than the one conceived by the totalitarian peoples, like Nazi Germany, that it would become in some way the property of Islam, is just such an amazing thing, so contrary to what everybody believed about politics. This demands an immense amount of thought, for there is no corresponding reflection about the coexistence of other religions with Islam and in particular Christianity. The religious problem is the most radical one in that it goes beyond the ideological divides – which of course most intellectuals today are not willing to let go of. And if this is the case, then our reflections will remain superficial with respect to 9/11. We must be willing to think in a wider context, and in my view this wider context is the apocalyptic dimension of Christianity. The apocalyptic dimension of Christianity is a threat because the very survival of the planet is at stake. Our planet is threatened by three things, all of which are the creation of man: the nuclear threat, the ecological threat, and the biological manipulation of the human species. The idea that man cannot be trusted with his powers is as true in the biological field as it is in the military field. So it is a triple threat of global proportions that has taken shape over the last century.

RD: I will return to the apocalyptic dimension in a moment. In a recent book, Zbigniew Brzezinski (National Security Advisor to President Carter) writes that "behind almost every terrorist act lurks a political problem. [...] To paraphrase Clausewitz, terrorism is politics by other means."[3] Though it may have other motivations, is terrorism not always in part political, to the extent that, no matter the actual target, it is always ultimately directed toward governments?

RG: Well, I think that it is not even by other means. Terrorism is a form of war, and war is politics by other means. In that sense, terrorism is political. But terrorism is the only possible form of war in the face of technology. The greatest mystery of what is going on now in Iraq is the confirmation of this immensely important fact. The superiority of the West is its technology, and it proves to be nothing in Iraq. Of course they put themselves in the worst possible situation by saying that we were going to turn Iraq into a Jeffersonian democracy, which was the stupidest thing to say! This is precisely what they cannot do; they are powerless before Islam. The divide between the Sunni and the Shia is infinitely more important. They manage to fight each other at the very moment when they are fighting against the West, which is truly amazing. Why should the West involve itself in this conflict within Islam? We don't even understand it. It appears to us like a reemergence of the quarrel between the Jansenists and the Jesuits. We don't see how enormously powerful it is in the Islamic world.

RD: Is it our incomprehension of the role of religion?

RG: It is incomprehension of the role of religion, and the incomprehension of our own world, of the weakness of the things that bind us together; for when we invoke our democratic principles, are we talking about things like equality and elections, or are we talking about capitalism, consumption, free trade and so on? One can say that in the coming years the West is going to be tried. The question is how the West will react: strongly or weakly? Will it dissolve itself? The West should start thinking about whether it really has principles, whether they are Christian or purely consumerist. Consumerism has no hold on those who engage in these suicide attacks. This is what America should be thinking about, because America has been expanding in the world, giving everyone what we consider more seductive than anything else. Does it really not work on the Muslim people? In other words, do they pretend that it doesn't work; is it resentment? Do they have a well-organized defense mechanism against it? Or is their religious view in some way more authentic and powerful? This is the real problem.

RD: Your original interpretation was that 9/11 was due to resentment.

RG: I'm much less affirmative than I was at the time of 9/11 that the reason was total resentment. I remember that I got carried away at a meeting held at the École Polytechnique when I agreed one hundred percent with Jean-Pierre Dupuy about the resentment interpretation of the Muslim world. But now I do not think it is sufficient. Can resentment motivate this ability to die like that? Could the Muslim world really be indifferent to the culture of mass consumption? Perhaps they are. I don't know. It is thus perhaps too excessive to attribute to them an envy of that. If the Islamists are really on a world domination kick, then they are beyond that. We don't know if there will appear something like rapid industrialization in the Muslim world, or if they will try to win on the basis of population growth and the fascination they exert. There are more and more conversions in the West. The fascination of violence certainly plays a role.

RD: But the resentment interpretation seemed logical in view of your thought.

RG: There is resentment there, of course. And this is what must have moved those who applauded the terrorists, as if they were in a stadium. That is resentment. This is obvious and undeniable. But is that the only force? Is that the main force? Can it by itself lead to the suicide attacks we see? I'm not sure. It is also true that the accumulated wealth in the West as compared with the rest of the world is a huge scandal, and that 9/11 in not unrelated to this fact. Thus I do not want to completely suppress the idea of resentment. There is certainly a strong element of resentment, but it cannot be the entire explanation.

RD: And the other force?

RG: The other force would be religious. Allah is against consumerism and so forth. What the Muslim really sees is that religious prohibition rituals are a force that keeps the community together, which has totally disappeared or is on the way out in the West. People in the West are united only by consumerism, good salaries, etc. The Muslims say: "their weapons are terribly dangerous but as a people they are so weak that their civilization can easily be destroyed." This is the way they think, and they may not be totally wrong. I think there is something right about it. Ultimately, I believe that the Christian view of violence will overcome everything, but we might consider this a great test.

RD: In his contribution to this volume, Jean-Pierre Dupuy calls 9/11 "a true sacrifice in the anthropological sense of the term."[4] Can 9/11 be thought according to a logic of sacrifice?

RG: I want to be very prudent in answering this question. One must be careful not to justify 9/11 by calling it sacrificial. I think that Jean-Pierre Dupuy doesn't do that. He maintains a kind of neutrality. What he says about the sacred nature of Ground Zero is, I think, perfectly justified. I would, however, like to quote from an insightful essay by James Alison, who has written on this very subject:

> And immediately the sacrificial centre began to generate the sort of reactions that sacrificial centres are supposed to generate: a feeling of unanimity and grief. [...] Phrases began to appear to the effect that "We're all Americans now" – a purely fictitious feeling for most of us. It was staggering to watch the togetherness build up around the sacred centre, quickly consecrated as Ground Zero, a togetherness that would harden over the coming hours into flag waving, a huge upsurge in religious services and observance, religious leaders suddenly taken seriously, candles, shrines, prayers, all the accoutrements of the religion of death. [...] And there was the grief. How we enjoy grief! It makes us feel good, and innocent. This is what Aristotle meant by catharsis, and it has deeply sinister echoes of dramatic tragedy's roots in sacrifice. One of the effects of the violent sacred around the sacrificial centre is to make those present feel justified, feel morally good. A counterfactual goodness which suddenly takes us out of our little betrayals, acts of cowardice, uneasy consciences.[5]

I think that James Alison is right to speak about *katharsis* in the context of 9/11. The notion of *katharsis* is tremendously important. People think that it is an Aristotelian word. This is not true. It's a religious word. It really means "the purge" as purification. In the Orthodox Church, for instance, *katharos* means purification. It's *the* word that expresses the positive effect of religion. The purge makes you pure. This is what religion is supposed to do, and it does it with sacrifice. I consider Aristotle's use of the word *katharsis* to be pure genius. When people condemn the mimetic theory, they don't see what formidable support it has in Aristotle. Aristotle seems to be only speaking about tragedy, but tragic theater is nothing but sacrifice reenacted as drama. This is why it is called "the ode of the goat."[6] Aristotle is always conventional in his explanations—conventional in the best sense. A very intelligent Greek seeking to justify his religion would, I think, use the word *katharsis*. Thus my answer to this question would place a great emphasis on *katharsis* and on Aristotle's understanding of the term.

RD: Certainly the spectacular aspect of 9/11 suggests an analogous relation to theater. But with 9/11 we could all be witnesses to a *real* event as it happened.

RG: Yes, with 9/11 there was television. Television makes you present at the scene, and thus it intensifies the experience. The event was *en direct*, as we say in French. You didn't know what was going to happen next. I saw the second plane hit the building not as a replay but as a live event. It was like a tragic spectacle, but real at the same time. If we hadn't lived it in the most literal sense, it would not have had the same impact. I think that if I had written *Violence and the Sacred* after 9/11, I would have most probably included 9/11 in this book.[7] This is the event that makes possible an understanding of the modern event, for it renders the archaic more intelligible. 9/11 represents a strange return of the archaic within the secularism of our time. Not too long ago people would have had a Christian reaction to 9/11. Now they have an archaic reaction, which does not bode well for the future.

RD: Let us return to the apocalyptic dimension. Your thought is generally considered pessimistic. Do you see 9/11 as a signpost on the way toward an apocalyptic future?

RG: The apocalyptic future is not something historical. It is something religious, and as such it is something that you cannot do without. This is what modern Christians don't understand. Because in the apocalyptic future, the good and the bad are mixed in such a way that from a Christian point of view, you cannot talk about pessimism. It is just being Christian. It is saying that all of the texts are part of the same totality. In order to understand this, you only have to quote the First Letter to the Corinthians: if the powers, meaning the powers of this world, had known what would happen, they would have never crucified the Lord of Glory— because it meant their destruction. Because when you crucify the Lord of Glory, the trick of the powers, which is the scapegoat mechanism, is revealed. To show the crucifixion as the killing of an innocent victim is to show the collective murder and to make it possible for people to understand that it is a mimetic phenomenon. Therefore the powers are ultimately going to perish from this truth. And all of history is simply the realization of this prophecy. Those who say that Christianity is anarchistic are somewhat right. The Christians are destroying the powers of this world, in the sense that they are destroying the legitimacy of all violence. From the point of view of the state, Christianity is a force of anarchy. Anytime it recaptures its old spiritual strength, this reappears in a way. Thus the conflict with the Muslims is really much more significant than even the fundamentalists believe. The fundamentalists think that the apocalypse is the violence of God. But if you read the apocalyptic chapters, you'll see that the apocalypse is the violence of man unleashed by the destruction of the powers, that is, of the states, which is what we're seeing now.

RD: But this understanding makes it possible for violence to continue on another level.

RG: Yes, but not as a religious force. The religious force is on the side of Christ, ultimately. However, it appears as though the real religious force were on the side of violence.

RD: What will it look like when the powers are defeated?

RG: Well, when the powers are defeated, violence will become such that the end will come. If you take the apocalyptic chapters, this is what they announce to you. There will be revolution and wars. State will rise against state, nation against nation. These are the doubles. This is the power of anarchy we have now, with forces capable of destroying the whole world. So you can see the coming of the apocalypse in a way that wasn't previously possible. In the early days of Christianity, there was something magical about the apocalypse. The world is going to end; we'll all be in paradise, and everything will be alright. The "mistake" of the first Christians was to believe that the apocalypse was going to be an instant affair. The first Christian texts, chronologically speaking, are the Letters to the Thessalonians, and they are an answer to the question: why is the world continuing when you announced its end? Paul says that there is something holding back the powers, the *katochos* (something that holds back). The most common interpretation is that it is the Roman Empire. The Crucifixion has not yet dissolved all order. If you look at the apocalyptic chapters of Christianity, they describe something like the present chaos, which wasn't there in the beginning of the Roman Empire. How can the world end when it is held so tightly by the forces of order?

RD: Then Christian revelation is ambivalent in that it has both positive and negative consequences?

RG: Why negative? Fundamentally it is religion that announces the world to come; it is not about fighting for this world. It is modern Christianity that forgets its origins and its real direction. The apocalypse at the beginning of

Christianity was a *promise*, not a threat, because they really believed in the next world.

RD: Then could one say that you are pessimistic in an a priori sense?

RG: I am pessimistic in the sense that everybody understands the word pessimism. But I'm optimistic in the sense that if one looks at the present world, it already verifies all the predictions. You can see the shape of the apocalypse increasing every day: the power capable of destroying the world, ever more lethal weapons, and the other threats that are multiplying under our eyes. We still believe that all of these problems are manageable by man, but if you take them all together you can see that this is not the case. They acquire a kind of supernatural value. Like the fundamentalists, many readers of the Gospels are reminded of the world situation when they read these apocalyptic chapters. But the fundamentalists believe that the ultimate violence comes from God, so they don't really see the relevance of what is going on now—the religious relevance. That shows how unchristian they are on a certain level. It is human violence that is threatening the world today; and this is in greater conformity to the apocalyptic theme in the Gospels than they realize.

RD: Can't we say that we have made moral progress?

RG: But the two are possible together. For example, we have less private violence. If you look at statistics from the eighteenth century, it was amazing how much violence there was compared with today.

RD: I was thinking about something like the peace movement, which would have been inconceivable just a hundred years ago.

RG: Yes, the peace movement is totally Christian, whether it knows it or not. But at the same time there is an unleashing of technological inventions that are no longer restrained by any cultural force. Jacques Maritain said that there is more good and more bad in the world all the time. I think this is an excellent formula. In other words, the world is both more Christian and less Christian, constantly. But it is fundamentally disorganized by Christianity.

RD: What you're saying, then, is in opposition to the humanist perspective of someone like a Marcel Gauchet, who says that Christianity is the religion of the end of religion.[8]

RG: Yes, Marcel Gauchet is the result of the whole modern interpretation of Christianity. We say that we are the heirs of Christianity, and that the legacy of Christianity is humanism. This is partly true. But at the same time,

Marcel Gauchet does not look at the world at large. You can keep everything together with the mimetic theory. As the world looks more threatening, religion is sure to return. And in a way, 9/11 is the beginning of this, for in this attack technology was used not for humanistic ends but for radical, metaphysico-religious ends, which are not Christian. That is why it is such an amazing thing for me, because I'm used to considering religious forces and humanistic forces together, not as if one were true and the other false; and then suddenly archaic religion is coming back in an incredibly forceful way with Islam. Islam has many aspects of the Biblical religions minus the revelation of violence as bad, as not divine but human; it makes violence totally divine. This is why the opposition is more significant than with communism, which is a humanism. It is a bogus humanism, the last and most incredibly foolish form, which results in terror. But it is still humanism. And suddenly we're back in religion, in archaic religion—but with modern weapons. What the world is waiting for is the moment when the Muslim radicals will somehow be able to use nuclear weapons. And the point you have to look at on the map is Pakistan, which is a Muslim nation that has nuclear weapons. And Iran is trying to develop them.

RD: Thus you see the Cold War as being superseded both in scope and importance by the conflict with Islamic radicalism?

RG: Totally superseded, yes. And the speed with which it was superseded was just something unbelievable. The moment the Soviet Union revealed that they were human is when they didn't try to force Kennedy's blockade, and from that time on they didn't scare anybody anymore. After Khrushchev you had to get to Gorbachev fairly quickly. The moment when Gorbachev came to power was the moment when the oppositions were no longer inside humanism. The communists had wanted to organize the world so that there wouldn't be any more poor people, and the capitalists had said that the poor were insignificant. The capitalists have prevailed.

RD: And this conflict will be more dangerous because it is no longer a struggle within humanism?

RG: Yes, though they do not have the same weapons as the Soviet Union— at least not yet. Things change so fast. However, more and more people in the West are going to see the weakness of our humanism; we are not going to become Christian again, but there will be more attention to the fact that the fight is really between Christianity and Islam, more than between Islam and humanism.

RD: You mean a conflict between the consciousness that violence is human and the consciousness that violence is divine?

RG: Yes, with Islam I think the opposition is total. In Islam, if you are violent you are inevitably an instrument of God. Thus it is really saying that the apocalyptic violence comes from God. In the United States the fundamentalists say that, but the big churches do not. However, they are not coherent enough thinkers to say that if violence does not come from God then it comes from man, and therefore we are responsible for it. We accept to live under the protection of nuclear weapons. This has probably been the West's greatest sin. Think of its implications.

RD: You're referring to the logic of mutual assured destruction.

RG: Yes, nuclear deterrence. But these are lame excuses. We are putting our faith in violence; we believe that violence will keep the peace. But this assumption is inevitably false. We are trying not to think radically today about what this confidence in violence means.

RD: What do you think the effect of another 9/11-like event would be?

RG: I think that more people would become more aware. But it would probably be like the first attack. There would be a period of great spiritual and intellectual tension followed by a slow relaxation. When people don't want to see something, they are pretty good at not seeing it. I think that there are going to be spiritual and intellectual revolutions in the not too distant future. What I'm talking about now seems totally mad, and yet I think that 9/11 is going to become more meaningful all the time.

RD: Has your view of the role of violence in Christianity changed?

RG: There are mistakes in *Things Hidden Since the Foundation of the World*[9]: the refusal to use the word sacrificial in a good way, for example. There was too much opposition between the sacrificial and the non-sacrificial. In Christianity, all sacrificial acts are intended to render violence more distant, to make it possible for man to do away with his own violence. I think that authentic Christianity completely separates God from violence; however, the role of violence in Christianity is a complex thing.

RD: At the time of *Things Hidden* you said that Christianity was a nonsacrificial religion.

RG: Christianity has always been sacrificial. It's true I gave the nonsacrificial interpretation too much importance – in order to be heretical. That is what was left of the avant-gardist attitude in me. I had to be against the Church in some way. The attitude was instinctive, since my whole intellectual training came out of surrealism, existentialism and so forth, which were all anti-Christian. It was probably a good thing, for the book might not otherwise have been successful.

RD: If you had appeared more orthodox?

RG: If I had appeared orthodox, I would have been silenced immediately, by the silence of the media.

RD: What is your current view of sacrifice in Christianity?

RG: One has to make a distinction between the sacrifice of others and self-sacrifice. Christ says to the Father: "you wanted neither holocaust nor sacrifice; then I said: 'Here I am.'" In other words: I prefer to sacrifice myself than to sacrifice the other. But this still has to be called sacrifice. When we say "sacrifice" in our modern languages it has only the Christian sense. Therefore the Passion is entirely justified. God says: If nobody else is good enough to sacrifice himself rather than his brother, I will do it. Therefore I fulfill God's requirement for man. I prefer to die than to kill. But all other men prefer to kill than to die.

RD: But what about the idea of martyrdom?

RG: In Christianity you are not martyring yourself. You're not volunteering to be killed. You place yourself in a situation in which the observance of God's precepts (turn the other cheek, etc.) will get you killed. But you will be killed because men want to kill you, not because you volunteered. This is not like the Japanese notion of the kamikaze. The Christian notion means you're ready to die rather than to kill. This is the attitude of the good prostitute in the judgment of Solomon. She says: Give the child to my enemy rather than kill him. Sacrificing her child is like sacrificing herself, for in accepting the equivalent of death, she sacrifices herself. And when Solomon says that she is the real mother, this does not even mean that she is the mother according to biology, but according to the spirit. This story is from the Book of Kings, which in some ways is quite a savage book. But I would say that there is no pre-Christian symbol of Christ's self-sacrifice that is superior to this one.

RD: Do you see this in contrast to the concept of martyrdom in Islam?

RG: I see it as contrasting Christianity with all archaic religions of sacrifice. Now, since the Muslim religion has copied Christianity more than anything, it is not openly sacrificial. But the Muslim religion has not destroyed the sacrifice of archaic religion the way Christianity has. No part of the Christian world has retained pre-Christian sacrifice. Many parts of the Muslim world have retained pre-Muslim sacrifice.

RD: Wouldn't spontaneous lynchings in the South be examples of archaic sacrifice?

RG: Yes, of course. You have to go to Faulkner to find the truth about this – to a novelist. Many people believe that Christianity is embodied by the South. I would say that the South is perhaps the least Christian part of the United States in terms of spirit, although it is the most Christian in terms of ritual. There is no doubt that Medieval Christianity was much closer to what fundamentalism has remained. But there are many ways to betray a religion. In the case of the South, it is very obvious, because there is such a return to the most archaic forms of religion. You must define these lynchings as a kind of archaic religious act.

RD: What do you think about the way in which people use the term "religious violence"?

RG: People use the term "religious violence" in ways that do not clear up the problems that my thinking is trying to clear up – that of a constantly moving relationship to violence, which is also historical.

RD: Would it be fair to say that according to your thinking any religious violence is necessarily archaic?

RG: Well, I would say that any religious violence includes a degree of archaism. But some aspects are so complicated. For example, in the First World War, what was Christian in the soldiers who accepted to be drafted in order to die for their country, many of them in the name of Christianity? There is something in this that is untrue to Christianity. But there is also something that is true. This does not, in my view, invalidate the fact that there is a history of religious violence, and that deep down, religions, especially Christianity, are continually influenced by this history, though its influence is perverted most of the time.

Notes

1. This interview took place, in English, on February 10, 2007 at Professor Girard's home in Stanford, CA. A brief follow-up interview was conducted on August 8, 2007, also at Girard's home.

2. Interview with Henri Tincq, *Le Monde*, November 6, 2001. (The interview is included in this volume. – ED.)

3. Zbigniew Brezezinski, *The Choice: Global Domination or Global Leadership* (New York: Basic Books, 2004), 28.

4. Jean-Pierre Dupuy, "Anatomy of 9/11: Evil, Rationalism, and the Sacred," *SubStance*, vol. 37, no. 1 (2008), 33-51.

5. James Alison, "Contemplation in a World of Violence: Girard, Merton, Tolle," http://www.jamesalison.co.uk/texts/eng77.html, accessed April 29, 2019.

6. The Greek word *tragoidia* is a combination of *tragos* (goat) and *ode* (song): "goat song" or "the song delivered at the sacrifice of a goat."

7. René Girard, *Violence and the Sacred* (Baltimore: Johns Hopkins University Press, 1977).

8. See Marcel Gauchet, *The Disenchantment of the World: A Political History of Religion,* trans. Oscar Burge, fwd. Charles Taylor (Princeton, NJ: Princeton University Press, 1997), 101.

9. René Girard, *Things Hidden since the Foundation of the World*, trans. S. Bann and M. Metteer (Stanford, CA: Stanford University Press, 1987).

CHAPTER 16
"I AM FIRST AND FOREMOST
A SOCIAL SCIENTIST."

*Pedro Sette-Câmara, Alvaro Velloso de
Carvalho, and Olavo de Carvalho/2008**

*On November 17, 2000, I participated in a conference given by René
Girard at Faculdade da Cidade in Rio de Janeiro. Soon after the event, I
was able to schedule a brief interview with Girard at Hotel Glória for the
next day. Alvaro Velloso de Carvalho, a colleague at O Indivíduo, and
the philosopher Olavo de Carvalho, who had been discussing Girard in
his private seminars, also took part in the interview. The interview was
published in O Indivíduo, which I launched as Brazil's first online student
newspaper at the Catholic University of Rio de Janeiro in 1997. The
publication became a platform for a wide range of young writers.*

—PSC

Olavo de Carvalho: Why is it that, even though you were the first to
reconcile the human sciences and Catholicism, twentieth-century Catholic
thought apparently had no influence at all on your work?

René Girard: I am first and foremost a social scientist, so it's not surprising
that I remained unaware of the philosophical and theological debates in
which Catholic thinkers were engaged. I am interested in the Bible mainly
as a sociological document. This is why they look at me with suspicion,
seeing me as a sort of sheep in wolf's clothing. They don't realize that my
work, even though it has no doctrinal or apologetic purpose, opens new
and unsuspected perspectives for Catholicism, to the extent that it shows its
moral superiority. We live in a society where everyone thinks the Gospels
are a myth, and that every myth is false; my work shows it is only possible

*From *O Indivíduo*, April 16, 2008. Originally published as "Interview with René Girard."
Reprinted with permission of *O Indivíduo*. Translated from the Portuguese by Pedro Sette-
Câmara.

to understand why myths are false in the light of the Gospel, and that the Gospels cannot be myths.

Olavo de Carvalho: In your system, punitive violence always appears as a collective act, an act of the masses, and in your latest book you claim to no longer believe in the possibility of a non-violent society. Do you believe at least within the human soul there is a sort of protected sanctuary, uncontaminated by violence?

René Girard: That depends on your view of the original sin. An Augustinian, or someone who believes in predestination, would say no. But I hope there is. It is evident that, both individually and collectively, we find essentially the same passions: envy, pride, etc. However, collectively they are magnified by the multiplying force of the mimetic mechanism.

Pedro Sette-Câmara: Would you agree that politically correct ideology, seeking state protection for every minority against everyone, represents an attempt of Satan to cast out Satan once again?

René Girard: Yes. What's interesting in this phenomenon is that it can only take place in a civilization that has already undergone the influence of Christianity. As the scapegoat mechanism has been revealed, we do not return directly to it, that is, we do not directly accuse the victim of having done something. We don't blame them directly. But the scapegoat mechanism continues to work, though in a different way: the politically correct movement accuses their opponents of creating scapegoats. They accuse them of victimizing others. It's like Christianity turned upside down: they take whatever is left of Christian influence, whatever is left of a Christian language, but to opposite ends, in order to perpetuate the scapegoat mechanism.

Pedro Sette-Câmara: I was reading an interview you gave in 1996 in which you defend the international intervention in Bosnia, stating it is not imperialist and only seeks to stop the killing of innocents. After stating that violence is the foundation of societies, would you still subscribe to that view? Or would you also say Christianity can provide a foundation for the organization of society?

René Girard: Christianity never had this goal. It never sought to organize society.

Pedro Sette-Câmara: But would you still subscribe to that view?

René Girard: Nowadays I would not be entirely favorable to the intervention in Bosnia. It is difficult to say where the world is headed today, with the perspective of the end of national sovereignty. If you look at cases like Pinochet's arrest, you will see that the whole procedure is completely outside international law. The thing is, international law has collapsed. What will come after this?

Some will say this is a new form of American imperialism, even if there are no specific plans, as imperialism can operate even without a direct goal, in a certain sense. For instance, when Putin spoke in private with Chirac recently, he said that De Gaulle would not act like him, would not accept to follow American foreign policy without question.

We could support this kind of intervention if we knew the international community would always intervene for the right reasons—but we cannot bet on that.

What worries me is the situation's potential to create new scapegoats, as we have clearly seen from the cases of Milošević and Pinochet: it is easy to hate them both from a distance, without knowing their particular situations, without listening to a single argument in their favor, just being dragged by the crowd's wave of hatred.

Pedro Sette-Câmara: I believe you said you today you would not be able to do the work you did if you had to do it in a university. Did you really say that?

René Girard: I did. If I were young today, and I had to join a university, I would be very worried. When I started, back in the 50's and 60's, the situation may not have been ideal, but it was good, it was different. There were errors, but people were honest, or at least they were trying to be honest. Today people in academia are not even trying to be honest. Everywhere— apparently everywhere in the world—is infested by ideology. Universities have become spaces for political propaganda.

Alvaro Velloso de Carvalho: In your book *When These Things Begin*, you make interesting observations about abortion and how its legalization represents a step back as regards some of Christianity's achievements. Could you elaborate?[1]

René Girard: In the United States abortion is still a matter of discussion, but in Europe, for instance, there is no discussion at all. Recently, I wrote an article for an European Catholic magazine where I mentioned abortion. One of my friends was shocked!

Alvaro Velloso de Carvalho: Abortion is never seen in a biblical context, or even in a broader anthropological context, right?

René Girard: Precisely. Even those who argue against abortion do not always take this view, because their view of the Bible is too rigid.

The protection of the children, newborn children, is essential in the Bible. The sacrifice of Isaac marks the difference between the old God and the new God: it's the old God who asks Abraham to sacrifice his son, and when Abraham is about to do it, the new God prevents the child's sacrifice, replacing it with an animal's sacrifice. The end of ritual infanticide is one of the features of our civilization, and we are losing this feature.

Recently I read a book where the author, whose name I can't remember, said abortion was the sacrifice of a child, and that he was in favor of this sacrifice. This is as horrendous as it can get.

It seems like the ancient, primitive fatalities, temporarily discarded by the light of the prophets and the Gospel, are coming back. In the Bible, the protection of children appears alongside the protection of the handicapped, lepers, cripples. These are the preferential victims of ancient societies, and we understand we must protect them. We still protect crippled people, handicapped people, but in the center of it all we find a sort of cancer growing, which is the return to infanticide. This is a decisive argument, which few people will take into consideration: those who defend abortion are trying to make our society go back to pre-Christian barbarism.

Note

1. From Michel Treguer's interviews with Girard in *When These Things Begin* (East Lansing, MI, 2014), 86: "Here we're in an absolutely tragic situation. It is perfectly true that, on the human level, the level of rational 'planning,' abortion and all the measures for limiting births are as justified as can be. The modern world seems to force people to choose between either, on the one hand, heroic renunciation, chastity, sobriety, poverty, and everything that was once deemed 'saintly' or, on the other, a blind descent into chaos and death. And this in an era that is increasingly unable to comprehend the positive nature of renunciation."

   "I already said earlier that the battle being fought by 'progressive' Christians to reconcile Christianity with contemporary society seemed to me to be out of touch with what people who have been uprooted by modernity are actually feeling. This way of confusing the Catholic Church with a political party that's a step behind its constituency is a loss of religious meaning."

   And elsewhere (page 85): "The attitude of the Catholic Church or let's say instead that of the Vatican, which today is very isolated at the heart of

Catholicism itself, disowned in an underhanded way by a good portion of the clergy, jeered by the entire universe, the practically official scapegoat of the media and of the whole world's intelligentsia, of every Nobel Prize winner and of every Nobel Prize nominee, has something heroic about it, all the more so because that heroism is itself unsung. We're increasingly unable to acknowledge or even to recognize true dissidence when we see it."

CHAPTER 17
"CHRISTIANITY WILL BE VICTORIOUS, BUT ONLY IN DEFEAT."
Cynthia L. Haven/2009*

Cynthia Haven: Just when people think they know what Girard is about, you surprise us. Your work has expanded into new and revelatory directions at several junctures in your long career. Now it appears to have changed again with your latest book on Carl von Clausewitz.

René Girard: *Achever Clausewitz* is a book about modern war, really. Clausewitz is a writer who wrote only about war; he was in love with war. He hated Napoleon, the enemy of his country, Prussia, but he also loved him because the emperor had restored war to its glorious nature after the eighteenth century, which weakened war by having conflicts that made maneuvers and negotiations more important than actual fighting. That is why Clausewitz's hatred for Napoleon was curiously united to a passionate admiration for the man who had restored war to its former glory.

CH: The love-hate nature of "mimetic rivalry" is apparent here, but is there anything else that attracted you to this offbeat topic?

RG: I found another interesting correspondence with my own work. Because Clausewitz talks only about war, he describes human relations in a way that interests me profoundly. When we describe human relations, we usually make them better than they are: gentle, peaceful, and so forth, whereas in reality they are often competitive. War is the most extreme form of competition. That is why Clausewitz says that business – commercial business – and war are very close to each other.

CH: You've pointed out that our whole contemporary society is reaching a point of "mimetic crisis." What, exactly, causes a mimetic crisis?

---

*From *First Things*, published online July 16, 2009. Reprinted with permission of Cynthia L. Haven.

RG: A mimetic crisis is when people become undifferentiated. There are no more social classes, there are no more social differences, and so forth. What I call a mimetic crisis is a situation of conflict so intense that on both sides people act the same way and talk the same way even though, or because, they are more and more hostile to each other. I believe that in intense conflict, far from becoming sharper, differences melt away.

When differences are suppressed, conflicts become rationally insoluble. If and when they are solved, they are solved by something that has nothing to do with rational argument: by a process that the people concerned do not understand and even do not perceive. They are solved by what we call a *scapegoat process*.

CH: You say that the history of scapegoating is suppressed by those who do the scapegoating.

RG: Scapegoating *itself* is the suppressing. If you scapegoat someone, only a third party can become aware of it. It won't be you, because you will believe you are doing the right thing. You will believe that you are either punishing someone who is truly guilty, or fighting someone who is trying to kill you. We never see ourselves as responsible for scapegoating.

If you look at archaic religions, it becomes clear that religion is a way to master, or at least control, violence. I think that archaic religions are based on a collective murder, on a lynch-mob murder, which unites the people and saves the community. This process is the beginning of a religion: salvation as a result of scapegoating. That is why the people turn their scapegoat into a god.

CH: You've said elsewhere: "I think ultimately the Christian view of violence will overcome everything, but we might consider this a great test." Do you really have that kind of confidence?

RG: Christianity will be victorious, but only in defeat. Christianity is the same scheme as archaic religions; it is an instance of scapegoating, but – and this difference is enormous – instead of blaming the victim, and joining the scapegoaters, it realizes that the victim is innocent and we all try to interpret this type of situation in the light of the innocent victim, that is, Christ himself. In a world that is no longer organized along the rigid lines of scapegoating and the sacrifices that reenact it in the penal systems, we have more and more disorder. More and more freedom, but more and more disorder.

CH: So tell us a little about this "great test"?

RG: History, you might say, is this test. But we know very well that mankind is failing that test. In some ways, the gospels, the Scriptures, are predicting that failure, since they end with eschatological themes, which predict the end of the world.

CH: You've said that, for modern societies, "the confidence is in violence. We put our faith in that violence, that violence will keep the peace." How can nations be strong without violence?

RG: Truth begins with the acknowledgement of our violence that Christianity requires of us. Well, the alternative is the kingdom of God, and the kingdom of God is, by definition, nonviolent. It never comes true, because people are not Christian enough and this is the same as what I said before: We must acknowledge our own scapegoating and we cannot do it.

CH: It's hard to imagine going to the negotiating table in the Middle East, without having the prospect of war as a last resort.

RG: I agree completely. But this is the same as our eternal deadlock. We must see history as a long process of education. God is trying to teach man to renounce violence. The kingdom of God would be no violence at all, and we do not seem capable of it. That's why you have the apocalyptic texts at the end of the gospels.

Right now, the world is moving more and more towards various types of catastrophes. It knows this very well; it talks about little else. Today we are in such a situation that we cannot distinguish the instruments of war and the instruments of peace.

When you look at the apocalyptic texts, they seem absurd and childish because they often mix up culture and nature. This sounded absurd until recently, but now it really happens. When there is hurricane in New Orleans, we wonder if it is not man rather than nature that is responsible. Unbelievers think that the apocalyptic texts of Christianity are antiscientific because they mix up nature and culture. But in our world it cannot be denied that man can interfere with the functioning of nature. The world has never known such a possibility before, but it does now and I think this situation is specifically Christian. So, far from seeing a Christianity that is outmoded and ridiculous, I see a Christianity that makes a great deal of sense. This sense is just too amazing to be understood by people who stick to conventional thinking.

CH: You've said: "More and more people in the West are becoming aware of the weaknesses of our humanism; we are not going to become Christian again, but there will be more attention to the fact that the fight is really between Christianity and Islam, more than between Islam and humanism."

RG: Yes. I believe it, you see, because Christianity destroyed sacrificial cults. Christianity reveals that our world is founded on violence. The main resource of government and civilization, in the archaic world, is the scapegoat phenomenon. The great paradox is that the scapegoat phenomenon operates only as long as it remains unperceived by the people it unites. The gospels make it visible that Jesus is a scapegoat. When people say there is no difference between a myth and Christianity, it is almost true. In both instances, the story culminates in a big drama: A victim is collectively killed and is divinized. But, in these two instances, the victim is not divinized for the same reason. Jesus is divinized because he suffers the Passion, in spite of his innocence, and he reveals their own violence to his murderers. In archaic religions, the guilt of the murderers remains invisible, unperceived. It's the reconciliation effect of scapegoating which is emphasized as the positive significance of the process. In Christianity, the criminal violence of the murderers is revealed as well as the innocence of the victim.

An archaic religion is nothing but a scapegoat phenomenon that succeeds, so to speak, as it is naively interpreted by the scapegoaters themselves. In the gospels, this scapegoat phenomenon fails and its meaning is revealed to the scapegoaters themselves, that is, mankind as a whole. Christianity destroys archaic religions because it reveals to us their reliance on scapegoat violence.

The self-denigration of the modern world, as well as its intellectual superiority, is rooted in this awareness of scapegoating. Unfortunately, we are not aware that the entire process is rooted in Christianity, which many people reject together with the false scapegoat religions.

In a way, the Western world has been sitting on its privileges, and paid not the slightest attention to Islam. It has been absolutely sure that – in all its ways, even the least Christian – it was superior, which in a certain sense is true, but it's due to something that Christianity has not earned.

CH: In what way superior?

RG: All the spiritual advantages it has because it knows the truth. It knows the sinfulness of man, the fact that man is a killer, a killer of God. In the East, their contempt for Christianity is due to the fact that they feel absolutely scandalized by the Crucifixion. What kind of God is it that will allow himself to be persecuted and killed by men? In a way, it's good to see because of the shock, you know. In a way I think what God is saying is that "I allowed these scapegoats. But you, I teach you the truth. So you should be up to that truth, and become perfect, and that is the kingdom of God." You are the chosen ones, in the Jewish sense.

CH: And you said Christianity had these advantages but had not earned them?

RG: It has not earned them, and it has not behaved as it should have. Christians are unfaithful to Christianity.

CH: You have said that this apocalypse is not necessarily a bang, or even a whimper, but rather a long stasis.

RG: In the Gospel of Matthew, it says: "Except those days should be shortened, there should no flesh be saved" – because it's an infinitely long stretch.

CH: So this is the period we're in?

RG: I think it may well be. We are proud of the achievements we call modern and there are scriptural indications that they coincide with the dangerous times we live in.

Some of the fundamentalist Christians think the eschatological themes show that God is angry with man and is going to put an end to the world. But the eschatological texts are more meaningful if you understand the situation as I just defined it. If man doesn't become more modest, his violence will increase in an unlimited way. This violence doesn't increase through physical fighting and wars only, but through the increase and multiplication of weapons, which now threaten the very survival of the world. Our violence is not created by God but by man; in a world that is practically more and more oblivious to God, if you look at the way nations behave with each other, at the way individuals behave with each other.

Before the invention of apocalyptic weapons, we couldn't see how realistic apocalyptic texts have become. Today we can see that, and we should be extremely impressed by this realism. Now only one thing is left to man if he wants to survive: universal reconciliation.

CH: Who is the antichrist in your interpretation?

RG: Well, we don't know, but there are many plausible candidates. Obviously there is something very insidious about the antichrist, who is a seducer. So it must not be someone like Stalin or Hitler since they failed miserably. And the antichrist doesn't seem to work by force. But I think you could see that it's a certain modern spirit—the spirit of power, the idea that man has become totally master of himself, and that he doesn't have to bow in front of powers greater than himself, and he's going to triumph in the end.

CH: So this crisis you see us constantly going through, how does it end?

RG: We're going through a slow increase in the symptoms of destabilization that characterizes the modern world.

CH: And then what will happen?

RG: I don't know. You have two conceptions of time to consider: the eternal return, which I think is the founding murder of a scapegoat, and therefore a new religion. The scapegoat phenomenon is so powerful, that a community can organize itself around it.

And then we have continuous time, which carries through to the destruction of the world, the Second Coming. Obviously, that withdraws the source of renewal, which is the sacrificial murder of a scapegoat. With the Bible there is no renewal, no new religion.

CH: Nietzsche noted that we've gone almost two thousand years with no new god.

RG: Nietzsche has some texts that are very interesting, because he would like to go back to the eternal return; therefore he is not really apocalyptic, because he is not really waiting for the kingdom of God. He would like to go back, and he hopes that there will be an end of Christianity.

CH: You point out that he hated the gospels, that he didn't see them from a theoretical or historical perspective.

RG: No, he didn't. He saw them as the worst possible thing for the world, because he saw it as a cause for decadence, of people becoming incapable of energy and moving in history in such a way that civilizations would not renew themselves and die. It was pre-Nazi. He was nostalgic for archaic religion.

CH: Did he have a point? Is there a kind of decadence to where we are now?

RG: Sure, he had a point. Because that long, endless period of apocalypse is getting a little tiresome. And, then, if you really look it is probably extremely noncreative. Today do you feel the arts are as productive as they were in the past?

The kingdom of God will not arrive on this earth, but there is an inspiration of the kingdom of God in our world, which is partial and limited. And there is a nonchristian, antichristian decadence in all its ways. We still have the prophesied "abomination of the desolation" to get through, undoubtedly.

CH: Given this long apocalypse we're going through, what do we do?

RG: Nothing spectacular.

CH: We just sit it out?

RG: We just sit it out. But we must try not to surrender to the spiritual decadence of our time and rise above the world around us.

CH: What about that quotation: "Except those days should be shortened, there should no flesh be saved: but for the elect's sake those days shall be shortened"?

RG: It means that the end times will be very long and monotonous – so mediocre and uneventful from a religious and spiritual standpoint that the danger of dying spirituality, even for the best of us, will be very great. This is a harsh lesson but one ultimately of hope rather than despair.

POSTSCRIPT
"RENÉ GIRARD NEVER PLAYED THE GREAT MAN," SAYS BIOGRAPHER
Artur Sebastian Rosman/2016*

Cynthia Haven and I met over An Invisible Rope: Portraits of Czesław Miłosz. *I provided the translation for one of the Polish essays in the book. We met at the Miłosz centenary in Kraków and have stayed in touch ever since. When I heard she was writing a biography of René Girard, published in 2018 as* Evolution of Desire: A Life of René Girard, *I asked to interview her, and we spoke shortly after the French theorist's death.*

—ASR

ARTUR ROSMAN: How did you become friends with Professor Girard? Did the prophetic intensity of his books carry over into his everyday life?

CYNTHIA HAVEN: I was on the Stanford campus in the 1980s, and I would occasionally see him, although I didn't know who he was. He was a memorable presence, even without knowing about his work. He was in his sixties then, and had one of the most remarkable and distinctive faces I had ever seen – typecast for the role of a great thinker, writing deathless books. Dark, deep-set eyes and shock of thick, wavy, salt-and-pepper hair. As I recall he carried a brown leather briefcase, the old-fashioned kind with buckles and stuffed with papers, letters, and folders.

The face was so memorable that I remembered it twenty years later, when I met him at last – by that time he was well into his eighties. He had been in my peripheral vision all along, and I had not known it.

So I wasn't immediately captivated by his "prophetic intensity." Later, I noticed that he would say the most astonishing things – prophetic, I guess – in a simple, non-bombastic way. Sometimes as a throwaway line,

*From the blog *Cosmos the in Lost*, January 19, 2016. Reprinted with permission of Artur Sebastian Rosman.

or undercut by a joke. He was one of the least pretentious or self-interested people I have ever met.

People who never knew René don't understand how much *fun* it was to talk to him. He was witty and charming and bracing and very, very smart. I found he would have a fresh and different take on pretty much everything under the sun. We became friends, in the usual sort of way.

And he would listen as much as he would talk. Given the great inequality of our friendship, this was *noblesse oblige* indeed. Yet he never made you feel this inequality. He never played the Great Man.

AR: Were you familiar with Professor Girard's theories before you met him? What did you think of them?

CH: His name was familiar to me as an important French theorist, but that was about all.

The more I learned and read, the more I was surprised that more hadn't been written about him in the American mainstream media. After all, he'd made his home in the U.S. since 1947.

Many felt his ideas were abstruse and difficult. On the contrary, I found the ideas to be pretty straightforward, and not hard to explain – although some of the applications of his ideas, and the research he uses to support them from the fields of, say, anthropology, can be challenging. I began writing a series of articles about him. He told me afterwards that this was the first time ordinary people understood what he was doing, although I think he was being overly generous. He signed my copy of *Mimesis and Theory*, "To Cynthia, with all my thanks for her splendid contribution to my scholarly reputation."

I find his ideas have enormous explanatory power not only for the world we see around us – but the world we find within us. People may question his reading of archaic societies or historical events, but the place to verify his theories is within oneself. We imitate each other. We are driven by competition and rivalry with the real or imagined "other." We struggle to acquire status symbols, which we fantasize will make us more like the one we idolize. We join in Twitter mobs, or Facebook mobs, that castigate and vilify the person or group we think is responsible for all our ills, and whose elimination will bring peace at last. The Democrats. The Republicans. Donald Trump.

This kind of "evidence" is much closer at hand than the Aztecs or the ancient Greeks. That said, I don't feel a need to force his template onto everything I see. Certainly he explains enough of our metaphysical dilemma that I thought his ideas should be much more widely known, and figure more prominently among the tools in our psychological tool kit. I don't see why his ideas can't circulate as widely as we those of Freud or Marx. Many people talk about the Oedipus complex without having read a word of Freud.

René wrote about so many aspects of human life and human nature: How much we imitate each other, and how our desires are not our own. We want what others want. Inevitably, then, our desires converge on the same objects or symbols. This leads to competition and rivalry, and ultimately violence, which spreads mimetically within a society. The all-against-all conflict devolves into all-against-one. A person, or group of people, are seen as responsible and blamed for all the trouble. The violent passions are assuaged only by the death, exile, or elimination of a scapegoat – often an outsider, or someone otherwise not in a position to retaliate and continue the cycles of violence. Archaic religions controlled the violence by the ritual of sacrifice – the sacrifice of the scapegoat would bring peace and harmony to the society, and a temporary, but only temporary, reprieve from its passions. But the Judeo-Christian tradition has gradually revealed the innocence of the victim, culminating in the most innocent victim of all.

I recently ran across this quote from René's *The Scapegoat*: "Each person must ask what his relationship is to the scapegoat. I am not aware of my own, and I am persuaded that the same holds true for my readers. We only have legitimate enmities. And yet the entire universe swarms with scapegoats." True for us all, still.

Speaking of "prophetic intensity," the first book I read was *Battling to the End*, his study of the military theorist Carl von Clausewitz, along with Franco-German relations, war, peace, the escalation to extremes, and the end of the world. Although many found it a dark, pessimistic, end-of-life effort, I found it riveting and persuasive. My review of it for the *San Francisco Chronicle* was well received and even spotlighted by the National Book Critics Circle. He was speaking urgently about what is increasingly clear to us each day: war no longer "works" to resolve our difficulties, and yet peace eludes us.

AR: That's quite a book to start with! It is something like Girard's equivalent of Solzhenitsyn's *Warning to the West*.

CH: *Achever Clausewitz* had just been published in Paris at the time I met him, so it was much on his mind then. In France, at least, the impact was major: French President Nicolas Sarkozy was citing René's words, and reporters were besieging him at his Paris apartment. At the time I met him, eight or nine years ago, the English translation was being prepared for publication, too.

Obviously, then, that book would have to have a special place in my approach to René's work, and so in my writing, too.

There are other reasons, of course. Although *Battling to the End* was a book that took on European history, it was also a book that was focused on the here and now, and had much to say about our current predicament: War no longer works, yet we don't know how to make peace. We don't believe, at least not entirely, in the guilt of the scapegoat, yet we keep repeating the process, hoping that it will bring peace. We keep hoping that the answer is to whack harder at our perceived enemies. Not such an easy sell when we can watch them killed on our TV screens, and watch their villages burn, knowing your government, and you, are responsible.

In previous centuries, a war was declared, the enemies fought, one side surrendered, and they came together to negotiate terms. A treaty was signed, and everyone knew roughly who won and who lost and by how much. Peace may not have been permanent – think of Alsace-Lorraine – but at least hostilities were suspended for the time being, and everyone knew where they stood.

When we wage war today, our aims are unclear, the enemies ambiguous, and the finale is muddied by troop withdrawals rather than treaties. We manipulate language in an Orwellian fashion to disguise the whole process. We long for peace, yet are trapped in reciprocal cycles of escalation. Carl von Clausewitz, the military theorist at the heart of *Battling to the End*, thought total war was only a theoretical possibility – but now?

AR: Has war really changed that much in since the nineteenth century?

CH: *The Guardian* published a respectful article on René's views after his death, focusing on what Clausewitz called "the escalation to extremes." The essay gets some things wrong, but this one right: "In a nuclear age, this modern *lex talionis* is the drumbeat of a future apocalypse." Now we have transnational actors who represent no government. No one answers for them. A single man with a large enough weapon can pretty much declare war on a major power unilaterally, thanks to modern technology.

Let me read what René wrote: "On September 11, people were shaken, but they quickly calmed down. There was a flash of awareness, which lasted a few fractions of a second. People could feel that something was happening. Then a blanket of silence covered up the crack in our certainty of safety. Western rationalism operates like a myth: we always work harder to avoid seeing the catastrophe."

A week after René's death, France suffered the greatest attack on its soil since World War II. René's Palo Alto Requiem Mass took place on a day of national mourning in France – how strange and apt for the man who wrote so much about violence. So often René was saying what we did not want to hear. Already the silence is beginning to settle like snow around the Paris atrocity. We find we can get used to just about anything. René said we are facing a whole new phenomenon, and that what we are watching with Islamic terrorism is in fact a new religion, an archaic one armed with modern technology.

Two decades ago, René said in *When These Things Begin*, an excellent book-length interview with Michel Treguer, recently published in English: "I think that historical processes have meaning and that we have to accept this, or else face utter despair." Clearly not a post-modern thinker – and he owed a little to Hegel. By the time of *Battling to the End*, he wrote: "More than ever, I am convinced that history has meaning, and that its meaning is terrifying." However, at least for me, perhaps the haunting cry that resounds through *Battling to the End* is René's offhand comment about the 9/11 pilots: "Who asks about the souls of those men?" And who does?

AR: Will the apocalyptic (in the original sense of revealing things hidden) *Battling to the End* be the focus of your biography? Will you also discuss the hidden connections that Girardian thinking reveals between seemingly unrelated disciplines such as theology, psychology, neurobiology, economics, history, literature, race theory, anthropology, literary theory, and political science?

CH: Given the news headlines, and the world we live in, of course *Battling to the End* was behind many of my thoughts – but so was *Deceit, Desire, and the Novel*. So was *Violence and the Sacred*.

Certainly I discuss his books at length, and the connections you mention are inherent in his oeuvre. However, *Evolution of Desire* is the story of the man, and the forces that shaped him – using his life as a vehicle for exploring our era and the evolution of his thought.

Above all, I'm writing for the general reader, not specialists. There are plenty of books for specialists, written by specialists. In the end my background is in literature – I'm not an anthropologist or neurobiologist or economist. As a journalist, I have a long track record of explaining complex ideas to a lay public. I'm writing for the intelligent, educated reader who, say, reads the *New York Times*, but has no prior exposure to René or his thinking. I wanted them to be haunted by his questions, and intrigued by his answers.

AR: What were the most formative experiences in Girard's life? How did they shape his thought?

CH: I once asked René what the most pivotal experience of his life was, and he replied that the major events were in his head. That's what everyone else said about him, too. However, events in our heads are put there by the things we see around us. Events in our head tend not to stay with us unless they explain what we see around us. Otherwise they'd be no use.

I pressed harder, and he responded emphatically, "Coming to America." That event in 1947, he said, made everything else possible. René is an American phenomenon, as much as a French one. Without America and the bigger vision it offered after the war, there would have been no books, no theories, and no academic career.

He had been trained as an *archiviste-paléographe* at one of France's *grandes écoles*, the École des Chartes in Paris. It was the same school his father had attended. It was a training ground for archivists, librarians, paleographers. The suit didn't exactly fit him. In the rigid French professional hierarchies at the time, the opportunities it provided were narrow.

And of course America led to other things. An exceptionally happy marriage, for example. Martha McCullough was in one of his first classes at Indiana University. The name stumped him midway through roll call. "I'll never be able to pronounce this name," he said. They met again a year or so later, when she was no longer his student. And he fixed the name problem for her in 1951, when they married. The stability and contentment of that 64-year marriage cannot be underestimated in supporting his very long, very fruitful career.

Let me add two more. Another formative experience was the "strange defeat" of France in 1940. Franco-German relations fascinated him throughout his life. It's a straight line from the toy soldiers he played with as a child, reenacting the Battles of Austerlitz and Waterloo, to his final book, *Battling to the End*. Certainly the topic frequently recurred in my own talks with him. Clearly he was pondering the real nature of the struggle for much of his life. It would be the centerpiece in *Battling to the End*.

And finally, of course, his conversion experience. "Conversion experience" is a mysterious, much-misunderstood term. He didn't say much about it – he said the subject was difficult to explain, and counterproductive to his work in advancing his mimetic theory. But one time he discussed it was in the book I mentioned earlier, *When These Things Begin*. Here's what he said about that period in autumn 1958, when he was working on his first book, *Deceit, Desire, and the Novel*, which discusses Cervantes, Proust, Stendhal, Flaubert, and Dostoevsky: "on the twelfth and last chapter that's entitled 'Conclusion.' I was thinking about the analogies between religious experience and the experience of a novelist who discovers that he's been consistently lying, lying for the benefit of his Ego, which in fact is made up of nothing but a thousand lies that have accumulated over a long period, sometimes built up over an entire lifetime."

"I ended up understanding that I was going through an experience of the kind that I was describing. The religious symbolism was present in the novelists in embryonic form, but in my case it started to work all by itself and caught fire spontaneously. I could no longer have any illusions about what was happening to me, and I was thrown for a loop, because I was proud of being a skeptic. It was very hard for me to imagine myself going to church, praying, and so on. I was all puffed up, full of what the old catechisms used to call 'human respect.'"

It changed him from being a very clever French literary scholar to something much more profound. And it also meant he lost an audience – yet he never backed off from what he understood then.

AR: What, if any, significance do you attach to Girard being born on Christmas Day?

CH: G. K. Chesterton said, "Coincidences are a spiritual sort of pun" – it's about the only Chesterton quote I know. I'd go with that one, but with some caution. After all, Isaac Newton and Humphrey Bogart were born on Christmas Day. So was Egypt's Anwar el-Sadat, Canada's Justin Trudeau, and Pakistan's Muhammed Ali Jinnah. So was Karl Rove, for that matter. That said, I'm tickled that René was born on Christmas!

CHRONOLOGY

1923	On December 25, René Noël Théophile Girard is born in Avignon, the second of five children, to Marie-Thérèse de Loye Fabre and a notable historian of the region, Joseph Frédéric Marie Girard, curator of Avignon's Musée Calvet and later the city's Palais des Papes, France's biggest medieval fortress and the pontifical residence during the Avignon papacy.
1939	On September 1, Germany invades Poland, leading Britain and France to declare war on Germany in retaliation.
1940 and 1941	Girard receives two *baccalauréats*, the first the one common for all students, the second in philosophy, with distinction.
	In 1941, he travels to Lyon to prepare for the entrance exam for the École Normal Supérieure, the foremost among the *grandes écoles*, but left after a few weeks. Instead, he prepares at home for entry into the École des Chartes, a training ground for archivists and librarians.
	On June 14, the Germans occupy Paris without a struggle. On June 22, France is partitioned into an occupied zone and an unoccupied zone (Vichy France).
1942–45	In November, 1942 the Germans extend their full occupation to the south of France, with the Italians occupying the small portion of France east of the Rhône.
	Girard is appointed to be a student at the École des Chartes in Paris in December 1942, and moves to Paris before his classes began in January 1943. He specializes in medieval history and paleography.

Paris is liberated during a military action that began on August 19, 1944, and ended when the German garrison surrendered the French capital on August 25, 1944.

On May 2, 1945, the German capital of Berlin surrenders to Soviet forces. On April 30, Hitler commits suicide, along with other members of his inner circle. On May 8, an unconditional surrender is officially ratified.

1947   Girard finishes his dissertation on marriage and private life in fifteenth-century Avignon, and graduates as an archiviste-paléographe in 1947.

In the summer, he and a friend, Jacques Charpier, organize an exhibition of paintings at the Palais des Papes from June 27 to September 30, under the guidance of Paris art impresario Christian Zervos. Girard rubbed elbows with Pablo Picasso, Henri Matisse, Georges Braque, and other luminaries. French actor and director Jean Vilar founded the theater component of the festival, which became the celebrated annual Avignon Festival.

In September, Girard leaves France for the United States to teach at the University of Indiana in Bloomington. He is first an instructor of French language, and later teaches French literature as well.

1950   He receives his PhD with dissertation on "American Opinion on France, 1940–1943."

1951   Girard marries Martha McCullough on June 18. They have three children: Martin, Daniel, and Mary.

1952–53   Girard becomes instructor of French literature at Duke University for one year.

1953–57   Girard becomes assistant professor at Bryn Mawr College.

1957   Girard assumes post of associate professor of French at Johns Hopkins University in Baltimore, where he eventually is promoted to full professor and chair of

the Romance Languages Department. While there, he
receives two Guggenheim Fellowships, in 1959 and 1966.

1958–59   While finishing his first book, published in English as
Deceit, Desire, and the Novel, Girard undergoes two
conversion experiences from the autumn of 1958 to
Easter, on March 29, 1959. The Girard children were
baptized, and René and Martha renewed their wedding
vows.

1961   Girard publishes *Mensonges romantique et vérité
romanesque* (*Deceit, Desire and the Novel: Self and Other
in Literary Structure,* published in English by Johns
Hopkins University Press, 1965), which introduces his
theory of mimetic desire.

He is promoted to professor of French at Johns Hopkins
University.

1962   Girard publishes an edited volume, *Proust: A Collection
of Critical Essays,* with Prentice-Hall (Englewood Cliffs,
N.J.)

1963   Girard's *Dostoïevski, du double à l'unité* is published with
Éditions Plon (Paris), later in English as *Resurrection
from the Underground: Feodor Dostoevsky* (Crossroads,
1997), reissued by Michigan State University Press in
2012.

1966   With Richard Macksey and Eugenio Donato, Girard
organizes international symposium from October 18–21:
"The Languages of Criticism and the Sciences of Man."
Lucien Goldmann, Roland Barthes, Jacques Derrida,
Jacques Lacan, and others participate in the standing-
room-only event. The conference marks the introduction
of structuralism and French theory to America; it
marked Derrida's debut in America.

1968   Girard is appointed Distinguished Professor at the State
University of New York, Buffalo, in the Department
of English. He begins a lifelong friendship and
collaboration with Michel Serres. These years also mark

the beginning of what would be a lifelong interest in Shakespeare.

1972   Girard publishes the groundbreaking *La Violence et le sacré* (Grasset) developing the idea of scapegoating and sacrifice in cultures around the globe (published as *Violence and the Sacred* with Johns Hopkins University Press in 1977).

1976   In September, he returns to teach at Johns Hopkins University as the James M. Beall Professor of French and Humanities, with an appointment to Richard A. Macksey's Humanities Center.

1978   With collaboration of French psychiatrists Jean-Michel Oughourlian and Guy Lefort, Girard publishes *Des Choses cachées depuis la fondation du monde* (Grasset), published as *Things Hidden since the Foundation of the World* in English (Stanford University Press, 1987), a book-length conversation in which Girard promulgates mimetic theory in its entirety. The book sells briskly in France—35,000 copies in the first six months, putting it on the nonfiction best-seller list.

Johns Hopkins University Press publishes *To Double Business Bound*, a collection of ten essays—seven of which Girard had written in English. The book of essays is selected by *Choice* as one of the outstanding academic books of the year, along with *Violence and the Sacred*, newly published in English.

1979   Girard is elected as a fellow of the American Academy of Arts and Sciences.

1981   Girard assumes post of inaugural Andrew B. Hammond Chair in French Language, Literature and Civilization at Stanford, effective January 1. With Jean-Pierre Dupuy, he organizes the "Disorder and Order" symposium at Stanford, which linked disciplinary domains previously thought to be separate. Participants included Nobel prize-winning scientist Ilya Prigogne and Nobel economist Kenneth Arrow, Ian Watt, Henri Atlan, Isabelle Stengers, Cornelius Castoriadis, Michel Deguy, Heinz von Forster, Francisco Varela, and others.

1982–85	Girard publishes *Le Bouc émissaire* in 1982 with Grasset (published in English as *The Scapegoat*, 1986) and in 1985 *La Route antique des hommes pervers* (*Job, the Victim of his People*, 1987), developing his hermeneutical approach to biblical texts based on premises of mimetic theory.
	He receives first *honoris causa* from Frije University of Amsterdam in 1985.
1988	Girard receives an honorary degree from the faculty of the University of Innsbruck in Austria.
1990–91	Girard publishes *A Theatre of Envy: William Shakespeare*, the only book he conceived and wrote in English. The French edition, *Shakespeare: les feux de l'envie*, received France's Prix Médicis in 1990.
1995	Girard receives honorary degree from the University Faculties Saint Ignatius Antwerp (Belgium).
1999	Girard publishes *Je vois Satan tomber comme l'éclair* (published as *I See Satan Fall Like Lightning* in 2001).
2001	Girard publishes *Celui par qui le scandale arrive* (published as *The One by Whom Scandal Comes* in 2014).
2003	A series of lectures at the Bibliothèque Nationale de France considers the Vedic tradition, and eventually becomes a small book of about a hundred pages, published as *Le sacrifice*, and in 2011 in English as *Sacrifice*.
	Girard receives an honorary degree in arts from the Università degli Studi di Padova in Italy.
2004	Stanford University Press publishes *Oedipus Unbound: Selected Writings on Rivalry and Desire*, a collection of Girard's essays.

He is awarded the literary prize "Aujourd'hui" for *Les origines de la culture* and receives an honorary degree from Canada's Université de Montréal.

2005   Girard is elected to the Académie Française, an honor previously given to Voltaire, Jean Racine, and Victor Hugo. He takes the thirty-seventh chair, vacated by the death of Ambroise-Marie Carré, a Dominican priest, author, and hero of the Résistance.

The Association Recherches Mimétiques founded in Paris.

2006   The University of Tübingen awards Girard the Dr. Leopold Lucas Prize.

2006   With Italian philosopher Gianni Vattimo, Girard publishes a series of dialogues on Christianity and modernity as *Verita o fede debole? Dialogo su cristianesimo e relativismo* (published in English in 2010 as *Christianity, Truth, and Weakening Faith: A Dialogue*).

2008   Scotland's University of St Andrews awards Girard an honorary degree.

On December 28, he receives received a lifetime achievement award from the Modern Language Association in San Francisco.

2009   On December 8, Girard receives a *doctorat honoris causa* from the Institut Catholique de Paris.

2013   On January 25, King Juan Carlos of Spain awards him the Order of Isabella the Catholic, a Spanish civil order bestowed for his "profound attachment" to "Spanish culture as a whole."

2015   On November 4, Girard dies at his home on the Stanford campus.

ACKNOWLEDGMENTS

My work on *Conversations with René Girard: Prophet of Envy* followed close on the heels of *Evolution of Desire: A Life of René Girard*. At that time, I was still responding to interview requests and invitations to discuss this first-ever biography of the French theorist, which was still getting reviews and publicity. However, although the publisher changed for the new volume, I was grateful much of the support continued. The Bloomsbury staff in London, especially publisher Colleen Coalter and her editorial assistant Becky Holland, have been outstanding in their resourcefulness, care, and patience with my overloaded schedule. My previous publisher, Michigan State University Press, also worked with me, securing permissions and providing support. I am most grateful to Prof. William Johnsen, Catherine Cocks, Julie Reaume, and Julie Loehr.

As with the earlier book, anthropologist Mark Anspach guided translations from the French, reviewing the existing translations, and occasionally intervening with French publishers for permissions. Moreover, Prof. Bruce Jackson of the State University of New York at Buffalo generously offered to share his excellent photos, an historically important record of Girard during his time on Lake Erie, just as he had for *Evolution of Desire*. I have an opportunity again to thank author Mary Pope Osborne for her generosity, support, and confidence in my efforts, and Hoover fellow Paul Caringella for friendship and guidance.

To my score of contributors—many thanks for grace under pressure, for meeting deadlines, for dealing with the imperious demands of an editor. To Trevor Cribben Merrill of the California Institute of Technology, I am indebted forever for help, guidance, and good sense over the years.

And gratitude, finally, to Imitatio for financially supporting this endeavor—from the beginning.

BIBLIOGRAPHY

Books by René Girard

Note: Works are given first in English translation, but are in chronological order of original publication.

(1961) *Deceit, Desire and the Novel: Self and Other in Literary Structure.* Baltimore, MD: Johns Hopkins University Press, 1965 [*Mensonge romantique et vérité romanesque.* Paris: Grasset].

(1962) *Proust: A Collection of Critical Essays.* Englewood Cliffs, NJ: Prentice Hall.

(1963) *Resurrection from the Underground: Feodor Dostoevsky.* New York: Crossroad, 1997 [*Dostoïevski, du double à l'unité.* Paris: Plon].

(1972) *Violence and the Sacred.* Baltimore, MD: Johns Hopkins University Press, 1977 [*La Violence et le Sacré.* Paris: Grasset].

(1976) *Critique dans un souterrain.* Lausanne: L'Age d'Homme.

(1978) *To Double Business Bound: Essays on Literature, Mimesis, and Anthropology.* Baltimore, MD: Johns Hopkins University Press.

(1978) *Things Hidden since the Foundation of the World: Research Undertaken in Collaboration with J.-M. Oughourlian and G. Lefort.* Stanford, CA: Stanford University Press, 1987 [*Des Choses cachées depuis la fondation du monde.* Paris: Grasset].

(1982) *The Scapegoat.* Baltimore, MD: Johns Hopkins University Press, 1986 [*Le Bouc émissaire.* Paris: Grasset].

(1985) *Job, the Victim of His People.* Stanford, CA: Stanford University Press, 1987 [*La Route antique des hommes pervers.* Paris: Grasset].

(1991) *A Theatre of Envy: William Shakespeare.* Oxford and New York: Oxford University Press.

(1994) *When These Things Begin.* East Lansing, MI: Michigan State University Press, 2014 [*Quand ces choses commenceront ... Entretiens avec Michel Treguer.* Paris: Arléa].

(1996) *The Girard Reader*, ed. James G. Williams. New York: Crossroad.

(1999) *I See Satan Fall Like Lightning.* Maryknoll, MD: Orbis Books, 2001 [*Je vois Satan tomber comme l'éclair.* Paris: Grasset].

(2001) *The One by Whom Scandal Comes.* East Lansing, MI: Michigan State University Press, 2014 [*Celui par qui le scandale arrive,* ed. Maria Stella Barberi. Paris: Desclée de Brouwer].

(2003) *Sacrifice.* East Lansing, MI: Michigan State University Press, 2011 [*Le Sacrifice.* Paris: Bibliothèque nationale de France].

(2004) *Evolution and Conversion. Dialogues on the Origins of Culture, with Pierpaolo Antonello and João Cezar de Castro Rocha*. London: Continuum, 2008 [*Les Origines de la culture. Entretiens avec Pierpaolo Antonello et João Cezar de Castro Rocha*. Paris: Desclée de Brouwer].

(2004) *Oedipus Unbound: Selected Writings on Rivalry and Desire*, ed. Mark R. Anspach. Stanford, CA: Stanford University Press.

(2006) *Christianity, Truth, and Weakening Faith: A Dialogue*. New York, NY: Columbia University Press, 2010 [*Verità o fede debole: Dialogo su cristianesimo e relativismo*, with Gianni Vattimo, ed. Pierpaolo Antonello. Massa: Transeuropa].

(2007) *Battling to the End*. East Lansing, MI: Michigan State University Press, 2010 [*Achever Clausewitz*. Paris: Editions Carnets Nord].

(2008) *Anorexia*. East Lansing, MI: Michigan State University Press, 2013 [*Anoréxie et desir mimétique*. Paris: Éditions de L'Herne].

(2008) *Mimesis and Theory: Essays on Literature and Criticism, 1953–2005*. Stanford, CA: Stanford University Press.

CONTRIBUTORS

Rebecca Adams is an independent scholar, poet, and teacher of feminist theory and theology. She is the author of the seminal "Loving Mimesis and Girard's 'Scapegoat of the Text': A Creative Reassessment of Mimetic Desire," in *Violence Renounced: René Girard, Biblical Studies and Peacemaking* (2000). She interviewed Girard for the *Journal of Religion and Literature* while a graduate student in English at the University of Notre Dame.

Mark R. Anspach is the author of *Vengeance in Reverse: The Tangled Loops of Violence, Myth, and Madness* (Michigan State University Press) and the editor of *Oedipus Unbound: Selected Writings on Rivalry and Desire* by René Girard (Stanford University Press).

Pierpaolo Antonello is Reader in Italian Literature and Culture at the University of Cambridge and Fellow of St John's College. He specializes in twentieth-century Italian literature, culture, and intellectual history, and has written extensively on the relationship between literature and science, futurism and the avant-garde, Italo Calvino, Italian cinema, and postmodern Italian culture. He has also published on French philosophy and epistemology, with particular reference to René Girard and Michel Serres. He has edited several collections of essays and books by or about Girard, including Girard's dialogues with Gianni Vattimo, *Christianity, Truth, and Weakening Faith: A Dialogue* (2010); *Mimesis, Desire, and the Novel: René Girard and Literary Criticism* (2015), co-edited with Heather Webb; and *How We Became Human: Mimetic Theory and the Science of Evolutionary Origins* (2015), co-edited with Paul Gifford. He is the coauthor of *Evolution and Conversion: Dialogues on the Origins of Culture* (2007).

Maria Stella Barberi is Professor of Political Philosophy at the Department of Cognitive, Psychological, Pedagogical Sciences and Cultural Studies (COSPECS) of the University of Messina. She has written about the anthropology of the sacred, political theology, political symbolism, and modern political thought from Thomas Hobbes to Carl Schmitt. She was editor of *La spirale mimétique: Dix-huit leçons sur René Girard* (2001), published in France simultaneously with *Celui par qui le scandale arrive*, which includes her lengthy interview with Girard. Her most recent book, coauthored with Giuseppe Fornari, is *Il riscatto dei fanti. Caporetto tra letteratura, storia e memorialistica*. She and Fornari recently brought out an Italian edition of the 1987 Stanford volume of conversations between Girard, Walter Burkert, and Jonathan Z. Smith, *Violent Origins: Ritual Killing and Cultural Formation*.

Thomas F. Bertonneau is an Emeritus Professor of English at SUNY Oswego. His articles have appeared in a number of scholarly journals. He is coauthor with Kim Paffenroth of *The Truth Is Out There* (2006), a study of religious themes in classic TV science fiction. At the time of the *Paroles Gelées* interview he was a third-year graduate student in the Program in Comparative Literature at UCLA doing research for his dissertation.

João Cezar de Castro Rocha is Professor of Comparative Literature at the Universidade do Estado do Rio de Janeiro. He is the Endowed Chair Machado de Assis of Latin American Studies (Universidad del Claustro de Sor Juana / Brazilian Embassy, Mexico, 2010), and he has edited more than twenty books, among which are a collection of six volumes of Machado de Assis's short stories. His most recent book is *Shakespearean Cultures: Latin America and the Challenges of Mimesis in Non-Hegemonic Circumstances* (2019). He is the coauthor of *Evolution and Conversion: Dialogues on the Origins of Culture* (2007).

Robert Doran is Professor of French and Comparative Literature at the University of Rochester and is the author of two recent monographs: *The Theory of the Sublime from Longinus to Kant* (Cambridge University Press, 2015, Spanish translation forthcoming in 2019) and *The Ethics of Theory: Philosophy, History, Literature* (Bloomsbury, 2016). He is the editor of five volumes, including a collection of essays by René Girard: *Mimesis and Theory: Essays on Literature and Criticism*, 1953–2005 (Stanford University Press, 2008).

Philippe Godefroid is a stage director, dramatist, doctor of musicology, graduate of political science, and teacher of performing arts.

Robert Pogue Harrison is Stanford University's Rosina Pierotti Professor in Italian Literature and a regular contributor to *The New York Review of*

Books. He founded and hosts the popular radio talk show and podcast series, *Entitled Opinions*, featuring the leading writers, scholars, and thinkers of our time. He is the author of *Juvenescence: A Cultural History of Our Age* (2014), *Gardens: An Essay on the Human Condition* (2008), *The Dominion of the Dead* (2003), *Forests: The Shadow of Civilization* (1992), and *The Body of Beatrice* (1988).

Élisabeth Lévy is a journalist, essayist, and a regular host and interviewer on radio and television talk shows in France. She studied at the Institut d'études politiques de Paris. She is the founder and editorial director of the Paris-based magazine *Causeur*.

Giulio Meotti is the cultural editor of *Il Foglio*, where he has worked since 2003. He has also written for the *Wall Street Journal*. He is the author of several books, including *Non smettermo di darmi* (2009), *Hanno ucciso Charlie Hebdo* (2015), *La fine dell'Europa, Cantagalli* (2016), and *Il suicidio della cultura occidentale: Così l'Islam radicale sta vincendo* (2018). He has a PhD in philosophy from the University of Florence.

Artur Sebastian Rosman is the editor-in-chief of University of Notre Dame's *Church Life Journal*. He formerly wrote about religion and the arts at the widely read *Cosmos the in Lost* blog. His published work includes six book translations from the Polish (most recently Tischner's *The Philosophy of Drama*) and essays in such periodicals as *The Review of Metaphysics*, *IMAGE Journal*, *The Journal of Religion and Literature*, *The Merton Annual*, and *Znak*.

Pedro Sette-Câmara has translated nearly seventy books, including titles by René Girard, Alice Munro, John Updike, and Pope Francis. He has written one play, published essays in the Brazilian press, and maintained ties with *O Indivíduo*, founded as a student website and now an independent blog dedicated to literature, religion, and politics. He has a PhD from the Universidade do Estado do Rio de Janeiro.

Laurence Tacou has directed Éditions de l'Herne since 2000. She has written about literature and foreign policy for *France-Soir*, *Le Monde*, *Vogue*, *Libération*, *Le Point*, and *L'Évènement du jeudi*. She is a Chevalier de la Légion d'Honneur and a Chevalier des Arts et des Lettres.

Henri Tincq has written for *Le Monde*, *La Croix*, and contributes regularly to the French-language magazine *Slate*. He is the author of *Larousse des religions* (2009). He is a recipient of the 2001 John Templeton award in journalism. In 2007, he was named a Chevalier de la Légion d'honneur.

Michel Treguer is a television producer, radio producer, journalist, and writer in Paris and Brittany. He is the author of scores of books, plays, and documentaries.

Scott A. Walter is Professor of Epistemology at the University of Nantes. At the time of his interview with Prof. Girard, he was an auditor of the latter's graduate seminar on "Myth and the Bible," and an occasional contributor to the literary magazine *Birth of Tragedy*.

INDEX

Index